# Postcapitalism

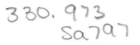

# POSTCAPITALISM
## MOVING BEYOND IDEOLOGY
## IN AMERICA'S ECONOMIC CRISES

RAPHAEL SASSOWER

Paradigm Publishers
Boulder • London

Copyright © 2009 Paradigm Publishers

Published in the United States by Paradigm Publishers, 3360 Mitchell Lane, Suite E, Boulder, CO 80301 USA.

Paradigm Publishers is the trade name of Birkenkamp & Company, LLC, Dean Birkenkamp, President and Publisher.

Library of Congress Cataloging-in-Publication Data

Sassower, Raphael.
  Postcapitalism : moving beyond ideology in America's economic crises / Raphael Sassower.
    p. cm.
  Includes bibliographical references and index.
  ISBN 978-1-59451-672-6 (hardcover : alk. paper)
  1. United States—Economic policy—2001– 2. United States—Economic conditions—2001– 3. Economic forecasting—United States. 4. Financial crises—United States.
I. Title.
  HC106.83.S27 2009
  330.973—dc22

                                                                      2008055961

Printed and bound in the United States of America on acid-free paper that meets the standards of the American National Standard for Permanence of Paper for Printed Library Materials.

Designed and Typeset by Straight Creek Bookmakers.

13 12 11 10 09   1 2 3 4 5

Dedicated to the memory of my teacher, Paul N. Rosenstein-Rodan

# Contents

# Preface

The response to what will become known as the financial crisis of 2008 has been that we are in an uncharted territory and, therefore, it is difficult to find our way out of it. This book suggests that this economic territory has been charted and traversed for more than two hundred years, but that most of us have ignored its signposts. Perhaps some economists and some financial pundits are finding themselves in a crisis mode, but philosophers and political economists since Adam Smith have always understood the intricate and delicate balance that must hold among various frameworks and constituencies, from the political, legal, and social to the economic and moral. In order to avoid and overcome, if not completely eliminate, economic crises and ensure the smooth operation of market transactions many other elements must be in play: legal protections of contracts, social sanction of profit-making, moral approval (utilitarian or not) of the benevolence enjoyed by society as a whole, and some level of political leadership that controls through regulation the extreme risks that might undermine the entire market system. This is not new. What is new is that the current financial crisis has been in fact a crisis in the confidence we have in the marketplace and its self-regulation insofar as its excesses and integrity are concerned. Turning to the historical and philosophical framing of capitalism is no longer the exclusive luxury of idle scholars but must become a necessary stepping-stone for every citizen whose future prospects have been put into question in this financial crisis.

The appeal to our cherished goals of "life, liberty, and the pursuit of happiness" should carry with it the force the goals were meant to have as an incentive to participate in our political life and the institutions we have created to ensure its survival and progress. But what do these words and concepts mean when we are jobless, penniless, and homeless? How can we endow them with meaning and craft policies that would ensure their protection? Just as we curtail the freedom of our children to play with matches, so we must curtail the freedom of some of our fellow citizens whose actions in the financial markets brought about a brush fire that has consumed the fruits of our labor. One cannot escape dramatizing that which deserves to be dramatic: The trauma of the current financial crisis will be felt for years to come by millions of Americans (and many across the globe) until we find the kind of delicate balance that retains our fundamental freedoms with some restraining policies. Although natural disasters, such as hurricane Katrina of 2005, are unpredictable and therefore test our national resolve after the fact, economic disasters are predictable and preventable if the resolve is there all along. If we are to regain our footing, we must move beyond glib ideological mud-slinging and design a pragmatic set of solutions and policies that would ensure a long-term prosperity we have learned to enjoy. Looking backward, as I do in this book, is a crucial step in being able to look forward to a stable and just future.

To be an antifascist and procapitalist after World War II seemed both reasonable and prudent. Socialist ideology was subsumed under the fascist umbrella that ranged from Italy and Germany to the Soviet Union, and it was contrasted with an American ideology that was simultaneously democratic and capitalist. The fact that the American ideological umbrella leaked here and there was overlooked, because at least it sheltered us from disasters and provided us hope for a better future, providing military protection and financial support. Using the vestiges of the Austrian School of Economic Thought (from Von Mises to Hayek), the Chicago School (of Friedman and company) put forth an economic model that set the tone for future political debates and policy decisions domestically and internationally for the remainder of the twentieth century. What seemed reasonable and prudent then is unreasonable and imprudent today, as we can see from the outcomes of recent natural disasters (hurricane Katrina) and the ongoing crisis in the financial markets.

The root of the problem, as far as I can tell, is first and foremost an ideological confusion that inevitably leads to inconsistent and harmful policies. By the time we enacted legislation that collected taxes from our citizens and enacted the New Deal programs in the 1930s, we had lost the pretense of having a "pure" capitalist model for the economy, however one defines this purity (classical or neoclassical, neoconservative or laissez-faire). Put differently, by the middle of the last century we were no longer capitalists, but rather social democrats of sorts, providing safety nets for the needy and coordinating our national economic efforts for the Great War and for the success of Big Science projects. It is not that we have never been capitalists, but that we always were compassionate capitalists or moral capitalists, inspired, as I shall demonstrate, by no other than Adam Smith, who cared about our personal virtues and the ways in which they played out in society as a whole. One recent book by Lawrence Brown and Lawrence Jacobs (2008) comes closest at least to diagnosing one of the maladies that afflicts us today if not to my own prognosis: the ideological confusion of wanting no government whatsoever in the name of market capitalism and needing the protection of government policies and regulations in order to foster the smooth operations of the markets. Though their concern is more specifically with policies regarding transportation, education, and health care of the past three decades and how their unintended consequences enlarged government agencies and budgets, their continued concern to dissociate themselves from utopian extremism in the name of realistic and pragmatic solutions puts them right at the heart of my argument. It is also reassuring to find economists and political scientists who share the philosophical concern and historical perspective I bring to this discussion, searching, for example, for antecedent statements made in the eighteenth century by Adam Smith and some of his colleagues.

What I propose here is a pragmatic middle ground of sorts between two extremes in the spectrum of capitalist analysis: On the one end is Robert Reich (2007) who recognizes the ways in which "supercapitalism" has damaged democracy but who shies away from blaming anyone in particular, and on the other end is Naomi Klein (2007) who indicts Milton Friedman's Chicago School for using political "shock therapy" in order to advance the causes and goals of its version of raw capitalism. They both have their hands on the pulse of the contemporary global marketplace, and they both acknowledge the ideological elements that loom over any discussion of this or that economic policy. And unlike Brink Lindsey who advocates an "implicit libertarian synthesis" of the political "center," which is the result of the "left-right ideological conflict" of the past century (Lindsey 2007, 319), my own suggestions revolve around a different sense of American pragmatism that transcends ideological convictions, and as such is neither libertarian nor collectivist.

It is with this in mind that I wish to argue for a more nuanced view of the past two centuries and offer some concrete suggestions for the organization of the economy in the twenty-first century, with an ongoing emphasis on collective and personal responsibility. Instead of trying to straighten out or clear the ideological confusions that permeate our contemporary cultural landscape and that are readily seen in our interactions in the marketplace, I suggest giving up any simpleminded adherence to or interpretation of the capitalist ideology. There are two reasons that explain, if not fully justify, my recommendation. First, American pragmatism has in fact been a more persuasive and prevalent intellectual commitment than any other, and it provides a way to skirt ideological principles and instead adopt whatever means are best suited for accomplishing our tasks, whether they relate to the economy or to our religious beliefs. American pragmatism as it applies to the marketplace is an organic approach that respects the changing conditions under which humans interact and the ongoing civic development of their sensibilities. Second, capitalist ideology as commonly ascribed to Adam Smith is much more nuanced and complex, more open-ended and morally grounded than it has been portrayed by contemporary zealots. As such, it demands eschewing any simplified vision of "no government intervention whatsoever," for example, and supports the cultivation of community-based benevolence that can ensure the well-being and happiness of all members of a community.

Some myths are worth preserving, and some must be debunked. I hope in some ways to debunk those myths that are detrimental to the social cohesion of contemporary society. The myths of equality and freedom are useful because they inspire individuals and provide goals that government agencies try to attain. So, we have a constitutional freedom of speech, though in many other areas of our interactions our freedoms are limited by considering the effects they might have on others. We are not free to use hate speech that might entice someone to hurt another. Likewise, we are motivated to work hard in an environment that promises equal opportunity, not equality, to everyone. In both cases, the myths of freedom and equality are important benchmarks we adopt as a democratic and progressive society where we respect all individuals alike and hope to fulfill their dreams.

But here is the rub: Can all the diverse dreams of all individuals be fully fulfilled? How come only some are and some are not? There are those who suggest that it is really up to individuals to achieve their goals, regardless of the conditions under which they live. Others maintain that certain conditions, like poverty and lack of access to basic resources, such as a library or the Internet, make it impossible for some individuals to take advantage of the opportunities that might be available. Both views have proponents who give ample anecdotal evidence to prove their respective cases. But at the heart of the debate, when one arises in academic circles or among policy makers, is the relation between the individual and the community. It is not which came first, but rather which part of this relationship should take precedence over the other and in what sense.

The history of social and political thought is home to intellectual giants who have tried to tackle the questions relating to the position of the individual in society. Whether we think of Socrates, who felt that his obligation to his fellow-Athenians was stronger than his ability to flee his death sentence, Rousseau, who recommended foregoing individual wills for the sake of the social contract and the establishment of a General Will, or Mill, who insisted on the centrality of individual rights and liberties, they all have worried about protecting the integrity of individual choices amidst the well-being of society as a whole. So, regardless of their particular recommendations, they all brought to the fore the political framework within which moral principles and quandaries should be examined. One question that comes up when discussing these issues relates to the alternative methods or strategies of accomplishing individual choices: competition versus cooperation. And at this juncture the social Darwinists are most vocal: The biological notion of natural selection and the survival of the fittest are the best metaphors or analogies to be used concerning what happens in the social environment. Cooperation or collaboration among individuals as a strategy for survival and political progress is considered socialist or communist and as such flawed to the core, whereas competition among individuals is perceived as the cornerstone around which capitalist success and progress are accomplished in a democratic, market-driven society.

This is one of the myths I am trying to debunk here, especially when refocusing on the political and moral foundations of the relations and interactions among individuals rather than on the economic or financial features that are commonly emphasized (income and wealth, subsidies and taxes). In order to fully appreciate the myth of competition as the salient thread that binds together social relations, I will use examples from the intellectual community and the academy, the scientific community and the business world, and the religious community. In their respective ways, all of these communities support individual initiatives that end up collectively improving their members' conditions (however one measures support and improvement). In other words, all of these communities, in their own ways, provide the conditions under which individual success or fulfillment can be achieved in principle (reaching for the stars) and in practice (well-grounded and educated individuals who appreciate their social relations with others in their own and other communities). The success, though, depends both on emotional and cognitive sustenance given by the rest of the community. Because I believe that the emotional conditions that offer a healthier basis for individual action are themselves bound up with and to a great extent reflect the cognitive or intellectual foundation provided by society to its members, I will limit myself to them.

One way to trace this intellectual or cognitive sustenance is to focus on what has been called of late the knowledge industry, however broadly defined, because it is around questions of the production, distribution, and consumption of knowledge that the community plays a vital role in the success of individuals. In this sense, a child who is born with minimal knowledge, despite reincarnation theories on the one hand (Greek or Indian) and a set of theories about deep mental and linguistic structures on the other (e.g., Noam Chomsky), can develop and thrive in an environment in which there is ready and free access to knowledge. And despite whatever genetic makeup constitutes each individual (shall we ever discover a genius gene?), or the specific ideological commitment of the state (democratic, totalitarian, capitalist, or socialist), the technoscientific and cultural environments in which knowledge is distributed and consumed has an important effect on the development and success of each individual. There is, then, an intellectual and cognitive context into which we are born and from which we develop our own traits and strengths, what some have attributed to a Jungian-like collective unconscious.

How does this relate to debunking myths? On one level, it is clear that the accumulated knowledge of any given culture provides the framework for, and springboard from which, each and every member of that particular culture, no matter how poorly exposed to that accumulation of knowledge, moves forward. For example, exposure to television programs is almost as useful to children as the wealth of knowledge stored at Harvard University's library. In the age of the Internet, rural residents can just as easily find answers to questions that interest and affect them, from medical diagnoses (which, incidentally, should be corroborated by actual nurses and physicians) to soil quality and climate trends for farming purposes, as can those in urban centers possessed of access to experts and libraries. This is not to say that everyone is an expert in the postmodern age of the Internet (where the plurality of data gathering and their unregulated distribution enriches and overwhelms at the same time). Rather, this is to remind us all that we are consumers of data at every juncture of our life, and that those data were produced and compiled by other members of our society who are willing to share them free of charge, in many cases, and for a fee, in others, as a form of social investment in our collective future. So, the first myth to be debunked is that the individual, however conceptually central he or she may be in a democratic society (retaining rights and duties in relation to the community as a whole), is disconnected from the community as if an island unto her or himself; on the contrary, every individual remains an entrenched member of a community on which she or he is fully dependent for (intellectual and social) survival, sanity, and nourishment.

The second myth relates to the notion of genius, namely, the premium we put on the singularity and uniqueness of individual activities and successes. This is not to say that no one can invent something new or make certain connections not seen before (see the long history of approved patents in this country as well as the artworks in museums around the globe), but rather that these cases should be celebrated within a context or framework that has been established by others as opposed to the cult-like focus on the uniqueness of celebrities. Whether an artist or scientist, the individual actor is part of a community that nurtures such an activity, that has provided even the most rudimentary tools with which to produce a mathematical formula or a piece of art, and that has established a tradition and a history of such activities. There is an implicit communal support that underlies the potential of these individual activities.

The third myth is related to the first two and has to do with incentives, motivation, and competition, which are talked about as if they are the benchmarks one must adhere to in order to excel at whatever endeavor she or he undertakes, or as if without them no individual would ever excel or succeed. This is not to say that people do not compete or that we cannot motivate people to do this rather than that (with praise and money). Instead, this is to suggest that on the one hand, we do not operate simply on the basis of our self-interest and rationality (as we shall see in the extensive work of behavioral economists) but rather on the basis of a variety of other, noneconomic and at times nonrational impulses and hunches; and on the other hand, competition is at times detrimental to our success whereas collaboration or cooperation among individuals may enhance the productivity and success of each individual within that group (with all the problems of measuring success and attributing personal rewards). These observations lead as well to the kind of American pragmatism we see around us on a daily basis.

Finally, there is a fourth related myth that claims that the relationship between the private and the public sectors is one of separation and antagonism. Instead, I suggest that without the public sector or domain the private sector could not survive, let alone thrive. Whether it is the legal or political system that provides the safeguards for the capitalist marketplace, what remains true is that without a proper and secure framework the marketplace would collapse (as we are seeing with the financial markets in the present day). The support is as much psychological and cognitive as it is legal and material. And the support comes in a variety of flavors, from direct (laws and regulations) and indirect (constitutional provisions) government intervention, all the way to national mottos ("In God We Trust") and cultural cues (the conquest of nature with plastic surgery) that are just as influential in informing the individual what expectations the community has of his or her behavior.

In debunking some of these myths I wish, among other things, to shift our attention from the contemporary divide between the scientific, artistic, economic, and religious communities as if those communities are hostile to each other and think poorly of each other (as is evident when creationism and evolution are pitted against each other in secondary education). The baffling facts of the increased membership in religious institutions and the belief in God in a materialist, capitalist, and democratic America should be taken seriously. Instead of jettisoning the importance of religion and relegating it to ignorance, we, in the academic and scientific communities, should figure out what religious communities offer their members that we regularly ignore or undervalue. The bad taste left in people's mouths and minds regarding the experience of post-Katrina New Orleans suggests an answer at least to politicians: People want to have a world order that makes sense, to belong to a community that loves and cares for them, and to know that through the community (and God) they have attained a spiritual transcendence that includes hope to improve their personal lot through communal assistance. The answers are given daily and are full of faith and optimism regarding the future. Whereas the scientific and political communities scare the public with predictions of doom and gloom about the environment and keep the public confused over their own self-critical and tentative pronouncements, religious leaders offer prayers and after-life salvation, certitude and compassion. I am not suggesting that we should ignore scientific realities and rely exclusively on faith communities when it gets to leading our life, but rather that in order to deal with natural (scientific) realities (such as floods and hurricanes) we might need to complement our social and economic strategies with those learned by religious communities that use the community as a base or foundation upon which individual salvation (or survival or success) can be achieved.

Before outlining the major arguments of this book and the ways in which I intend to support them within chapters, I would like to briefly explain the term in the title of this book: *Postcapitalism*. In contrast to Robert Reich's *Supercapitalism* (2007), in which he argues for seeing our current economic situation as the latest stage in the evolution of capitalism (and one that undermines democratic institutions and principles), and to Jürgen Habermas's *Legitimation Crisis* (1975), which finds some historical similarities between postcapitalism and postmodernism as principles of organization, I see postcapitalism the way Jean-François Lyotard (1984) sees postmodernism. For him, postmodernism is not really "post" in any chronological or organizational sense—modernism first and then postmodernism—but rather a state of affairs that is and has always been parallel with modernism. This means that postmodern tendencies and principles—multiplicity of viewpoints, nonhierarchical comparisons, reconfiguration of existing data, case-by-case judgment without a permanent foundation, to name some—have been operational alongside modernist tendencies and principles all along. In the present context this means that postcapitalist features that promote collaboration and collegiality, that appreciate the social, political, and moral frameworks that legally protect the marketplace interaction among people, have been present from antiquity. These features must be acknowledged and cherished to ensure the prosperous and peaceful future of our planet. As such, these features constitute the kind of pragmatism that overshadows any strict adherence to a narrowly defined capitalist ideology. This kind of pragmatism, to be sure, transcends the specific commitment of any ideology (capitalist or socialist) and allows for the practical assessment of the efficacy of this or that government intervention in the affairs of its people: rescue schemes, bailout offers, regulations, and oversight commissions.

The first chapter deals with the original formulation of classical economics, or capitalism, as we have come to know it, so as to remind ourselves of the beliefs and ideas held by Adam Smith as opposed to their more contemporary, subverted variations in popular media of the West. Of course, when we deal with particular contemporary models of capitalism we tend to forget the extent to which they overlook the need for public support of private industry, whether it relates to mortgages or the knowledge industry. Reviewing Smith's own words about the need for communal and personal benevolence in order to ensure the operations of the marketplace and the happiness of individuals, we appreciate the intellectual trajectory that moved neoclassical economists to consider development projects in less-developed countries. What I wish to emphasize here is the entrenched political dependence of the marketplace on the legal and social frameworks that protect and subsidize it. In this sense, the classical marketplace model of Adam Smith and its current transformation into "supercapitalism" (in Reich's sense) must be acknowledged as a politically infused model with tax breaks and bankruptcy laws, for example, so as to find a pragmatic middle ground for policy purposes, one that acknowledges the responsibility of the state to protect and motivate its citizens. I use the philosopher Karl Popper to envision particular policy solutions to some current practical national problems.

The second chapter is devoted to a brief survey of the knowledge industry and its genealogy from purely academic endeavor that included skill-acquisition to an economic force that underlies productivity in the computer age. In looking at some of the features of this industry, I will focus on the production, distribution, and consumption of knowledge as if it were an economic model, so that the financial aspects of this industry will be understood. For example, should government subsidized research (Global Positioning System) be eventually turned over free-of-charge to corporations that profit from it? If the answer is yes, then citizens in fact pay twice for the same knowledge-based technology: once through their taxes when the Department of Defense, for instance, funds academic research, and the second time when they buy a device that uses this technology (cellular phones or dashboard maps). This example can move us back to reconsider the ways in which information and data are circulating in the marketplace, and the ways in which lifelong learning is attained. This might be an extension of or a contrast to the view that it is important to acquire knowledge for knowledge's sake, the view that promotes the love of learning, or the Greek ideal of the love of wisdom (philosophy). Contemporary academic institutions are being transformed from institutions of higher learning and the custodians and repositories of knowledge to factory-like assembly lines that feed the labor market. This transformation is sanctioned by the marketplace and guided by government agencies and the state, illustrating the kind of inevitable and inherent political entanglement with corporate needs and financing.

The third chapter delves more deeply into the relationship between individuals and the community in which they live, shifting our focus from competition to cooperation and collaboration. Beginning with a different appreciation of the survival of hunters and gatherers who needed each other's help, we shift to contemporary examples of intellectual-industrial production that is team based. The focus on venture capital firms and the system that supports them is meant to bring to light the extent to which capitalist ideals are themselves being transformed in the contemporary environment of investment in the production of knowledge. From domestic cases we move to national boundaries as being too restricted in the age of globalization, where international cooperation now becomes a necessity and no longer a luxury. Just as the unit of measurement in the corporate world is no longer the individual worker but the company as a whole, so in the larger context the unit of measurement is no longer a company or even a country but the entire globe. This move is in turn not limited to natural sources and labor availability (as we will see in Chapter 1 in relation to developmental economics) but also relates to ecological issues that end up affecting us all, regardless of our economic developmental stages (the Kyoto Accord, for example). But when the focus remains the knowledge industry, we must recall the postmodern notion of interlaced strands of data and insights that are recycled around the globe, from ancient herbal therapies to the conservation of land use, and as such may escape the traditional framework of intellectual property. As global networks of knowledge sprout and proliferate, private property-like claims are difficult to sustain, and in their stead we find ourselves in a new world order of "open-source" Internet communities whose global interaction and collaboration would have been impossible to envision a few decades ago.

The fourth chapter takes a different tone and tries to complement the focus on the intellectual wealth of knowledge and the cognitive enrichment offered by contemporary society with a discussion of the sociopsychological elements or features that enhance this richness. But here certain problems loom large, as individual gratification sometimes is not as immediate as desired or expected. Can one personally enjoy collective relief or rewards? That is, does the individual need to personalize the benefits that are present in society as a whole, or is it more likely that these benefits would be taken for granted (sanitation comes to mind in advanced societies)? Are we just as content or even happy when the group gets recognized (our club, team, or city) as when we individually win a prize (for beautifying a park or designing a landmark)? The complexity of these issues is fruitfully analyzed by behavioral economists and psychologists who explain human tendencies for reciprocal altruism, their ambivalences in regard to collaborative strategies (The Prisoner's Dilemma), and the inevitable concerns over free riders (those who contribute less than they take from the collective effort of their community). The issues are complex, because there is a tension between motivating and rewarding individual excellence while recognizing that the individual works within a group and therefore is always only as good as the company, corporation, or government agency is.

The fifth chapter takes the themes developed in the previous four chapters and attempts to pull them together in dealing with collective and personal responsibility. This issue dates back to biblical times when questions of guilt and culpability came up (the exodus from Egypt, the sins of Sodom and Gomorra in later times, for example), were revisited during the Nuremberg trials of the Nazis after World War II, and haunt us in the current environment of corporate crime (the corporation as a legal entity no longer shields its officers and directors, as seen in the Enron case). The importance of ethical questions in contemporary society is an issue that should be raised only if we believe that the community is the foundation of our existence and survival, of our past, present, and future. The individual actor is responsible to the community as a whole, and if there is higher accountability to one's conscience or one's God, it is a way of expressing the profound responsibility that ought to be ever-present in our lives. By the same token, indiscretions (whether personal, as in the case of personal bankruptcy, or corporate, as in the case of bailouts) are treated by the federal government as if they should be forgiven or at least taken care of. It is in this sense, then, that the community—with its obligations and rights, its responsibilities and interventions—seems to be the final guardian and arbiter of individual actions (successes and failures), rather than a superfluous burden (with taxes and regulations).

Concluding with these recommendations, as seen in the sixth chapter it seems that the American pragmatic landscape is ready to go beyond any ideological confines of the right and the left of the political spectrum and adopt a postcapitalist attitude and set of policies that respect individual choices and freedoms, while recognizing that their preservation requires the guiding hand of a government that respects the needs and aspirations of the rest of the community.

*   *   *

I would like to thank Prof. Steve Fuller of the University of Warwick, Dr. Thomas Basboll of the Copenhagen Business School, and Prof. David Levine of the University of Denver for their feedback on the initial direction of this project. I am also indebted to Prof. Sam Gill of San Francisco State University, Prof. Joseph Agassi of York and Tel-Aviv Universities, Dr. Dolores Byrnes, and Perry Sanders Jr. who provided valuable comments on the overall arguments and some of the details of this project. Dean Birkenkamp's encouragement has sustained my research and writing over the past year, especially as I tried to respond to the current economic crises. Drew Hutchinson has meticulously read numerous drafts and steered me clear of unnecessary missteps. As always, I am grateful to the officials at my home institution, the University of Colorado at Colorado Springs, for staying out of my intellectual way.

*—Breckenridge, Colorado*
*October 2008*

# CHAPTER 1

# From Supercapitalism to Postcapitalism

As the twenty-first century unfolds, some, like former Labor Secretary Robert Reich, have commented on the transformation of our domestic economy into a global economy (Reich 2007). In using the term *Supercapitalism,* Reich emphasizes the shift from merely a capitalist or hyper-capitalist economy as the United States has developed it in the twentieth century with a certain level of democracy to a supercapitalist nation whose democratic institutions fail to catch up with the economy. In making his argument and illustrating the concentration of capital in fewer and fewer corporate hands, Reich decries the failure to ensure the good old liberal values upon which our democracy was founded. Though a centrist at heart—fiscally conservative and socially progressive—Reich seems to be following the basic lines of argument already proposed by the so-called Chicago School. Its founder, Milton Friedman, in turn, follows the neoclassical Austrian School and has always believed that with numerous free consumers interacting in the marketplace, decision-making processes (voting with one's pocketbook), including political ones, would remain democratic instead of becoming totalitarian (Friedman 1982).

Using numerous statistical data, Reich demonstrates that there is instead an inverse relationship between the triumphs of capitalism and the protection of citizens: We have moved from "democratic capitalism," where corporate interests worked in tandem with political and social interests ("what is good for GM is good for America") to a system where the economy is divorced from social and political concerns and corporate America seems disinterested in the welfare of the state (Reich 2007, 46–47, 126–127). In Reich's words, "The triumph of Supercapitalism has led, indirectly and unwittingly, to the decline of democracy" (224).

More specifically, supercapitalism thrives not only because of the concentration of capital in fewer hands, but also because of the advantages of deregulation. This alleged advantage, as we saw with the 2008 financial crisis is coming into question: The question is no longer how much deregulation, but how little, because the excesses of the past decade might prove impossible to fix. The push to deregulate this or that segment of the economy is a result of the competitive diversion of great sums of money to entice political campaigns and politicians toward policies of deregulation so that a competitive edge can be legally guaranteed to specific corporations or industries (Reich 2007, ch. 4). This line of argument goes deeper than the accusation against the abuses of Halliburton, for example, a corporate giant headquartered in Dubai that has continuously received no-bid contracts from the Department of Defense in supplying our troops in Iraq and Afghanistan. On the one hand, it offers a refutation to the classical and neoclassical economic models that have suggested that the more capitalist-like our markets become, the better off we would all be. On the other hand, it suggests that the kind of inside information regarding predictable government needs and specific regulatory exemptions benefit some corporations more than others and in the process co-opts political institutions to perform the will of financial giants, all without consideration of the welfare of the state and its citizens. As Reich brilliantly summarizes, "the fundamental problem does not, for the most part, involve blatant bribes and kickbacks. Rather, it is the intrusion of Supercapitalism into every facet of democracy—the dominance of corporate lobbyists, lawyers, and public relations professionals over the entire political process; the corporate money that engulfs the system on a day-to-day basis, making it almost impossible for citizen voices to be heard" (211).

Tony Judt's assessment of Reich's book suggests that the presentation of Supercapitalism as an inevitable next stage of capitalist growth, based as it is both on technological advances and an increased international marketplace, fails to address fully enough both its political and its personal dimensions (2007). The profound commercialization of human behavior, whether as consumers, investors, or producers, takes the social and moral dimension, however attractive it may be, away from the analysis, so that we end up with a picture of a world seen only through the prism of commercial growth. When economic problems arise, Judt reminds us, there is no responsible party at whose feet we can lay the blame for any crisis, for any kind of inequality in wealth (narrowly or broadly construed), because the inevitable march of capitalism is presumed to be value-neutral. But at some point we do object and might even protest. At some point the financial crisis becomes a national disaster, as even billionaire George Soros admits. And when this happens, a call for government regulation and intervention becomes reasonable if not necessary for the protection of the very system Reich calls Supercapitalism (Soros 2008). Cynically, this could be the only response aimed at protecting the continued growth and success of supercapitalism as bailout offers and government-backed guarantees and securities abound; logically, this is a call to reassess the political, social, and moral context within which the marketplace operates; and practically, this is a call that must be heard across the nation, a call to revise our outdated definitions and views of capitalism, super or not.

Perhaps it is this reassessment that Naomi Klein undertakes in her *The Shock Doctrine*. In general, her argument is that the Friedman-Chicago School "fundamentalist form of capitalism has always needed disaster to advance" (2007, 9). When natural disasters happen, as she demonstrates the world around, or when political crises are deliberately set in motion, there are opportunities for the private sector to usurp the powers of the public sector and thereby ensure financial gains, whether in Chile in the 1970s or in the current war in Iraq. She calls "these orchestrated raids on the public sphere in the wake of catastrophic events, combined with the treatment of disasters as exciting market opportunities, 'disaster capitalism'" (6). Although one can read her analysis as one large conspiracy theory where Milton Friedman and his cohorts are the villains, and although one might dismiss her analysis because it is overly polemic, her collection of data is so overwhelming that one must take pause. Unlike Reich's survey of the inevitable historical march of capitalism from one stage to another, following in broad outlines Marx's own original version, Klein's survey lays blame on a specific form of capitalist progress that is not simply exploitive in the old-fashioned Marxian sense (workers get paid less than they deserve, while the capitalists reap large profits) but coercive and cruel. In her words:

> This book is a challenge to the central and most cherished claim in the official story—that the triumph of deregulated capitalism has been born of freedom, that unfettered free markets go hand in hand with democracy. Instead, I will show that this fundamentalist form of capitalism has consistently been midwifed by the most brutal forms of coercion, inflicted on the collective body politic as well as on countless individual bodies. The history of the contemporary free market—better understood as the rise of corporatism—was written in shocks. (2007, 18–19)

In demystifying the capitalist myth of deregulation and freedom, Klein also explains that the Chicago School was not simply fighting the ghosts of

Marx and Marxism, but that in fact it was fighting the ghosts and realities of Keynes (who believed in the intervention of the state to overcome recessions and depressions and whose ideas were implemented in the United States as the New Deal of the 1930s), the social democrats in Europe (about whom more later), and the developmental economists (who set policies in the so-called Third World) (2007, 53). She is right on target here, for Marx and his ideas are always relegated to such an extreme interpretation as to make any policy consideration laughable; but the Keynesians had some success after the great depression, the social democrats are still dominant in post–World War II Europe, and developmental strategies are being revised and reassessed to this day. Could an unbridled capitalist marketplace thrive under all conditions? Is the promised freedom of all indeed protected once supercapitalism reigns? And is it appropriate to use the classical economic model of the eighteenth century as the blueprint for contemporary capitalism in a democratic state, especially in light of the fact that, according to Emma Rothschild, "the 'state' and the 'market' were not yet understood as the two imposing and competing dominions of society" (2001, 30)?

And it is exactly with this in mind that I move to reconsider Adam Smith. What we see with Reich and Klein as well as with other politicians and policy makers is a confusion regarding the success and prospects of capitalism, in its superform or otherwise. It is becoming more apparent that policies and laws (the political and legal systems) in fact support or undermine the growth of the marketplace (the economic and financial systems), whether through the regulation of workplace safety and pollution or through tax incentives. In short, the pretense that the marketplace is an isolated enterprise in our midst is more clearly seen as false; instead, it is an intricate system of checks and balances, of gives and takes, of signs and signals, all of which promote certain behaviors and transactions and prevent others. There are some who are sensitive to the complexities of the marketplace and the insights of behavioral economics (drawing heavily on psychology and experiments regarding human behavior, from incentives to the influence of others) and who suggest, as Richard Thaler and Cass Sunstein do, that perhaps there is a middle-way, an alternative way, or what they call a "new path" (Thaler and Sunstein 2008, 13ff). Their version of "libertarian paternalism" attempts to retain a great deal of choices for all consumers (regarding all facets of life) in the marketplace, while having the government provide a set of "nudges," literally pushing us to behave in some ways rather than others (on choices that range from diets and obesity to energy use and pollution), so as to improve our individual well-being and that of the entire country (4–6, 252–253). I mention this middle-ground variant, not in order to promote its specific new path, but rather to illustrate the extent to which the marketplace remains a centerpiece for most policy discussion, and its very existence is never fully questioned. This factual reality, then, sets the stage for our consideration and can therefore not be ignored or dismissed out of hand. Instead, I will be working through the origins of this standard-bearer of the modern agora, where all commerce takes place, where daily exchanges of goods and services, of goodwill and gossip, all take place.

When focusing on the marketplace, the centerpiece of the contemporary world of ideas and material possessions, the person in whose name both the protocapitalists and their critics advocate their respective agendas is being stereotyped and misrepresented. In what follows, I wish to remedy this situation and use Adam Smith's own insights to shed light on some potential remedies to our current maladies. Unlike Shakespeare's eloquent words in the hands of Mark Antony, I do not come to bury Adam Smith, but rather to praise him, honor the subtlety of his pronouncements, and see their lasting insights more than two centuries later. And in doing so, I am keenly aware of the assessment of some, like John Kenneth Galbraith, who admitted that Adam Smith "was categorical about almost nothing, and ever since economists have been at their best when they adhered to his example" (1958, 16). This is what is praiseworthy about Smith and what makes his insights so relevant to the landscape of American pragmatism.

## The Capitalist Framework Revisited: Adam Smith's *Moral Sentiments*

At the heart of the argument of this book is the need for communal cooperation and collaboration in order to achieve personal success. Whether one speaks of the "knowledge industry" (more on this in the second chapter) in general terms or the specific ways in which the cumulative knowledge of a society provides the foundations for the education of present and future generations, one must recognize the communal nature of accumulating knowledge. The image of a lone inquirer or genius, detached from any contact with other members of society and its knowledge repositories (such as libraries and databases in the World Wide Web), is both false and misleading. I hope to explain in more detail this argument in the next chapter. In what follows here, I wish to reexamine the personal and social conditions under which this unfortunate image came into being. A convenient place to start is the works of Adam Smith, in part because of Rothschild's assessment that our contemporary world, not only owes much to the revolutionary and postrevolutionary times of the eighteenth century, but is in fact "defined, in important respects, by the events" of that period (5–6).

In league with other intellectual giants of the past, such as Karl Marx and Charles Darwin, Adam Smith (1723–1790) has captured the imagination of his contemporaries as well as that of generations after him, with the simple coinage of the idea of an "invisible hand" that oversees the marketplace without any regulation. The appeal of this image is twofold: On the one hand, it conjures the image of divine intervention as a benign yet sanctioning oversight that goes far beyond any human power, and on the other hand, it is comforting to know that everything in the marketplace works out smoothly without any laws and regulations, and without any palpable force of any arbitrary authority. As with religious institutions and conventions, the appeal is to a remote and divine authority whose worldly application remains open to sanctioned interpretations by powerful and dominant leaders. The very questioning of their interpretation of divine intervention or withholding becomes blasphemy. So, it is with the invisible hand that Smith ensures the workings of the marketplace, where individual actors find themselves interacting with all other actors according to simple principles that bring about some equilibrium if not harmony. The point here, as Rothschild reminds us, is "the pursuit of self-interest within rules, and the transformation of wealth into political power, including the power to transform rules" (5).

The image of the invisible hand has had the same effect on the collective psyche of Western culture as the image of the "survival of the fittest" or some sort of "natural selection." The image of our survival as a long and continuous battle among all the individuals within the human species, as if we indeed had to fight our way to survival each and every day of our miserable lives, has allowed the social Darwinists, as Richard Hofstadter (1992) reminds us, to explain and justify certain economic and social experiences that could be morally objectionable. For example, if the "fittest" indeed survive and the "less fit" perish, then it makes sense to see the rich among us as the surviving fit and the poor as the condemned unfit. This is not merely an empirical observation, but indeed serves as a moral judgment as well. Two steps downward in this slippery logical slope one can find the basis for the theory of eugenics (e.g., Francis Galton 1869) and for forcible euthanasia of physically and mentally infirm people. The point here is not the reality or the scientific foundation of biological theories and principles, as we shall see in the case of economics, but the power of images and metaphors, platitudes and sound-bites that misrepresent methodological debates or overshadow the fallible character of any scientific idea, theory, and principle. Unlike Rothschild's judgment that this particular image of the invisible hand is a "mildly ironic joke" (116) or that it is "the expression of Smith's faith in a Stoic providence" (131), I take it to be indicative of his scientific views (which Rothschild acknowledges repeatedly when speaking of the appearance of this image in his "History of Astronomy," 116). What distinguishes the scientific enterprise in general, and the scientific community at its best, in particular, is an eagerness to question everything, to be critical of everything posed, and to self-police any proclamation by the most powerful leaders of the scientific establishment. But such an image, a catchy one at that, is difficult to unseat or erase from memory.

When Adam Smith writes about the invisible hand in his 1776 landmark text *An Inquiry into the Nature and Causes of the Wealth of Nations,* it is within the context of the contribution that each individual makes to society without intending to do so. He says that "every individual necessarily labours to render the annual revenue of society as great as he can. He generally, indeed, neither intends to promote the public interest, nor knows how much he is promoting it" (*WN,* 423) In this sense, then, the individual actor, according to Smith, is not an altruist sacrificing himself on behalf of society, neither does he have a clear intention with regard to the results of his action. He is, for all intents and purposes, ignorant of the consequences of his actions, oblivious to the larger picture of the marketplace and how the Gross National Product (GNP) of his society is calculated. Smith continues to say that "by preferring the support of domestic to that of foreign industry, he intends only his own security; and by directing that industry in such a manner as its produce may be of the greatest value, he intends only his own gain, and he is in this, as in many other cases"—here is the image—"led by an invisible hand to promote an end which was no part of his intention" (*WN,* 423). So, is the fact that he is unaware of the invisible hand a bad thing? Should he have noticed it? Would his awareness contribute to a greater "public interest"? Smith responds that "nor is it always the worse for the society that it was no part of it. By pursuing his own interest he frequently promotes that of the society more effectually than when he really intends to promote it" (*WN,* 423).

But as we read along his construction of the image of the invisible hand, we should notice how nuanced his argument is. I would say that it is not tentative, but qualified. He says "nor is it always the worse," rather than saying that it is always better, and likewise he says "he frequently promotes," rather than saying that he always promotes the interest of society as well as his own. I want to emphasize these slight modifications to Smith's own argument or construction of a vision in order to set the tone of what makes his vision at once so powerful and so misleading; powerful, because we immediately grasp the seeming contradiction that from self-interest public interest arises, and misleading, because we might thereby believe that the well-being of society as a whole depends on nothing more than the aggregate of the self-interests of its members. But we should remember here Rothschild's astute observation that Smith's concern with order is not necessarily one that is designed, either by government officials or the divine (135). This is similar to Jean-Jacque Rousseau's warning in his *On the Social Contract* that the general will of a community is not simply the aggregate of all the wills of its members (and is therefore not designed in particular ways nor can it ever be fully anticipated), but rather an emergent quality or framework that transcends individual wills ([1762] 1978). In fact, sometimes self-interest can hurt the society, when, for example, greed and cheating undermine public trust and the smooth operation of the marketplace.

Perhaps another reason why the invisible hand image is so useful and appealing at such a late stage in Smith's book (it appears on page 423) is that is helps explain an earlier discussion of the division of labor, which is the linchpin of Smith's entire book. The opening line of the book says, "The greatest improvement in the productive powers of labour, and the greater part of the skill, dexterity, and judgment with which it is any where directed, or applied, seem to have been the effects of the division of labour" (*WN*, 3). The division of labor makes a society more efficient and thereby allows it to increase its production, enlarge its marketplace, and eventually increase the wealth of its members. And here Adam Smith brings into play his sense of the "propensity in human nature" to "truck, barter, and exchange one thing for another" (*WN*, 13). Propensity, as we know, is a tendency and not an ingrained characteristic, so that even here, Smith is careful and qualified, not certain and dogmatic. Even if we grant Smith his view of human nature, what incentive would one member of society have to trade with another?

According to him (and this, once again, is an oft-cited passage), "it is not from the benevolence of the butcher, the brewer, or the baker, that we expect our dinner, but from their regard to their own interest" (*WN*, 14). Smith removes here any sense of the mysterious or of divine intervention. Our commerce with each other is neither magical nor contrived. Instead, it is a logical consequence of the manner in which each member of the community *promotes,* to use Smith's term, his own interest. There is nothing wrong with this, he reminds us, and we shouldn't expect more than we are getting. The demystification of this process of exchange that eventually allows me to eat my dinner also allows me to enjoy it without pride or guilt. The emotional and moral dimensions seem absent in this context. As he continues to say, "we address ourselves, not to their humanity but to their self-love, and never talk to them of our own necessities but of their advantages" (*WN*, 14). This sounds almost like strategic manipulation, for we do have needs that can only be fulfilled, under the conditions of the division of labor, by others; yet, for Smith, the trick is to let the others believe that their "advantages" are the only ones that allow me to have my dinner. And sure enough, Smith the populist mentions meat first (as an expensive delicacy enjoyed by the rich), mentions bread last (which remains the basic nourishment of the poor), and positions beer in the middle (the lubricant that, when consumed in large quantities, gets the rich and the poor alike drunk).

"Nobody but a beggar," he admonishes his readers, "chuses [*sic*] to depend chiefly upon the benevolence of his fellow-citizens" (*WN*, 14). So, hard as he tries to keep morality out of his image of the butcher and brewer and baker who supply me my dinner, he ends up mentioning benevolence nonetheless. So, if it isn't "benevolence," then what is it? Can one simply close up the argument with "self interest"? Something else must be at hand to support this exchange, to ensure a certain common foundation that is logically and morally sound. When Immanuel Kant (1724–1804) sets up his "categorical imperative," he suggests that the reciprocity of human relations would follow the classical "golden rule" of doing unto others that which you want or expect them to do unto you (and vice versa). Speaking of "self love," Kant brings to bear reason and rationality, the means by which all humans can come to an agreement regardless of their differences: "reason, which should legislate for human nature, is used only to look after the interest of inclinations, whether singly or, at best, in their greatest possible harmony with one another" ([1785] 1981, 19). And with reason on our side, we can appreciate the "law" Kant proposes: "I should never act except in such a way that I can also will that my maxim should become a universal law" (14). Given his insistence that humans respect and not exploit each other, Kant explains that his maxim should be, "act in such a way that you treat humanity, whether in your own person or in the person of another, always at the same time as an end and never simply as a means" (36).

The dual notions of a moral law of behavior being imperative, that is, incumbent on all without exception, and categorical, that is, related to the form of one's action rather than its intended result, explain quite a bit about how Kant navigates between human nature as it is and social relations as they should be. Any action that is instrumental, that strategically seeks to accomplish some end at the expense of someone else (assuming a zero-sum game), is suspect because it could harm someone in the process without any assurances that its result will benefit all those involved. In his words: "the categorical imperative would be one which represented an action as objectively necessary in itself, without reference to another end" (25).

It is here that Kant's procedural and objective proposal comes into play, for he insists that if the process is fair and judicious no matter what the results end up being (given that they cannot be predicted in advance with certainty), then our actions could be justified both to ourselves and to others. So, he rephrases his maxim, his universal law, or norm: "act only according to that maxim whereby you can at the same time will that it should become a universal law" (30). It is with this in mind that we think of Adam Smith and how much he was influenced by and related to the moral thinking of past scholars. Was the invisible hand an image for a universal law or oversight committee that watches over the transactions in the marketplace? Kant's maxim would ensure that one would not cheat another because he or she didn't want to be cheated in return, namely, if they licensed themselves to cheat, they would also sanction someone else to cheat them in return. Here one's own interest, be he a butcher, brewer, or baker, is aligned with that of all others so that some harmony of interests—such as to be honest or to remain trustworthy—regulates each of his or her actions in the marketplace. As focused as Kant and Smith are on the individual actor, they immediately appreciate that there is a social context for personal decisions and behavior, regardless of emotions or intentions.

The strength of this rationalistic approach to human interaction is that it can be explained, discussed, and even debated. The common denominator is reason, which is easily generalized or universalized. Thus, one's own psychological makeup can be subsumed or regulated according to it. Reason is not a substitute for one's feelings or inclinations, but rather a procedural mechanism that provides common understanding among individuals and thereby reduces fear (of the unexpected and unpredictable) and the inherent distrust or alienation we have when encountering a stranger with whom we exchange goods or services in the marketplace. Perhaps what we have here is a false dichotomy between cold rationalistic calculations and human emotions, because, as Rothschild eloquently reminds us, during the late eighteenth century the "life of cold and rational calculation was intertwined with the life of sentiment and imagination," so that the one contributed rather than stood in contrast to the other (1).

What follows Smith's explanation of the exchange among people, and what remains overlooked by those who quote his line about the self-interest of the butcher, brewer, and baker, is the following startling line: "in civilized society he stands at all times in need of the co-operation and assistance of great multitudes, while his whole life is scarce sufficient to gain the friendship of a few persons" (*WN*, 14). This extraordinary admission points to two insights that, in my view, provide the foundation for Smith's actual view of exchange: On the one hand, there must be a sense of cooperation, and on the other hand, real friendship is difficult to come by. Whereas the former is the precondition for the smooth operation of the marketplace, an implicit assumption about the need for the help of others, the multitude, the latter points out his resignation about the few friends one can hope to make in a lifetime. Both insights, then, are about human relationships and to some extent transcend whatever simplistic assumptions are commonly made about human nature and the strategies with which individuals interact with others.

It seems that because the *Wealth of Nations* was written seventeen years after *The Theory of Moral Sentiments* (1759), Smith felt comfortable to use one book as the basis for the other. And those of us who ignore his *Moral Sentiments* might be missing the very foundation on which his classical model of the free exchange in the marketplace, the supply and demand features that determine prices, was built. But is the image of human nature similar in the *Wealth of Nations* and in the *Moral Sentiments*? As D. D. Raphael reminds us, this question was already posed by scholars in the nineteenth century. Citing some scholars of that period, Raphael explains that they all agreed that human actions were ascribed to selfishness in the *Wealth of Nations* and to sympathy in the *Moral Sentiments* (1985, 88). Were these two sentiments complementary or contradictory? Instead of finding Smith inconsistent, their consensus was (from a sociological rather than a psychological perspective) that the one feature of human nature was supplementary to the other, "so that, in order to understand either, it is necessary to study both" (Raphael 1985, 88). Whether one's rational "self- interest" is a higher or a lower moral sentiment in comparison to "benevolence" remains an open question; but what becomes clear is that both texts complement each other and that the chronological priority of the moral discussion provides a solid foundation for the economic one.

If my concern with the cooperative nature of the marketplace is correct, and if this presupposition is essential in allowing individuals to interact with a sense of economic self-interest, then their behavior is not only efficient (given conditions of freedom), but also sanctioned by the social conditions of their interaction. Put differently, if one assumes a harmonious social bond among individuals, however implicit, then any expression of self-love (or self-interest) can be tolerated, for it will not descend into a feeling of greed with its attendant negative connotation. My self-interest will be appreciated, in a Kantian sense, as a way for me to express my needs and for you to recognize them as such, no more and no less; and thereby you will be granted permission to express your needs and the ways in which I, or anyone else in the marketplace, might be able to meet them. We thus confront one another as a mutual-benefit society, a group of people who can identify with one another's needs, rather than as a group of suspicious or skeptical people whose every thought and action is perceived as strategic and possibly injurious to me in preying on the desperate expression of my needs.

Because Raphael's approach is to compare the two books from a sociological perspective, he can say that "sympathy and imagination in the *Moral Sentiments* are the cement of human society in forming socializing attitudes," whereas a "different kind of social bond, mutual dependence, is produced in the division of labor" (93). In both cases, then, the emphasis is on the conditions that bring about the bond among people; in both cases, the "cement" that glues together individual wills and actions allows us to see beyond ourselves and consider ourselves as part of a greater whole, a social fabric in which every move is related and responded to by others. Although Smith uses a different kind of cement in each book, and his emphasis and explanatory models are different, they are not inconsistent or contradictory: They are complementary elements that move us from the individual to society. Kant used reason; Smith uses emotions. One could think of Smith as reverting to some of Rousseau's notions about pity and human compassion being the basic human instincts as they were in the "state of nature" (thus before being corrupted by reason and civilization) that bind us together (Rousseau [1750] 1964). Or one could think of Smith as responding to Thomas Hobbes's dreadful view of humans in their raw and frightful brutality (Hobbes [1651] 1968). Instead, Smith constructs an ethical foundation, with moral sentiments, that could set the tone for how we have become the civilized people we are, exchanging our goods and services in a harmonious fashion with freedom and prosperity.

E. G. West reminds us (when editing the *Moral Sentiments*) that instead of seeing Smith's two works as containing an inconsistent view of human nature, one should appreciate that "in Smith's comprehensive and panoramic view of society, self-interest lives with perfect propriety side by side with Benevolence" (Smith *MS*, 30). Thus what Smith sets up as the three cardinal virtues of prudence, justice, and benevolence remain in the public domain, much like the ancient Greeks' sense of the social context in which such virtues can be tested and displayed. Hence, West explains Smith's economic motivations as they come up in the *Wealth of Nations* as "multidimensional," so that the "stoical instinct for self-preservation, was to him obvious enough. What was more interesting, however, was why men worked so hard *beyond* the requirements of their basic (caloric) needs" (*MS*, 41). And here what comes forth is a certain sociological analysis that is rooted in morality and aesthetics, where a certain balance or harmony among one's virtues provides, as we see later in the *Moral Sentiments,* social approbation.

In Smith's words:

> And hence it is, that to feel much for others, and little for ourselves, that to restrain our selfish, and to indulge our benevolent, affections, constitutes the perfection of human nature; and can only produce among mankind that harmony of sentiments and passions in which consists their whole grace and propriety. As to love our neighbor as we love ourselves is the great law of Christianity, so it is the great precept of nature to love ourselves only as we love our neighbor, or, what comes to the same thing, as our neighbor is capable of loving us. (*MS*, 71–72)

Right away Smith brings to the fore the Golden Rule and the sense of harmony that ought to guide our virtuous life. His sense of self-love is such that it must be condoned by our neighbors so that our fear of them or greed when interacting with them would not overrule our moral and economic behavior. When Smith brings up the benevolence of the butcher and the brewer and the baker, he is right in saying that it is not this particular virtue that is at work at the moment of exchange, but rather the virtue of prudence that guides and tempers their self-preservatory needs. In doing so, Smith does not diminish their other virtues, nor does he turn them into selfish human beings; rather, he reminds us that what accounts for the harmony of marketplace exchanges as a whole is a certain inner level of harmony among our virtues and the ways in which we give credence to them all.

It is with this in mind that Smith keeps on coming back to the theme of the social context in which humans interact and according to which our human nature is informed and receives feedback from others. I quote him here at length so as to dispel misconceptions about what he actually said and what he wrote in his two major texts. In an age of sound bites, one must stop and read carefully and at length. Here is Smith:

> The state or sovereignty in which we have been born and educated, and under the protection of which we continue to live, is, in ordinary cases, the

greatest society upon whose happiness or misery our good or bad conduct can have much influence. It is accordingly by nature most strongly recommended to us. (*MS*, 372)

He continues to explain that not only is the safety and prosperity of the state dependent on our behavior, but that because we have been protected by the state and therefore owe it our best behavior, "its prosperity and glory seem to reflect some sort of honour upon ourselves" (*MS*, 372). We can appreciate right away the reciprocal relationship Smith draws between the individual and the state, where *safety* and *prosperity* and *glory* are interchangeable terms that should motivate us to behave honorably.

Instead of continuing with a close reading of the text, I shall round up this discussion with the image that Smith uses in this text. Whereas the image of the invisible hand from the *Wealth of Nations* provided generations of commentators with the justification for a prohibition on government intervention in the marketplace and for the free-for-all mind-set of classical capitalism, in the *Moral Sentiments* there is another image. This image is of the "impartial spectator," as Smith calls it (*MS*, 422). Smith admits once again, "concern for our own happiness recommends to us the virtue of prudence; concern for that of other people, the virtues of justice and beneficence." But these two sets of virtues are not separate: "Regard to the sentiments of other people, however, comes afterwards both to enforce and to direct the practice of all those virtues," so that the one does not overwhelm the others or does not make us forget them altogether. In his words, then, "no man ... ever trod steadily or uniformly in the paths of prudence, of justice, or of beneficence, whose conduct was not principally directed by a regard to the sentiments of the supposed impartial spectator, of the great inmate of the breast, the great judge and arbiter of conduct" (*MS*, 422).

Worried about restraining the passions and acquiring in each and every one of us a level of balance among all our virtues, Smith keeps this image of the impartial spectator as if it were both a social and a psychological factor or constraint in our behavior. Raphael mentions this parallel (6, 41–43), but draws attention to some differences between Smith's image and Sigmund Freud's view of the superego as both parental and censor-like. Yet, if we cast this parallel in sociopsychological terms, then we can immediately appreciate Smith's concern for an "intimate" impartial spectator, but also one that can watch over all of us, and not only over this or that individual. However personal the admonition remains, its universality (in the Kantian sense of being categorical, that is, generalizable to all of us) means that it has the power for "self-approbation" as well as social approbation. We measure ourselves against this standard, as Smith says, because "it is this inmate who in the evening calls us to an account for all those omissions and violations, and his reproaches often make us blush inwardly" (*MS*, 422–423). This sounds very psychological indeed! But what are we blushing about? What are we accounting for? According to Smith: "both for our folly and inattention to our own happiness, and for our still greater indifference and inattention, perhaps, to that of other people" (*MS*, 422). So, it is not about some set of rules or moral standards we have violated, but rather that we have in the process also hurt others. The social dimension is ever-present in Smith's mind.

So much so, concurs West, that he brings the political dimension or context into the foreground without losing respect for individualism. Using the metaphor of "the great chess board of human society," quotes West, Smith acknowledges that "every single piece has a principle motion of its own," so that individual wills and desires are always present. (West 1976, 126) And sounding almost Popperian in his summary, West explains Smith's political vision as "a kind of pragmatic negative liberty which sees politics, in the constitution-making sense, as an attempt to reach compromise between individuals with admittedly different values. He had arrived, in other words, at the threshold of the open society" (127). Though "open," this society can function only if all participants recognize the differences of all others and allow them to interact as part of a "society."

It would be overstating the case if we were to move on to the next section and leave the impression that the image of the impartial spectator as a moral superego of sorts overshadows the image of the invisible hand. Perhaps the invisible hand belongs to the impartial spectator, and as such, it does influence or guide its oversight. And perhaps this is what Smith has in mind when he says the following:

> Though the standard by which casuists frequently determine what is right or wrong in human conduct be its tendency to the welfare or disorder of society, it does not follow that a regard to the welfare of society should be the sole virtuous motive of action, but only that, in any competition, it ought to cast the balance against all other motives. (*MS*, 482)

I take this statement to be crucial in appreciating not only how we should be reading the advice of Adam Smith in the twenty-first century, but also how we should think of all of our economic and social policies. That is, that one should not foreground one element or set of elements in relation to all others, but rather find a balance among them so that virtue can flourish. If there is competition, and if competition can bring about prosperity, it should do so while maintaining a certain balance with the welfare of society as a whole. Perhaps it would be helpful to recall, as Rothschild implores us, that "the interdependence of commerce and government, in this setting of regulated markets and interested officials, is at the heart of Smith's theory of economic reform, as it was for Turgot and Condorcet" (2001, 32). This kind of interdependence during the eighteenth century was more tilted toward the power of government officials, and therefore Smith's call for individual freedom was so essential at the time; it remains an open question, on pragmatic grounds, whether his call is as crucial still today.

## Planning: Complementing the Marketplace

When speaking of the welfare of a society and the pragmatic strategies that would bring it about, one is not necessarily speaking of the welfare state as we know it today. It is true that the welfare of members of society can be protected or enhanced with legal regulations regarding safety and prudence and by social programs that provide some safety nets or that ensure some fairness in the distribution of income and wealth in the broadest sense of the term. This would include the provision of public goods, such as roads and bridges or what we consider the infrastructure of a nation, as well as security in the form of military forces and police and fire departments. The appreciation of Smith's concern for the well-being of others while maintaining a vibrant marketplace that allows for economic growth should ideally lead to a constellation of economic and political powers with a delicate balance between them. Should the marketplace be completely unregulated, or should there be some government measures that ensure the safety and welfare of society as a whole? With this question in mind we come to reexamine the foundation of the capitalist system as it has been tested and experienced over the past century in the Western world.

As one example, we examine the spectrum of time lines that is bracketed between the old Soviet model of the Five Year Plan and the quarterly American corporate report. Though it maintains a focus on current operations, the quarterly report is both shortsighted (failing to account for changes that take time to appear on the balance sheet) and misleading (representing financial conditions in the best possible ways to ensure favorable stock market trading). The peculiarities of quarterly corporate reports are such that some financial analysts refuse to rely on them and find their ongoing pressure on corporate officers to be detrimental to healthy planning and implementation. So, let us focus instead on longer-term planning and see the extent to which it counterbalances and provides an alternative to the standards of American financial markets. The advantage of the Soviet-like model in planning any sort of expenditure is, of course, that it allows for some infrastructure to be built before any results, in manufacturing or in agriculture, can be measured. The disadvantage, of course, is that at times this horizon may be too long under changing market conditions. A long-term commitment of this sort to capital and human resources alike might turn out to be misguided: How can one tell the future? How can one predict with accuracy what will happen in five years? By the time the plant is built its products might no longer be needed. This is true especially, as we have seen in the past few decades, when we build nuclear power plants that take up to twenty years between the submission of plans and the onset of operation at the facility.

The advantages of long-term planning, on the other hand, are numerous as well. A worker can plan on working in this or that factory for a long time (equivalent, in some cases, to the lifelong employment guarantees of the Japanese system). As a result, the worker can comfortably plan to buy a house (with a thirty-year mortgage), enroll the kids in the local school, and take out a five-year car loan that he feels secure in paying in full. This allows for a stable real estate market, proper planning for school districts (in terms of budgets and physical plant), and for the business community (from car dealers to hardware stores and restaurants) to know what to expect in the future. It is in this sense that long-term planning is useful and even essential for a stable economy.

The models of developmental economics throw light not only on what should be done in less-developed countries, but also on what can be done within developed countries. Though the issues might seem on the surface quite different—less-developed countries need an infrastructure, for example, that is already in place in developed countries—when considered in terms of the technological transformation of the economy and government intervention, it seems that there are more rather than fewer parallels that help reassess a "pure" capitalist system. For example, Kevin Murphy and his associates analyze the situation of an "imperfectly competitive economy with aggregate demand spillovers," so that a "good equilibrium" can be reached (Murphy et al. 1989). In other words, both the classical and the neoclassical models are too "pure" or "perfect" in their model presentations and are therefore less than "real." One solution to this problem, as Lawrence Boland has argued, is to revise the very conception and methodological approach to economics and turn them, if not on government intervention, then on an appreciation of a foundational "disequilibrium" of markets that may or may not eventually lessen (Boland 1986). This, incidentally, is more in line with Smith's own conception of the need for government intervention under certain conditions so as to ensure the fairness of the marketplace (see Rothschild 2001, 82). According to these qualifications, one can more readily appreciate the ongoing disequilibrium from which markets suffer, whether because of imperfect competition or poor foresight (inefficiencies and price fluctuation, economic cycles and crises). It is with this in mind that I am turning now to consider the lessons learned from developmental economics.

Paul Rosenstein-Rodan, in a couple of his landmark essays for the early past century, argued about these two main features of planning (e.g., 1943, and Murphy et al. 1989). Couched in terms of his own experience in the World Bank post–World War II and as a member of the Committee of Nine of the Alliance for Progress, this was not a choice between socialism (long-term planning) and capitalism (short-term reports), but rather between chaos and order, between coordinated development and haphazard infusion of capital in counterproductive ways. Though his own concern was in the area of developmental economics, this came as a logical consequence of what he saw during the middle of the last century as an international division of labor, where capital and labor could be supplemented in different markets, and where large-scale planning could be warranted (Rosenstein-Rodan 1943). Four main themes come out of his work: First, in order to enjoy a successful developmental effort there must be, up front, a commitment to building an infrastructure; second, the key to successful planning is a coordinated exchange of information, rather than the dictates of this or that agency; third, the developmental global map is north versus south, rather than west versus east; and fourth, the idea that the doctrine of development should consider the "transfer of financial and technological resources to less-developed countries (LDCs) as an international income tax" (Rosenstein-Rodan 1981). For our purposes, the first two themes are most relevant.

As for the infrastructure, his concern was that foreign aid would fixate on building a shoe factory, for example, and forget about its dependence on raw materials and their dependence, in turn, on a usable road reaching this factory. Likewise, without electricity, no machines could be operating, and without some warehousing depot, no efficient shipping could be undertaken. In short, unlike the recommendations of Schumacher (1973), for example, where "small is beautiful," namely, where local, small-scale intervention seems sufficient to ensure economic health and growth, Rosenstein-Rodan suggests that a "big push" is necessary to achieve any economic health and growth (see also 1961). Incremental intervention might temporarily help this or that individual, this or that village (as has been practiced by the 2006 Nobel Peace Prize recipient, the Bangladeshi economist Muhammad Yunus (2007), who has initiated microcredit, or small loans, in poor areas), but will never have an overall impact that will change the course of the economy. In some countries after the Industrial Revolution, this meant bridges to connect one region with another (UK); in others it meant the construction of a railroad system that allowed goods to be shipped cheaply enough from coast to coast (as allowed for by an 1862 congressional appropriation in the United States). But a bridge cannot be built by a small village alone, nor can a railroad be built by a town here and there. Instead, a coordinated effort must be made to acquire land and ensure the most effective routes through a region, with the approval and consent of all those involved. Once in place, this kind of infrastructure can enhance the development of many small factories and businesses and provide the conditions for their growth and prosperity. In many cases this kind of Big Push is provided by government agencies rather than by corporations, but this need not be the exclusive model. Some companies are big and wealthy enough to undertake an entire development of the infrastructure, as can be seen with land developers who provide their plats with sewer and water systems, roads, and electrical wiring ready to connect to the rest of the grid.

What is of interest in the case of developmental economics is that its main doctrines and principles draw from the insights as well as the critiques of neoclassical economics and provide a continuum for current discussion of any economic theory or economic policies (e.g., Scitovsky 1954 on "external economies"). This makes sense because some parts of the country, and at times some segments of the economy, could benefit from being approached as if they existed under the conditions of "less-developed" countries. This means that taking a more "macro," rather than "micro" view of the economy is necessary at times: A city provides tax incentives for a manufacturer to move into town under the assumption that it will provide jobs and increase spending in town on goods ranging from housing to clothing and food. There is a methodological issue here that requires a comment: Though the classical and neoclassical models favored growth both as a condition and a goal for the efficient operation of the marketplace, "economic theory can determine the necessary though not the sufficient conditions of growth. The so-called 'non-economic' factors account for the gap . . . " (Rosenstein-Rodan 1969, 6). This means that concern with external factors of the economy, be they political or legal, is essential for the appreciation of the conditions that enhance or retard development and growth. Whether this should push us toward a coordinated planning of the economy or of any country in the international marketplace remains an open, but intriguing question.

This way of thinking was on Rosenstein-Rodan's mind when he shifted his own concern from the efficiency of the capitalist marketplace to the global marketplace, for what would be these external factors? How would we have access to them? And, more specifically, who would have access to these noneconomic factors? Are they available to all of us, or only those more closely aligned with government officials and the captains of the financial markets? It is with these questions in mind that he suggested that "the first and primary purpose of planning is to make available additional information to decision-makers of a type which market forces cannot possibly provide" (1963, 3). Though the markets provide substantial information about what past behavior was like and at times give a quick read on economic conditions at the present (great new computers can churn a great deal of data and thereby increase labor productivity), they are bound to be less useful for predicting future trends. But planning, as envisioned here, can provide future-oriented information that is invaluable: who plans to hire more workers or close a plant, who is planning to infuse cash into the financial markets or withdraw it and transfer it into foreign markets. In his words: "This information alone would reduce risk, change investment decisions in the direction of improving both the amount and the composition of investment" (3).

Smith already appreciated the dynamic nature of the economy and its need to be monitored if not regulated, and since then it comes as no surprise that the shift toward an ever-more technologically sophisticated economy would require a collaborative effort. "Large-scale planned industrialization," according to Rosenstein-Rodan, would create a "complementary system," and as such would "reduce the risk of not being able to sell, and, since risk can be considered as cost, it reduces costs" (Rosenstein-Rodan 1943, 249–250). How true these words ring today with the present financial crisis in the United States (more on this in the next section). For those skeptical of this recommendation, Rosenstein-Rodan continues to explain elsewhere: "Even if neither direct instruments of planning (public investment) or [*sic*] indirect means (incentives and disincentives for private investment) were to be used, a purely 'indicative' planning would improve the risks of economic operations" (Rosenstein-Rodan 1963, 4).

As far as Rosenstein-Rodan and most of the economists in this field are concerned, the main ingredient by which the marketplace should be supplemented is access to information. The Smithian model was predicated on individual (hence small) actors whose own behavior was so marginal in terms of the entire performance of the market that their personal risks and by extension the risk to the entire system was minimal. Likewise, their knowledge was limited by their limited personal exposure to but a few market transactions. This, of course, was the main virtue of this classical model: No individual would be powerful enough to affect the entire marketplace. Of course, in time capitalism tended toward growth, consolidation, and monopolistic behavior by large companies, such that the barriers to entering the marketplace to begin with were getting higher and higher. Likewise, weighing the risks and benefits became more complicated because of the disproportionate impact one company might have relative to others in the marketplace. The great freedom and equality that characterized the classical model was evaporating before our eyes, and this, oddly enough, was happening at the same time as a greater premium was put on democratic institutions and social programs. In addition to capital, collusion among the more powerful in the market could be enhanced by their preferential access to information; for the planner in the developmental model, the issue is not abandoning capitalism as such (with its division of labor and promised growth), but rather modifying it enough to ensure sustained and fair growth in cooperation with the public and private sectors. (This, in fact, is the core of Reich's book mentioned at the beginning of the chapter.) So, what is under consideration here is not a comparison between socialism and capitalism, but rather between the painful and painless varieties of planned capitalism. Perhaps one way of thinking about this mechanism or process would be to bring it back to the political and moral fold and revisit the pragmatic insights of Karl Popper or his insights within a pragmatic strategy.

## The Middle Ground: Popperian Influence

Though some of Karl Popper's disciples and critics claim that his thought and academic work have been absolutist in the sense of being rigidly rule-bound methodologically and conservative politically, and though some have used this characterization as an excuse to label, categorize, and in some cases dismiss everything he said or wrote, I would like to suggest an alternative. From my perspective, there is more to Popper's thought and work than is usually given credit, because in every case his thought and work are more nuanced and subtle, more open-minded and ready to accommodate novel factors and variables as they come about, in a pragmatic way similar to what we have seen in Smith's and Rosenstein-Rodan's works. Moreover, as I have suggested in the preface, Popper's views could be compared to the kind of American pragmatism associated with thinkers, such as Charles Sanders Pierce or William James, even though they did not address economic issues the way Popper did. So, of particular interest to the present discussion, the appreciation of Popper's collaboration with and influence of the Austrian School of Economic Thought did not preclude him from realizing that there might be a role for government intervention. It seems that for him, it was always a question of degree—a question of the practical conditions that affect the theoretical principles—a very Marxian attitude, if you wish, but also one that is exemplified by the pragmatic promoters of the welfare state who have found a way to combine social concerns within the marketplace or use market strategies to achieve social goals.

In what follows, I suggest embarking on what have been traditionally called "thought experiments," insofar as these are idealized narratives of contemporary questions (in a Weberian sense of Ideal Types) that are answered in Popperian terms. I turn now to examine briefly three major issues that plague the American landscape: immigration, mortgage funding, and universal health care insurance. Though some critics would object that addressing these issues could render my discussion obsolete or make it dated within a few years, I say that there are three main reasons to focus on these particular cases. First, these cases are both symptomatic of a particular set of conditions in the American economic and social landscape and of the structural problems that are inherent in a confused or inconsistent capitalism marketplace, where appeal to political and legal protection is coupled with a rejection of any government interference. Second, as we have seen in Smith's own work (*WN*), when he focuses on tariff issues and specific legislation of his day, his theoretical concerns come to life; his model comes to life and makes sense in light of these particular illustrations and not despite them. Smith's concerns were real enough to his contemporaries so that we today, more than two hundred years later, can relate to what he wrote. And finally, in order to anchor my philosophical examination, however historically informed it might be, in reality and in real-world problems that require solutions, I find it compelling to give concrete examples of policy matters that set the tone now and will for some time in regard to the peculiarities of the capitalist marketplace in a modern democracy. As we shall see in Chapter 3, these issues are symptomatic of larger, international problems and shed light on what might be ways of approaching the global economy.

As I write this book within the time period of the 2008 presidential election debates, these issues are paramount, even if the rhetorical devices employed by candidates of either of the major parties, Democrats and Republicans, are simpleminded and superficial. Unfortunately, we are less likely to find in present-day debates historical icons, like Thomas Jefferson, who were both intellectually engaged and politically astute (with all the reservations associated with the hypocrisy of being a freedom lover who owned and preyed on slaves). It is because our contemporary society has the weight of legal and political precedents that Popper's middle ground, so to speak, is quite attractive. From my perspective, though viewed by good old-fashioned liberals as a reactionary conservative, Popper had no problem with congressional legislation and government control of policies, as long as they retain their mediating status among individual citizens and the corporate community. Perhaps his approach makes sense if one assumes, in the manner Smith has done, the participants to be indeed responsible individuals (and corporations) and not greedy and irresponsible ones who respect each other and the minimal rules of the marketplace. But to be sure, my intent here is not to defend Popper or ensure a positive legacy for his intellectual contributions; instead, I wish to illustrate the extent to which someone's ideas and philosophical principles could be useful in approaching and even solving practical economic and social problems, and the solutions in turn transcend simple ideological commitments (that reveal themselves in political propaganda).

Let us begin with immigration to the United States. In a country that numbered roughly three hundred million citizens in 2007, there are claimed to be anywhere from eight to twenty million undocumented or illegal residents (according to the Center for Immigration Studies 2007 that uses data from a variety of sources, such as the Department of Homeland Security and the brokerage firm Bear Stearns). No matter what source one consults, this figure of undocumented or illegal immigrants in the United States is high enough to warrant concern by public officials. The distribution of this group of people is primarily in the southwestern states that are along the Mexican border (even though they are also numerous in any large metropolitan center), and the majority of this group is reportedly Mexican in origin (even though it includes other nationals both from central and south America as well as from eastern Europe and southeastern Asia). Some are recent arrivals, whereas others have been in the country for more than one generation. The spectrum of views concerned with "what to do with them" ranges from "do nothing," on one extreme, to "expel immediately," on the other. Obviously, many alternative proposals are offered in between, such as "legalize their status with fines," "expel and invite them to apply for immigration within five years," and so on.

The arguments that are used from the two extremes can be delineated into two camps, here called "law and order" and "fairness": The first worry about the legalization of an illegal, even criminal, act of smuggling people across national borders (allowing post hoc something that was not allowed to begin with), whereas the second casts the matter in humanitarian and pragmatic terms so as to acknowledge the contribution of this group of people to the maintenance and functioning of the economy (most are hard-working individuals who perform menial and manual jobs others will not). So, between the hard-core legalists and the soft-core humanists, there is a wide range of opinions and proposals to resolve our very own *Gastarbeiters* problem. One should note here that President Bush proposed a "guest worker program" in January 2004 that was considered a veiled amnesty of sorts that would have a humanitarian appeal (although the president himself remains a staunch conservative).

This, of course is not the first time the United States has faced immigration debates, especially because its very growth and success has historically been driven by waves of immigrants, whether through New York's Ellis Island on the East Coast some one hundred years ago or California's Silicon Valley on the West Coast more recently. The Europeans have been supplanted in this role by Asians, and the refugee status claimed by some of the former has been replaced by an entrepreneurial spirit of some of the latter (including the Israeli brain drain and the wave of digital-genius Indian immigrants). How do Mexican laborers fit into this continuous wave of immigration? How should we conceptualize their plight and our responsibilities in philosophical as well as practical terms? Invoking Popper at this junction might be of use.

Aligning his political economy thought with the Austrian School of the early previous century (especially Friedrich Hayek), and having a fairly laissez-faire attitude toward the marketplace, with an overriding distaste for anything resembling socialist central planning, Popper would encourage the free flow of labor across national boundaries (akin to what we observe today among the members of the European Union, where work permits are no longer hindrances to relocation). Let us recall, in this context, that Hayek understood the need for state intervention in order to provide the conditions of competition: "In no system that could be rationally defended would the state just do nothing. An effective competitive system needs an intelligently designed and continuously adjusted legal framework as much as any other" (Hayek 1944, 39ff.). And here one might suggest that Popper sounds a bit more like Karl Marx, in his *Communist Manifesto* of 1872, urging the international working class to unite across the world, than Adam

Smith, in his *Wealth of Nations* of 1776, who worried about the free flow of goods from one country to another, even while encouraging open markets. Likewise, Popper would welcome any infusion of relatively cheap labor that is underemployed in its home countries into a growing foreign economy, what Marx called the reserve army of unemployed labor, and what others call today our Western hemisphere's "outsourcing" opportunities abroad, so as to improve the lot of the unemployed (or underemployed) while keeping in check rising labor costs. And finally, it would stand to reason that given his own experiences before, during, and after World War II, the protection of immigrants' rights and the accommodation they deserve in their respective host countries would be legally enshrined.

Now, of course, this line of thinking, this attitude toward the labor marketplace can be seen as being a bit more complex than presented so far. As we have seen in the previous section, some developmental economists, such as Rosenstein-Rodan, have perceived the labor market internationally rather than domestically and had no problem considering the transfer of technologies to underskilled labor pools across national boundaries. Though it would seem that there is an inherent contradiction between Rosenstein-Rodan's "big-push" for infrastructure and Popper's "piecemeal engineering" (see Popper 1943 vol. 2, 158ff.), it is easily overcome when we appreciate the conditions set by Rosenstein-Rodan: Government agencies do not dictate what should be done, but rather provide the forum for the exchange of information according to which banks and corporations, individuals and local communities, decide how to go about implementing a change in investment strategies. As we have seen previously, providing the conditions for coordinated market knowledge reduces risk-taking and the pain of market cycles and ensures, to some extent, a more efficient market mechanism without thereby taking away the importance of individual actors in the marketplace (the kind of responsibility mentioned previously). It is in this sense, then, that piecemeal economic engineering is made possible. It would therefore seem that unlike the position that the conservative right wing in the United States holds in the current debates over immigration, Popper would strike a more liberal stance, perhaps in the classical British nineteenth-century sense, that would see the infusion of cheaper labor not only in economic terms but also as a humanitarian issue deserving some government intervention, thereby providing the legal and economic frameworks within which individual actors can safely work.

One must remember that for Popper, police-like regimes, whether fascist or totalitarian, are anathema; it is the *open society* in the broadest sense of the term that he valued and promoted. The openness is not limited to philosophical debates and theories and the occasional political change of guard without violence, but is intended to be *practical* so as to allow for the free flow of humans from one country to another (given changing economic or social circumstances) as well, treating them as individuals whose choices regarding homeland and occupation would be defended socially and morally and protected economically and legally. His concern, therefore, would remain with the individual immigrant, young or old, male or female, who makes the decision to cross a border and establish a new life for herself or himself. But beyond this general theoretical and practical principle, Popper would always be on the side of those who suggest incremental changes in policy, so that his famous piecemeal engineering principle would become operational (Popper 1943 vol. 2). If you juxtapose the respect for protecting individual decisions and choices as an ultimate value of some sort with a deep appreciation that every social policy (government coordination that is seen as planning or engineering) must be tentative and gradual, allowing for mistakes to surface so as to correct them, then you have a Popperian recipe for immigration policy in the United States.

We can turn now to the second case I wish to examine here, namely, the latest mortgage-loan debacle that has crippled the financial markets and that is threatening to bring about a fatal recession in the United States with ripple effects that are already reverberating across the globe. The origins of this debacle are innocent enough at some level and have become more egregious as time has gone by. At the end of his first presidential term, President George W. Bush encouraged home ownership by all Americans as a way to motivate the middle class to have a stake in the economy and take advantage of the private property rights democratic capitalism offers every citizen. In some sense, this is a laudable ideological commitment by a president whose own intellectual sophistication has been questioned throughout his presidency. But, as the chairman of the Federal Reserve Board, Ben Bernanke, testified before the Congressional Committee on Financial Services, the issue of making house ownership affordable has deeper origins than merely a cyclical downturn in this particular market.

As part of the New Deal, there was a great push toward home ownership with government support, such that Fannie Mae and Freddie Mac were established as independent but government-backed entities that guarantee or ensure the payment of interest to lending institutions. As time goes by, one can see the extent to which these institutions themselves have come under closer scrutiny in terms of their independence, government-dependence, and the role they play in the financial markets. As both institutions have been taken over by the government (as of September 2008), the general argument proposed here for a pragmatic solution to economic crises has been validated. To simplify an awkward and arbitrary system, standard credit scores were established to assess the creditworthiness of individual borrowers, and local banks and mortgage companies were allowed to enter this market for financing home purchases. "Subprime mortgages," explained Bernanke, "are loans intended for borrowers who are perceived to have high credit risk" (Bernanke 2007). Credit has been extended on those terms for more than twenty years, but because of national standards for credit scoring, risk assessment became easier for lenders, and the market expanded from its traditional small base into wider national and international markets. "Regulatory changes and the ongoing growth of the secondary mortgage market increased the ability of lenders, who once typically held mortgages on their books until the loans were repaid, to sell many mortgages to various intermediaries, or 'securitizers'" (Bernanke 2007). This meant, in turn, that these institutions could bundle mortgages of various risks and sell them to investors whose sole concern was the anticipated cash flow of these bundled securities. This innovative process, explained Bernanke, increased the number of households that could and in fact did own their homes in the 1990s.

So far the narrative sounds positive. But let us retell this narrative from a different perspective. In order to purchase a house one needs to have sufficient funds, and if not, be able to borrow the funds to purchase the house. This prospect seems daunting to most people, because coming up with a few hundred thousand dollars up front is unrealistic; hence, borrowing is the only way to fulfill the American Dream (with the post–World War II image of a white picket fence, etc.). The qualifications for house purchases were reasonable and ensured that buyers did not buy expensive homes they could not afford (matching dreams with realities). Buyers had to come to a closing with a down payment of up to 20 percent of the purchasing price (so that they had to save their money if they were committed to buying a house), show evidence of steady employment with sufficient income to pay the mortgage (that included interest on the borrowed money plus some principal spread over, traditionally, thirty years). But what if the push is to purchase a home even though one fails to meet these qualifications?

Assuming the presidential mandate and playing off the American consumerist dream of personal property ownership, while also being financially sophisticated, financial institutions began calculating their risks of lending money to less and less qualified borrowers, so that their own risk assessment would justify what eventually became known as "subprime interest" (as was explained previously). Moreover, to skip the saving period that would take borrowers to come up with down payments, borrowers would be promised 100 percent of the purchase price as their loan, and income records were less rigorously scrutinized. The risk of this practice, as we have seen, was mitigated in a variety of ways, not the least of which was the ingrained belief that the housing market would continue to grow and display price increases indefinitely. This meant, for example, that the increasing value of a home (by anywhere from 5 percent to 10 percent annually) would render the original loan a lower percentage of the total value of the house, so that in case of default, the full amount of the original loan could be realized (even if the house sold at a foreclosure for 10 to 20 percent discount from the going market prices).

The increase in borrowing and the reduction in direct risk to lenders who immediately sell their loans to the secondary markets created a double effect. On the one hand, great incentives were posed to provide as many loans as possible and receive transaction fees regardless of the responsibility to provide full risk assessments of individual borrowers (because the scoring mechanism seemed trustworthy), and on the other hand, adjustable-rate mortgages were offered with initial low rates that increased much more quickly than anyone anticipated (partially because "teaser" rates were unrealistically low). If the scrutiny of potential borrowers is compromised, and if the rates are so high that borrowers cannot afford to make monthly payments, foreclosures are bound to happen more often than under otherwise normal market conditions. Add to this mixture falling house prices, so that lenders cannot even be repaid the value of the loan (regardless whether some amount was paid as a down payment), and default cases become even more problematic because lenders cannot simply liquidate the loan and be made whole. With increased losses by primary and secondary lenders, the whole housing market has been rapidly collapsing insofar as lenders become more reluctant to underwrite the new loans that usually fuel the market for new homes (though there are other factors that account for an expanding economy, such as wars). The purchase of a home occasions other economic activity, for instance, the purchase of durable goods (such as refrigerators, washing machines, furniture, and all other goods that are needed to provision a home). With the decrease of the former, the rest of the manufacturing markets feel the stress. This snowball effect is what has alarmed the United States and the rest of the world, given, incidentally, that close to 70 percent of the U.S. gross national product is based on consumer spending, which dramatically decreases with any whiff of a presumed "crisis." Sometime in the middle of 2007, the subprime mortgage market collapsed, when more and more foreclosures threatened to ruin some large financial institutions.

Inventory of unsold houses was increasing, prices of existing and new houses were declining (following the classical model of supply and demand), and tearful citizens were interviewed across media outlets. The actual number of families who might be losing their homes because of the current crisis comes close to two million (Center for American Progress 2007). What should be done?

Some would argue that greed drove the housing markets, on the part of both financial institutions and mortgage banks, whose fee-collection alone was astronomical, and homebuyers, who set their sights too high and bought what they could not afford. Regardless of how we got to this point, should individual borrowers suffer the consequences of their own actions? Should they have been alerted to the potential for changes in the financial markets and the increase of their adjustable rates? Should the financial institutions bear the burden of their own reckless behavior? Or should the government intervene? Some would suggest that, if we do indeed have a capitalist economy with marketplaces that find their equilibrium (or not) because of the fluctuation of supply and demand and with prices that move in tandem with such fluctuations, then a collapse of a commodity (mortgage) can happen and should not be interfered with by government agencies (Utt 2007). If a few giant companies declare bankruptcy, so be it. If a few thousand homeowners lose their homes, so be it. This is the price of enjoying capitalism as a system of free choice (even when the choice is a bad one). Others have clamored for government intervention, for the rescue of the financial institutions and the borrowers who might be losing their homes. Government guarantees will keep interest payments from becoming delinquent, and the rest of society, through their taxes, will subsidize the greed or lack of foresight of fellow citizens. What would someone like Popper say? It should be noted here that my use of Popper is meant as a useful thought experiment relating to potential thinkers and advisors who might help solve some of the problems facing our nation, and by extension, the rest of the world (not because we are at its center, but because the capitalist system has become globally interconnected).

For a pragmatist like Popper, it is never an "all or nothing" endgame, but rather an understanding that there is a spectrum of choices we can all make, and that these choices have political or moral frameworks within which they are protected. The "we" in the previous sentence applies both to the individuals who make decisions and to the government and its agencies that make decisions for the welfare of society as a whole. So, Popper would encourage some government intervention to temporarily support a failing mortgage market if there were guarantees that that market would benefit from the intervention and soon become healthy again. The government has the fiduciary responsibility to regulate large corporations so as to protect individual citizens who come in contact with them (as is seen with the Food and Drug Administration that ensures the safety of our food supplies). This is different from dictating what financial instruments should or should not enter the financial markets. Rather, it would be a regulative mechanism that would protect the markets from abuses or from the pain suffered when cyclical fluctuations disrupt the lives of millions at a time. It is a way of finding a middle ground between the extreme absolutes of no government intervention whatsoever, called for by the classical capitalist model, and an overly oppressive government intervention of the socialist kind that would directly own and control all banks and financial institutions.

The key to this decision would be the rational arguments mustered on behalf of intervention. By this I mean the way to interpret market forces and market cycles so as to smooth the ups and downs of the economy in order to cause as little human suffering as possible. This is different from eliminating market cycles, which is only possible if one were to abandon capitalism altogether and endorse centrally planned socialism. But the freedom to enjoy economic prosperity is moderated by the risk of failing to enjoy any prosperity at all, because one might have chosen wrongly, even when the choice was freely undertaken. So, the rational questions to ask before acting would be: Will it work? Are the effects of the intervention temporary or permanent? Will the intervention restore public confidence and strengthen the markets overall? Or, by contrast, would government intervention exacerbate the situation (as is repeatedly debated in the case of the Federal Reserve Board's increasing or decreasing the prime rate)? Because housing market conditions are constantly changing, and because their changes are linked to the conditions of other markets (e.g., manufacturing), one must eschew, once again, absolute ideological or philosophical principles and endorse the Popperian "situational logic" (see Sassower 2006, ch. 3). By this I mean the recognition that many regulators express of finding solutions that pertain to the particular context within which they are made. The problem, of course, is that the "situation" or the context is itself a moving target, so that whenever a solution is proposed, its application (given the shift in time and circumstances) might be already a misapplication.

Incidentally, the 2007 Bank of Sweden prize in economics in memory of Alfred Nobel was given to three economists who developed the "mechanism design theory," which attempts to systematically take into account the realities of economic life so as to structure economic incentives and institutions to enhance social welfare. The appreciation of the need for and influence of institutions (government agencies as well as private clearinghouses) overcomes the basic shortcoming of the idealized competitive marketplace that cannot, for example, deal with the need to reduce pollution. Some have called this approach to applied economics Institutionalism, whereas others have tried to retain it within the mainstream of economic theory (see Hodgson 2004). The only "solution" to this and many other social or global problems is the vigilant continuation of providing and adjusting incentives as partial solutions, so that no single solution is ever solidified or revolutionized. One could say, then, that it is in this Popperian spirit that the Federal Reserve Board meets regularly and that its presidents bring to the forum their diverse data from their respective regions of the United States. Likewise, this follows my argument in the first section of this chapter, where I suggested that Smith always understood his model of the invisible hand as being supported by the impartial spectator who ensures some form of social benevolence.

The last item that I will examine here, and of paramount interest in the United States, perhaps differently construed from the European experience of socializing many public goods and services, is health care. To some extent, health care insurance has become the litmus test of how Americans view their society. Out of three hundred million citizens, there are close to fifty million who are working but uninsured (e.g., Bernasek 2007). There is no mandatory insurance provision at the federal level, even though some states, such as Massachusetts and California, have enacted legislation that attempts to mandate health insurance the way all other states mandate car insurance for drivers. Whether you like it or not, by law you must have car insurance, namely, you can be fined and your driver's license can be suspended if you do not have insurance. This illustrates an approach to the public domain and our interactions within it that commits us to being responsible for the consequences of our actions, may they be car accidents or sickness, and ensuring that the public burden is fairly shared by all citizens.

Should citizens in a democracy be forced to have health insurance? Should the government mandate that they get it directly or through their employers? What should be done with the unemployed or with children? Do we have a responsibility for taking care of all the citizens of this country? On some level, we already do, because when services are rendered to the uninsured, the premiums of the insured go up proportionately to cover such costs. On another level, there are fewer incentives for insuring oneself if it is commonly known that hospitals cannot legally deny care to indigent or uninsured patients. But perhaps we should reflect for a moment on what the very term *health insurance* means, because like all kinds of insurances, it provides guaranteed access to health care, regardless of the circumstances of one's ailment. Does it matter if the national government collects the premiums and guarantees payment to clinics and hospitals, or if it directly owns and operates them? Should health insurance in a capitalist society be of necessity or by definition in the hands of private corporations? Can large corporations self-insure? In 1880s Germany, Bismarck tried out this idea (of national insurance), but the United Kingdom developed the first national health care system in 1948. Most developed countries (from Western Europe to some in Asia) have some sort of a universal health care provision, except for the United States. So, what should be done in America today?

Some politicians from both parties are proposing specific measures in order to find solutions to our mounting health care problems (or *crisis*, as some have termed it). The minute social programs are suggested, Popper would readily agree, there is a hint of socialism in the air, and the inefficiencies of government agencies are brought to the fore. For example, there is some question as to whether the European system is indeed superior to the one in the United States. The measurement used by some is based on a Commonwealth Fund study that compared the quality of the American health system with those of five other countries and found that "despite spending twice as much per capita, the U.S. ranks last or near last on basic performance measures of quality, access, efficiency, equity, and healthy lives" (Capell 2007, 1). The trick, of course, is the definitions used in assessing "quality" and the numerical or statistical data provided by various national or private agencies. In the United States, we spend more money on health through government budgets (close to one-third) and private organizations (close to 15 percent of our gross domestic product), but our life expectancy is lower than that in most European countries and our infant mortality rate is higher. Moreover, the World Health Organization rated the French health care system in 2001 the best in the world, whereas the United States was ranked thirty-seventh; likewise, whereas the French spent about $3,500 per capita on their system, the United States spent $6,100 per capita. The differences are so great that they invite more serious questioning (Dutton 2007).

Instead of using "single-payer insurance" or "universal health insurance" or a "national health system," the American model has opted to rely on a mixture of private insurance companies and government safety nets. But relying on the private sector is problematic as well, for a variety of reasons. To begin with, if the ultimate goal in a capitalist system is profit maximization, then (all things being equal) the less they have to pay for care, the better off the corporation (whereupon denying coverage or reimbursement for medical procedures and services is the norm, rather than the exception). Moreover, as capitalist entities, insurance companies are prone to assess risk and are likely to deny access to insurance to high-risk clients (thus creating the reality of about 15 to 20 percent of the American population being without any coverage). Along the same lines, as participants in the marketplace, insurance companies are prone to seek low-cost solutions to medical problems, so as to decrease their own costs and thus "cut corners" or compromise on the quality of care (for instance, to use less-qualified professionals and avoid specialists). Finally, any financial speculations by insurance companies that collect premiums today in order to pay out for future services will be paid by current policyholders (in the case of speculative losses) in the form of increased premium fees. Should private insurance companies be regulated? Should we intervene in their operational methods and impose government guidelines?

Once again, the questions plaguing health care provision in developed democracies with capitalist marketplaces must be framed in terms of capitalism versus socialism. The Popperian approach has traditionally favored reliance on market mechanisms rather than the wisdom (or lack thereof) of government agencies and their functionaries. But is this true only of consumer goods, such as food and clothing? Should this be true also of our health? In the United States we at least regulate pollution and believe that it is the government's duty to mandate and enforce clean breathing air for the citizens. But what should we do about preventive medicine? We know that it is cheaper to invest in the health of a pregnant mother than wait until she has some complications during or after delivery. If uninsured, the mother will find her way to the emergency room and be treated at the expense of the rest of the insured community, or at times the city or state (which is the case in some hospitals that are city-owned or subsidized by the state), rather than investing much less in making sure her pregnancy and her offspring are healthy (and thus cost less to care for). The relationship between the individual citizen and her or his entitlement to health care, on the one hand, and the duties or responsibilities of the state to care for all citizens equally and fairly, on the other, remains a political as well as an ethical issue (more on this in Sassower and Cutter 2007).

Popper would approach hospitals and pharmaceutical companies as free agents in the marketplace and therefore try to impose as little regulation on them as possible, except to ensure their compliance with state and federal laws that protect the lives of patients and ensure their safety in the hands of medical professionals. But at the same time, he would also appreciate the extent to which the private sector benefits from being protected by political and legal frameworks (as Karl Polanyi recognized in 1944) that allow certain tax deductions, for example, for the research and development of new drugs and instruments (for more on Polanyi, see Stehr 2008, 26–28, 55–57). Perhaps Popper would favor a private-sector framework for insurance as well, as long as insurance agents would not deny access to insurance or funding procedures that are needed, with excuses that are based on greed and profitability. Put differently, using his piecemeal engineering concept, Popper would suggest incremental policy changes that could be tested practically and improved on over time. This would not mean the switch of health care in the United States from capitalism to socialism overnight, but rather an ongoing experimentation with and testing of the overall national commitment to take care of all the citizens in a reasonable fashion. When insurance companies abuse their role in society, the government must be watchful and take measures to correct these abuses and prevent their recurrence. When patients abuse their rights and overtax the health care system, they too must be accountable for their behavior. And within this gradually changing framework, rights and duties can be reassessed, and quality of care expectations can be modified.

As I have tried to argue in this chapter, the customary labels of old along with those of contemporary media pundits fall short of the nuances and complexities of life. Moreover, there is a treasure trove of classical texts with a great many insights that could be of help in the contemporary setting. To see Adam Smith simply as the father of classical capitalism, or worse, as the champion of greed and fear, is to miss his greatness. Likewise, to see developmental economics as a subfield of research confined to bleeding-heart liberals who care about under- or less-developed countries and who plead for foreign aid, is to miss their own indebtedness to neoclassical economics. And finally, to miss the political and moral underpinnings of any intellectually interesting thought is to ignore what makes that thought exciting and applicable. The ideas of Smith, Rosenstein-Rodan, and Popper are used here with all the critical reverence they deserve, so as to be pragmatically applied in an economically confused period in our history. We can learn from them, we can critically apply some of their ideas without buying into their entire framework, appreciating all along the kind of detached engagement that keeps us intellectually alive. Most of all, as we shall see in the third chapter, though considered here within the American domestic level, these problems are international in scope and therefore warrant a broader application in the age of globalization. Institutional support for global initiatives is much more effective if it is mirrored on the domestic level, that is, if there are national institutions that can maintain and affect policies and regulations that are rational and critical, compassionate and efficient. Incidentally, there are in place numerous regulatory agencies whose work and effectiveness have been recently challenged, such as the Securities and Exchange Commission, the Office of the Comptroller of the Currency, the Office of Thrift Supervision, the Federal Reserve, the National Credit Union Administration, and the Commodity Futures Trading Commission. Smith's original pragmatism should not be cloaked in some extreme version of capitalism to which he himself never adhered. Neither should it be ignored in the name of a sanctified or petrified sacred doctrine. Instead, it should be appreciated for the delicate balance it offers between the financial and economic systems of market capitalism and the social and moral systems of benevolent citizens.

## CHAPTER 2

# The Knowledge Industry

### *The Academy and the Internet*

The shift from the invisible hand to the impartial spectator, as we have seen in the previous chapter, is a shift from a prudent or selfish worldview of the marketplace to one that pragmatically acknowledges our personal and social benevolence. But the way to make this shift seamless is to appreciate what kind of a society we have become by the twenty-first century. We are no longer toolmakers who exchange their wares and their labor power, but rather members of an international community who consume information through many means, including the Internet. In other words, the shift we could detect already in Smith's eighteenth century has been amplified in an era where the "cement" of which Smith speaks is made of visual pixels on screens and other manifestations of speedy communication. We have moved from the industrial age to the information age, so that in the age where data collection and dissemination are so important, we can see how the concerns of developmental economists (from the previous chapter) come to the fore.

If knowledge is not only the means by which we exchange goods and services but in fact becomes the foundation on which such exchanges even take place (both personally and technologically), then we should turn our attention to the production, distribution, and consumption of knowledge. Perhaps it should be said at this point that the mere collection of information or data is not the same as the production, distribution, and consumption of knowledge (more on this distinction later). The difference is at once onto-logical and methodological. Ontologically speaking, the question is: When does something become a fact? Under what conditions does a blade of grass or a butterfly become bits of information? Some would say that the very question of what is out there in the world is meaningless without the added variable of who is asking the question and for what purpose. Pragmatically, we approach any set of data with a question or purpose in mind, and therefore our classifications, as Michel Foucault reminds us (1970), are suited for particular purposes. This is true when we see the global financial markets collapse before our very eyes, when we are confronted by natural disasters, or when we wish to figure out what we own. At times, says Foucault, the classification or taxonomy can be quite entertaining:

> Animals are divided into: (a) belonging to the Emperor, (b) embalmed, (c) tame, (d) suckling pigs, (e) sirens, (f) fabulous, (g) stray dogs, (h) included in the present classification, (i) frenzied, (j) innumerable, (k) drawn with a very fine camelhair brush, (l) *et cetera,* (m) having just broken the water pitcher, (n) that from a long way off look like flies. (1970, xv)

As exotically charming as this old "Chinese" taxonomy may seem to us, as weird and incomprehensible as some would see it, this way of organizing data and ordering the world around us is probably no more nor less exotic and weird than some of our own classifications and taxonomies. We usually explain and justify our own methods and criteria with historical antecedents or changed circumstances that dictate this or that preference in choosing our criteria. But our classifications, like those of others, can be easily criticized and dismissed. How would we classify the current financial crises? Should we compare them to previous historical instances? But would such a comparison hold when we have shifted to a global rather than a domestic economy? What do billions of dollars mean in relation to one's own annual earnings or in relation to the national debt? Are these "real" numbers or just symbols of some value assigned to assets and liabilities? In the hands of politicians, even the most rigorous figures and tables find a way of being misrepresented and therefore misunderstood.

Methodologically speaking, there are various ways in which we can collect data, classify them, compare them, and then categorize or synthesize them. The inductivists suggested that we collect as much information or samples as possible and then generalize from them about the major or salient characteristic of our observations: for example, the reasonable assertion that all swans are white. The hypothetico-deductivists suggested we form some hypothesis about swans and then try and confirm or refute it: in the latter case proclaiming, hey, there is a black swan over there! Obviously the black swan would refute the hypothesis of all swans being white. If we cherish this particular hypothesis we can either kill the black swan (by extension, ignoring an experimental result in laboratory experiments) or kill the report (that is, to refuse to publish the report in scientific journals).

Without elaborating on all the methodological debates of the past two centuries among scientists and philosophers, and without detailing the statistical issues emanating from "Black Swans," as Nassim Nicholas Taleb details them in his work (2007), let me suggest that the importance of information gathering as a stage in the acquisition of knowledge is not the same as knowledge itself. This might seem like an insignificant distinction at this point, but when we discuss the conditions under which the stock market, for example, operates with partial knowledge or with misinformation or with basic uncertainties, this kind of distinction becomes more pronounced. In other venues we are clear about the distinction: When you use Google to find something, you are more likely than not to find a great deal of information, most of it useless, and you are not yet in a position to know anything about the topic or question that interests you. The sifting through the information, its assessment, and the criteria by which you prefer to focus on a subset of the available data are the relevant ingredients that move you from being informed to actually knowing something of interest to you. In what follows, I focus more on the economic dimension of knowledge, rather than its philosophical or pedagogical dimensions, so as to keep with the issues outlined in the first chapter.

## The Production, Distribution, and Consumption of Knowledge

The two extreme positions of the educational spectrum (and of the main "factory" of the knowledge industry), from an economic perspective, end up being labeled socialist and capitalist (as we have seen in the first chapter). But in examining the two extreme positions we should be careful to distinguish between the three stages or components of the educational market: first, its production in laboratories, universities, and on the streets; second, its distribution through traditional institutions, such as schools, as well as through corporate mechanisms, such as workshops and seminars, all the way to self-education via the Internet; and finally the various modes of educational consumption, from traditional means to more esoteric ones. So, let us begin with the socialist position, as mentioned by Karl Marx in *The Communist Manifesto*. When describing in 1872 what would be achievable goals and pragmatic ways to measure the success of the communist stage of economic development, Marx included, as his tenth item, the following: "Free education for all children in public schools. Abolition of children's factory labour in its present form. Combination of education with industrial production, etc. etc." (Marx 1988, 75). Sounding much less radical today than it did at the time, Marx's concern for free universal education was right away connected with and dependent on the place of education in the marketplace. To begin with, education is free to citizens, because the state is paying for it. Second, if kids are in school, then they are not on the factory floor, and this way their exploitation is avoided. And third, education is linked to the industrial sector of the economy, so that the former contributes to the latter; one could call this instrumental education, it is education with a training purpose in mind. The Marxian ideal has been fully implemented in the United States, with mandatory education and labor laws that protect children from being abused at the workplace. Likewise, as we shall see in what follows, even the university system has been keen on seeing itself as a partner in the world of commerce, training generations of productive citizens who will join the marketplace.

Though Adam Smith wrote about education about one hundred years earlier than Marx, and although we would expect him to be much less sympathetic to public education, he ends up surprisingly close to Marx. In his *Wealth of Nations* of 1776, he appreciates the fact that his recommendation for the division of labor would split society into two main groups, one of laborers and one of the gentry. It would seem that with this division of labor the laborers would need no education at all, because their main contribution to the marketplace is the sale of their labor power. But, here is Smith's concern with both their productivity and their dignity:

> The man whose whole life is spent in performing a few simple operations ... has no occasion to exert his understanding ... and generally becomes as stupid and ignorant as it is possible for a human creature to become.... His dexterity at his own particular trade seems, in this manner, to be acquired at the expense of his intellectual, social, and martial virtues. But in every improved and civilized society this is the state into which the laboring poor, that is, the great body of the people, must necessarily fall, unless government takes some pains to prevent it. (Smith, *WN*, 734–735)

So, there is a role not only for education per se, but for publicly financed education. Even though the laboring citizens might not be able to have the time and money for their own education, he suggests that: "for a very small expense the public can facilitate, can encourage, and can even impose upon almost the whole body of the people, the necessity of acquiring those most essential parts of education [read, write, and account]" (*WN*, 737). He speaks in the same breath about the necessity for acquiring some basic skills and the establishment of local schools for young people. Smith ends his argument about the benefits of the various educational systems (and their historical or traditional failings) by openly declaring: "The expence [*sic*] of the institutions for education and religious institutions, is likewise, no doubt, beneficial to the whole society, and may, therefore, without injustice, be defrayed by the general contribution of the whole society" (*WN*, 768). For Smith and Marx alike, education, the acquisition of knowledge for the purpose of improving general social conditions, was important enough to set aside ideological differences and personal attitudes. They both realized what made education a unique feature in the marketplace, an essential ingredient in making humans more efficient and thoughtful, more productive contributing members of society, while at the same time being a means by which the dignity and self-worth of society can be more easily measured and honored. Whether from compassion or expediency, the two extremes of the spectrum of opinions are joined in a uniform exaltation of the importance of educating the whole of society.

If one were to transform this attitude about education to a more focused question about the economy, then, as Friedrich Hayek reminds us, we should limit ourselves to a "rational economic order," and then approach our economic problems rationally. This would be quite simple, namely, "purely one of logic," he explains: "*If* we possess all the relevant information, *if* we can start out from a given system of preferences, and *if* we command complete knowledge of available means" (Hayek 1977, 5). The issue, then, is making sure that all these conditions are fulfilled, which, as anyone reasonable would admit, is quite impossible. What is missing, of course, is access to full knowledge about all the variables that would go into deciding what the best course of action would be. As we have seen in the previous chapter, sharing information on the most basic level about potential investments and preferences would take risk out of the marketplace and allow greater stability and growth (because of reduction of those costs associated with risks). Hayek, of course, is in line with this quest for sharing knowledge, but, as always, he is wary of it being centralized in the hands of government agents and planners, trying as they do to anticipate changes in the economy (1977, 11).

So, for Hayek, the miracle of the price system, as he calls it, ensures that "the knowledge of the relevant facts is dispersed among many people," eventually allowing for separate actions to be materialized in the form of prices for goods and services that act as coordinating agents (1977, 13). But instead of needing to know more and more, instead of being able to ascertain the "relevant information" (which itself is a feat of sorts), Hayek advocates a contrary approach to the "economy of knowledge," namely, "how little the individual participants need to know in order to be able to take the right action" (1977, 14). This view is either naive or misleading, for the less one knows the more one might be manipulated, or by contrast, the more intricately one corporation understands the ignorance of consumers, the more likely it is to set prices that are irrelevant to actual production costs. Put differently, though the ongoing neoclassical presumption is that humans are rational by design and therefore act rationally most of the time (and especially so when acting in the marketplace), new studies in behavioral economics illustrate not only that we act irrationally, but that we do so persistently, and in fact, so persistently that our irrational behavior is predicable.

Dan Ariely, for example, compiled the results of numerous experiments at MIT and other leading academic institutions and documented the predictability of our irrational behavior. One of my favorites, among the many examples he cites, is an instance where Williams-Sonoma introduced a high-end bread machine priced at $275. This machine sold poorly until such time as the vendor introduced another bread machine that cost 50 percent more. The (now) cheaper machine then sold very well. The point Ariely makes by this example is that "people didn't have to make their decision in a vacuum" (Ariely 2008, 14–15). Rather, people have a need for relative values to be present in order to make so-called rational decisions; but now their decisions are contextualized irrationally, thereby providing an artificial logic in terms of which to make choices.

Does the consumer make decisions in an information vacuum? Yes, probably most of the time, for unless comparisons are available, no basic information about costs and values are available. However, this allows for anyone to fabricate comparisons or a set of false contexts within which choices are made, devoid as they are of any sense of reality (in the sense of the raw materials and labor and shipping and marketing that go into bringing a product to market). Ariely's conclusion about what he terms our *irrational behaviors* is that they are "neither random nor senseless—they are systematic and predictable," and they arise "because of the basic wiring of our brains" (239). For him, then, there is room for improvement on the assumed standard economic model of rational behavior allowing for people to learn from their own mistakes, appreciate their own decision-making patterns, and watch out for their own follies. Surely for someone else, such as marketing and public-relations companies, this would be an opportunity for manipulation.

Instead of continuing to discuss human nature or the way our brains are "wired," Ariely's examples and arguments make it clear that we should focus on the context within which our decisions are made. This context is made up of all the variables that provide for the operations of the marketplace, and the ones we focus on here are knowledge or information. The first sustained study of the production and distribution of knowledge was undertaken by Fritz Machlup in 1962. As the economy changed, as it grew and relied more and more on advanced technologies that themselves were driven by advances in knowledge, he found it appropriate to study the function of the knowledge industry not as an exogenous variable (as we saw in the first chapter was done in most developmental models that excluded social or political variables) but as an endogenous variable (which can be measured and plays an integral part in the construction of the economic model). His main concern was to go beyond the basic assumptions that have driven economic thinking as to the knowledge individuals have of market conditions (the equilibrium prices of goods and services) or that producers have regarding their production opportunities (the best available technology and their lowest material and labor costs). Being modest, Machlup gives credit to Adam Smith as the one who first noticed that individuals who have been highly educated or trained could be seen as if they were "expensive machines" both more expensive and productive than uneducated ones, or what we would call today human capital (Machlup 1962, 5).

Machlup goes one step farther than considering exclusively those kinds of knowledge that are "instrumental in increasing the efficiency of the economy" (6). For him there are other kinds of knowledge that might seem at first less directly related to the increase of economic efficiency, but that indirectly have a great impact on society. There are five kinds of knowledge, according to Machlup, which might be worthwhile to list in full:

(1)  Practical knowledge: useful in his work, his decisions, and actions; can be subdivided, according to his activities, into
    a)  Professional knowledge
    b)  Business knowledge
    c)  Workman's knowledge
    d)  Political knowledge
    e)  Household knowledge
    f)  Other practical knowledge
(2)  Intellectual knowledge: satisfying his intellectual curiosity, regarded as part of liberal education, humanistic and scientific learning, general culture; acquired, as a rule, in active concentration with an appreciation of the existence of open problems and cultural values.
(3)  Small-talk and pastime knowledge: satisfying the nonintellectual curiosity or his desire for light entertainment and emotional stimulation, including local gossip, news of crimes and accidents, light novels,

stories, jokes, games, etc.; acquired, as a rule, in passive relaxation from "serious" pursuits; apt to dull his sensitiveness.

(4) Spiritual knowledge: related to his religious knowledge of God and of the ways to the salvation of the soul.

(5) Unwanted knowledge: outside his interests, usually accidentally acquired, aimlessly retained. (21–22)

But this general classification is only one way of appreciating the different kinds of knowledge we all acquire along the way. How to see these kinds of knowledge in an economic model requires that we consider knowledge either as a "final product or as a necessary requirement—as a cost element—in the production of other goods and services" (Machlup, 29). If knowledge is considered a final product, then it is either consumed or invested; it is an investment when it comprises scientific research, for example, and it is similarly consumption when we read a novel (Machlup, 29–30). It is from this perspective that Machlup wants us to appreciate the different kinds of knowledge we encounter and how we make use of these differently for multiple purposes. These classifications, admittedly, are not as clear-cut and sharp as they are presented, as Machlup himself admits, but are designed and laid out for heuristic purposes.

As far as Machlup is concerned, there are eleven reasons for embarking on this analysis of the production, distribution, and consumption of knowledge, whether understood as a product or an investment or a consumptive activity. Though outlined more than fifty years ago, these reasons seem to ring true today.

(1) It is a fact that increasing shares of the nation's budget have been allocated to the production of knowledge.

(2) It can also be shown that a large portion of the nation's expenditures on knowledge has been financed by government, so that much of the production of knowledge depends on governmental appropriation.

(3) One may strongly support the judgment that the production of knowledge yields social benefits in excess of the private benefits accruing to the recipients of knowledge.

(4) It is probable that the production of certain kinds of knowledge is limited by inelasticities in the supply of qualified labor, which raises questions of policy, especially concerning the allocation of public funds.

(5) The facts that the production of knowledge of several types is paid for by others than the users of the knowledge, and that these types of knowledge have no market prices, raise questions of their valuation for national-income accounting as well as for welfare-economic considerations.

(6) The production of one type of knowledge—namely, technology—results in continuing changes in the conditions of production of many goods and services.

(7) One may advance the hypothesis that new technological knowledge tends to result in shifts of demand from physical labor to "brain-workers."

(8) There is evidence of a change in the composition of the labor force employed in the United States, in particular of an increase in the share of "knowledge-producing" labor in total employment.

(9) There is ground for suspicion that some branches of the production of knowledge are quite efficient, although it is difficult to ascertain input-output ratios and to make valid comparisons, especially since the very wastefulness is held to be productive of psychic incomes and social benefits.

(10) It has been suggested that some of the growth in the production of knowledge may be an instance of "Parkinson's Law," which implies that administrators tend to create more work for more administrators.

(11) There is probably more validity in the hypothesis that the increase in the ratio of knowledge-producing labor to physical labor is strongly associated with the increase in productivity and thus with the rate of economic growth. (9–10)

From any of these reasons, it becomes clear why Machlup embarks on the project, and why, as time has passed, the study of knowledge as part of economic analysis has grown all the way, as we have seen previously, to the sociopsychological variables that make up behavioral economics, which in my mind, is part of the study of the knowledge economy. It is not only the knowledge we acquire about the marketplace, but also the knowledge we bring to the marketplace in order to operate it more efficiently or to be more efficient within it.

Knowledge acquisition, according to Machlup (what we call education), can be found or distinguished in various places or institutions: home, school, job-training, church, military, media, self-education, and personal experience (51). Regardless of how or where knowledge is acquired, it can be argued that "most of the outlays for education can be regarded as investment in human capital because they are expected to yield returns in future years" (63). This way, education or knowledge acquisition can be simultaneously investment and consumption, because it relates partially to future benefits and partially to current enjoyment (108). So, education can be viewed as either a productive force for present or future ends, or as a pleasure one derives in the present or in the future (115). One could reform schools, for example, to minimize costs and derive the most from future productivity, or one could appreciate the importance of the pleasures derived from education and then be more hard-pressed to put a price tag on its value. Machlup tabulates all the relevant statistical data available to him so as to illustrate the significance of this sector of the economy: This is no longer a philosophical issue but an economic one.

There are some, like James Cates, Sam Gill, and Natalie Zeituny (whose distinction between knowledge and information was mentioned at the opening of the chapter), who have turned this general discussion into a more operational manual that helps business leaders figure out how to use information. In their model, one can move from facts (events in the real world), to data (which organize facts), to information (which is data that are organized to answer specific questions), to knowledge (which consists of information and its usage rules), to understanding (knowledge that is shared), and finally to enabled intuition. These stages of comprehension and data organization move us from diverse and independent facts all the way to a level of understanding that can put things together, that has logical or cognitive rules that can be explained and predicted. The final goal, for them, is the level of what they call "enabled intuition," which they define as "a higher level of understanding that facilitates decision makers to intuitively choose the right course of action that will benefit the business in any situation. With enabled intuition decision making is refined to an art" (Cates et al. 2007, 3–5). To me this model is an example of how to take the general discussion of knowledge acquisition and make it operational: Facts are not collected in a vacuum, and eventually the ways we put them together and learn to understand the information and knowledge to which we have access lead us to a level of decision making that is both informed and intuitive. Whether one follows this model because it is descriptively accurate or because it provides a prescription for business leaders remains an open question. But what makes this model compelling for the present discussion is the ways in which philosophical and methodological issues, as developed, for example, by evolutionary epistemologists (e.g., Radnitzky and Bartley 1987), are turned from the abstract to the concrete, how ideas about knowledge acquisition become tools in the hands of businesspeople.

Regardless if this remains on the level of philosophical abstraction or moves to market implementation, what becomes clear from Machlup's concerns of the past century and those of contemporary writers is the need for communal cooperation. Just as classical and developmental economists always recognize the need for a social context for economic activity, whether it was moral or political or legal (and probably all of those combined), so, too, we can appreciate that the knowledge industry is a collective effort. The collective nature of knowledge production, distribution, and consumption is evident not only when we speak of public schools that educate the youth, but also when corporate leaders make decisions that affect their businesses. Just as exchanges in the marketplace, as we have seen in the previous chapter, hinge on the invisible hand of an impartial spectator, so does the genius of a single individual depend on the acquired knowledge of previous generations or of those collecting and organizing data in the present. Robert Merton, one of the leading sociologists of science of the twentieth century, has devoted an entire book to the oft-quoted phrase attributed to Newton that the reason he has been able to have his insights (otherwise put, to see farther than others) is because he has been standing on the shoulders of giants (Merton 1965). One could say that Newton was modest, but one could also say that Newton realized that his own ideas were embedded in and were the results of the ideas of others. This is in line with the view of the accumulation of knowledge and the general rules and laws that come out of such an accumulation.

Moreover, this view also acknowledges the need for group effort rather than the effort of a single genius. Contemporary believers in this view, such as Nathan Myhrvold (former head of Microsoft's research division), put their belief into practice, in this case, by founding Intellectual Ventures, LLC as a mechanism to bring together the insights of many intellectuals and provide a cooperative environment for scientific and technological discoveries. The history of science and technology has taught us that multiple inventions are not rare, but rather common, because, as they claim, the ideas are in the air, and it is only by accident who comes to be credited with bringing them to fruition (Gladwell 2008). Now, of course, in financial terms, there is much at stake when one does or does not get credit for an invention, for an idea that can be commercially produced and sold. These concerns of Intellectual Property will be addressed more fully in the next chapter. In the meantime, I wish to pull together what I see as a consensus extending from Adam Smith to some in the present in regard to the communal foundation of our knowledge and education as they bring about a more productive, and if you wish happier, marketplace.

But when speaking of cooperation and collaboration among many thinkers and researchers, data collectors and analysts, we might find out that there is not as much cooperation as we may have expected. What is it that prevents more, rather than less, interaction and intellectual cooperation? Perhaps the term is *trust,* as Nicholas Rescher aptly reminds us:

Only through cooperation based on mutual trust can we address issues whose effective resolution makes demands that are too great for any one of us alone. In the development and management of information, people are constantly impelled toward a system of collaborative social practices—an operational code of incentives and sanctions that consolidates and supports collective solidarity and mutual support. In this division of labor, trust results from what is, to all intents and purposes, a custom consolidated compact to conduct their affairs in friendly collaboration. (Rescher 1989, 43)

Rescher brings up the classical economic model that promotes division of labor, but sees this particular sector of the economy, and perhaps our educational life as a whole, as being dominated by mutual support and collaboration. Perhaps some tasks are too big, as we have seen in the last century with Big Science projects, like the Manhattan Project that delivered us the atomic bomb; perhaps even when the tasks are smaller, the human mind cannot cope with so much data at once and therefore needs the help of others; finally, perhaps the interdisciplinary collaboration among specialists in different areas of research might be more productive than staying within one's own narrow area of expertise. (For more on this issue, see Sassower 1993.)

We have seen in the history of philosophy how important Socrates' dialectical method of questions and answers was in developing our inquiries and the human mind. Continuing this line of argument, we can document the developments in the history of ideas as a process whereby one innovation after the other is indeed a response to previous thinkers, ideas, texts, and intellectual frameworks. But instead of trying to prove that collaboration is in fact what we are used to, perhaps we should ask why it never was the prescribed method of producing knowledge (even when it was in use)? Among the many answers, I venture to claim that the disclosure of one's ignorance and the disclosure of one's limited knowledge can be appreciated as the main reasons for withholding information or being leery of collaborating. Socrates prided himself on his ignorance and on his quest for intellectual exchange, and Newton claimed to be merely the beneficiary of the genius of his predecessors; but how many of us are embarrassed to say: I do not know, instead of fabricating half-truths and skirting the question altogether? How many of us welcome full exposure of our state of knowledge? With this in mind, I wish to return for a minute to Rescher, himself a philosopher, who frames collaboration as an economic prescription, rather than dwelling on the psychopathologies that might plague some of us. Admitting that knowledge is power, as so many before and after him have agreed, he continues:

But the hoarding of knowledge—monopolization, secretiveness, collaboration avoidance—is generally counterproductive. In anything like ordinary circumstances, mutual aid in the development and handling of information is highly cost effective. The way in which people build up epistemic credibility in cognitive contexts is structurally the same as that in which they build up financial credit in economic contexts. Considerations of cost effectiveness—of economic rationality, in short—operate to ensure that any group of rational inquirers will in the end become a community of sorts, bound together by a shared practice of trust and cooperation. (1989, 33)

Rescher not only uses the economic terminology to explain the rationale for collaboration, he almost makes it sound inevitable when comparing it to building credit in the financial markets. You must have money or assets to be creditworthy, but your money is deposited somewhere, and your assets are designated as such based on public records. Before you know it, your financial worth is defined by others, and not simply by your own declaration. As explained in the first chapter, credit scores might allow you to buy a house (get a mortgage) or might, conversely, prevent you from getting a car loan: They determine who you are in the marketplace and what role you are licensed to play in it. Likewise, our intellectual work is sanctioned by others, is quoted in others' work (such as with mine here), is paid for when the research can yield financial benefits, and is understood more communally than individually. It is true that this or that person will get credit here and there, or that his or her name will make the headlines; but only a wholly egomaniacal person will ever deny that others contributed to her or his success.

## Taxing Knowledge: Why Pay Twice for GPS?

As mentioned previously, one of the areas in which credit to individual researchers or practitioners is broadly divided or treated as a group effort is so-called Big Science undertakings. During and after World War II, military needs, perceived or real, provided infrastructure and funding for enormous projects, like the Manhattan Project for the development of the atomic bomb. Instead of reviewing the history of this project (see, for example, VanDeMark 2003) and all the unintended consequences related to it (see, for example, Rabi 1970), what interests me here is the way in which we have shifted as a culture from focusing on individual scientists and their research to large laboratories funded by government agencies through academic or private institutions. When Big Science projects began to dominate the scientific scene, they also shifted our focus from the theoretical research undertaken, as Einstein used to quip, where a pencil was sufficient to scribble insights, to the need for large sums of money to organize experiments and analyze their results. The shift is indeed a movement toward what has been termed *technoscience,* where science and technology are enmeshed in a reciprocal relationship, so that the insights of the one inform the other without any sense of chronological or logical priorities. The Manhattan Project (primarily but not exclusively undertaken in Los Alamos, New Mexico) was the major exemplar of such a success, because theoretical scientists and engineers collaborated daily in order to achieve a specific goal.

Though I have argued elsewhere (Sassower 1997) about the transformation of technoscientific ambiguity into anxiety and anguish and tried to relate the technoscientific feat accomplished during the Manhattan Project to the ultimate responsibility borne by its community, I said little about the sense of collaboration among the group. Perhaps in part because of this particular case, and perhaps because of the appreciation of the emergence of Big Science projects around the world, philosophers, historians, and sociologists of science stopped talking about science as such and instead began talking about the scientific enterprise and the scientific community. Once you move the discussion from science to scientists, once you move from the pristine confines of theoretical exploration to the practical application of principles and theories, certain complexities come to light. This is not to say, as was seen in the previous section, that individual research is not informed by the research of others, and that there are not some ethical considerations that must be appreciated, but rather that the consequences might be more radical and dangerous, as was the case when bombs were dropped on Hiroshima and Nagasaki.

The concern with the scientific community, its budgets and oversight, is a concern that is not limited to what Thomas Kuhn (1970), among others, understood in terms of the education and socialization of young researchers into existing paradigms—at least in the context of normal science where no revolutionary ideas break down the existing paradigm and everyone contributes to solving given puzzles—but is also related to public relations concerns for congressional appropriation, for example, or the potential for future success. I have studied these concerns elsewhere (Sassower 1995) and shown that in the case of the Superconducting Supercollider the rhetoric of those soliciting funding as well as local groups that vied for the project to be built in their backyards as economic bonanzas depended less on the technoscientific substance of the project and more on the images that could be conjured on its behalf. In one instance the proposed project of colliding subatomic particles in a fifty-two-mile long tunnel was compared to the manned landing on the moon and in another to the building of the pyramids (Sassower 1995, ch. 1). Eventually the project was not funded because of the uncertainties of its ballooning budget (from $2 to $11 billion), but not before it received all the necessary political endorsements and those of the parties that could benefit from its funding. Such examples of Big Science, including, more recently, the Human Genome Project, illustrate that by the end of the twentieth century the United States was providing funding under the guise of National Security or on behalf of the national interest so as to maintain its global image as a leading scientific and economic power in the international community. As long as these projects conform to the criteria under which national funding is justified, we consider them as public goods, namely, those activities and services that are paid by taxation and benefit, without exclusions or differentiation, by all members of a society. Though each individual might not see the direct benefit from this or that project, she or he can appreciate how all of these projects collectively ensure the safety and well-being of society.

The case of the Global Positioning System (GPS) could well fall within this broad category of public projects that are paid for by society as a whole for our collective benefit. Just as nuclear fission was originally used for the purpose of building a bomb for military use, eventually this knowledge about the behavior of subatomic particles and the way their energy could be harnessed was used by utility companies in the construction of power plants. The transformation from military to civilian use could be easily justified because this new technology benefited society, and the enormous investment undertaken by the Department of Defense transcended its original intent. A public utility company, according to *Black's Law Dictionary*, is a

> privately owned and operated business whose services are so essential to the general public as to justify the grant of special franchises for the use of public property of the right of eminent domain, in consideration of which the owners must serve all persons who apply, without discrimination.... To constitute a true public utility, the devotion to public use must be of such character that the public generally, of that part of it which has been served and which has accepted the service, has the legal right to demand that service shall be conducted, so long as it is continued, with reasonable efficiency under reasonable charges. (1979, 1108–1109)

So, five elements make up this particular definition of a utility company: First, it is privately owned; second, it has access to private property on behalf of society; third, being entrusted with the provision of a public good, it cannot discriminate against any individual or class of individuals; fourth, the recipients have rights in regard to how the company is run; and fifth, no monopoly abuse would be allowed in terms of fees being charged (see also, Pace et al., 1995, 184–186). Utility companies are therefore regulated differently than other private companies, so that their monopoly status and of course the economies of scale such a monopoly enjoys (in terms of efficiency) do not adversely affect consumers. There are, of course, some utilities that are publicly owned (e.g., in Colorado Springs, Colorado, and Sacramento, California) even in the United States, and in many other countries it is much more prevalent that the state owns its utilities, primarily, one could surmise, for national security purposes.

The case of nuclear power plants parallels the kind of concerns that have been brought up by GPS: What are the policy concerns we should have with the multiple uses that both military, transportation, civil, and commercial interests have? Is there potentially a conflict among these multiple uses? The Critical Technologies Institute of RAND prepared a report for the Executive Office of the President, Office of Science and Technology Policy in 1995, in which these concerns and many others are carefully discussed. It is fascinating to see, given it is an independent entity, how national security concerns permeate the report, both in domestic and international terms. Incidentally, the United States is not alone in developing technologies that are global in scope, as can be seen with the Galileo project undertaken by the European Community (with whom an agreement was signed in 2004 to ensure communication cooperation). The main problem from their perspective is the rapid proliferation of the technology and its application across boundaries that were initially more easily delineated: As a military project, GPS was exclusively used for naval navigation and antimissile detection, and the kind of personal use we are accustomed to enjoy today, from cell phones and personal computers to cars and the Internet, was hardly anticipated. Instead of reviewing the technical history of the GPS or its detailed functions (which are changing as we speak), I would rather focus on the commercial or financial elements that make this technology and the knowledge-basis it enjoys problematic in terms of costs and fees.

Obviously, as a Department of Defense project, GPS was financed through funding appropriation from collected taxes. Taxpayers paid $10 billion over a couple of decades to get to a point where commercial use was available at the consumer level. From the RAND report we learn first that there should be a "national GPS policy that will provide a predictable environment for future business decision" and second that "the 'no-fee' approach is a technical necessity arising from the nature of GPS signals" (Pace et al. 1995, xxi). As we can see, Rosenstein-Rodan's ghost is still with us: We would like to share information in such a way so as to ensure low risks for future investments, and a national policy regarding GPS would help create a business environment where companies would more readily invest, knowing that a "predictable environment" is being established. For example, this would mean, as we see in regard to the "no-fee" policy, that a business plan that outlined capital needs for infrastructure could assume no fees for signal acquisition, even though they would need to invest in transmission technologies. Whenever business decisions have to be made in an unpredictable environment, it is safer not to make them or to decide not to invest at all, rather than face high fees that cannot be passed on to the consumers as final users. It is with this in mind that the report recommends that "the United States should issue a statement of national policy (e.g., a Presidential Decision Directive) on the Global Positioning System to provide a more stable framework for public and private sector decision-making" (xxv and 147). Incidentally, according to the authors of this report, after Soviet interceptor aircraft shot down a civilian airliner KAL 007 in 1983 in restricted Soviet airspace, killing all 269 passengers and crew on board, President Reagan announced that once the GPS was completed it would be available for civilian use. This disaster, in retrospect, could have been avoided had the pilot accurately known the position of the aircraft, so as to avoid restricted foreign airspace.

As we see from the debates about GPS, "commercialization and privatization of all or parts of the GPS" might not be "consistent with U.S. security, safety, and economic interests" (6), and, therefore, might warrant relying on government agencies for the construction and maintenance of such a system. As the authors observe, the case of GPS really falls in the gray area between clearly defined boundaries of the public and private sectors, and, therefore, it helps challenge our standard views of the superiority and exclusivity of the American capitalist system. In their words,

> In one sense, GPS is a model dual-use technology in which military development leads to civil and commercial benefits beyond what was originally intended for the program. In another sense, GPS is a commercially driven information technology, like high-speed data networks and mobile communication, which is affecting the nature of national and international security. (11)

What this ambivalence in approach brings to light, from this perspective, is how "original equipment manufacturers" (who are contracted by the

Department of Defense but remain privately owned) "cooperate when common interests are at stake" so as to remain competitive (despite government contracts) and efficient (to increase their profits) (33). But those manufacturers are not the only ones affected by policies related to GPS, as the authors acknowledge, because the chain of connections is much longer and more complex (41), and decision-making processes cannot be limited to Department of Defense directives or to commercial entities that wish to maximize their profits through an ever-expanding market for their products. Moreover, the balance of diverse interests of those participating in and affected by the proliferation of GPS devices will itself be shifting over time, because the share the military uses in the aviation and marine areas is shrinking relative to the share of civilian consumers. Finally, the report surveys the increase in patent application both domestically and internationally in all GPS-related areas so as to illustrate the shrinkage of the dominance of military research and development of GPS technology (114–127).

As we observed in the previous chapter, there are some areas of research and development that would make no commercial investment sense, and some that would. Judgment about these situations is left to individual companies in the marketplace, given the classical and neoclassical capitalist models. However, as we see in the case of the GPS, no commercial entity, no matter how large, would have invested some $10 billion over two decades in the hope of reaping some profits in the future, especially because at its inception no civilian applications were apparent. The military, by contrast, brings into its calculations a set of security and autonomy concerns that supersede any concern for financial viability or a return on investment: Maintaining military superiority in the global arena is not measured by dollars and cents, but rather by how many lives can be protected or saved or as some would term it, how this affects national security concerns. If the military deems an investment essential for national security, and if it can convince Congress to appropriate funding for such an investment, then it will undertake to complete such a project. Some projects fail, and we might never hear about them; some succeed, but remain classified; and some, like the GPS, eventually have commercial applications that transcend anything military in nature. Bringing them into focus under financial calculations alone would be difficult in many ways, because direct fee collections by the government (in addition to already collected taxes) would be expensive and perhaps not worth it at all (150–154, 168–175). To put this in perspective, the annual cost to the Air Force of maintaining the GPS is about $400 million, which is a fairly insignificant amount in relation to other costs of maintaining national security (174).

It is interesting to note here that the Internet was also initially developed as a military research program, but unlike the initial investment in satellites, monitoring stations, master control stations, and ground antennas required of the GPS, there was no hardware required for development of the Internet. Instead, what was required to make everything operational was an agreement on a set of standards and protocols that would allow global communication. There remain, in both cases, legal and security issues, as well as access and fees concerns, so that the use of the systems will remain uninterrupted. The GPS can assist in knowing *where* one is, and the Internet can help in discovering *who* one is. But what makes these two kinds of knowledge both useful and enlightening makes them also problematic: Who else could know where you are and who you are? What kind of surveillance is inadvertently available to a third party about whom you know nothing? As we have seen after the September 11, 2001, catastrophe, Congress was quick to grant the executive branch of the government broad measures and a great deal of latitude to conduct whatever secret inquiries regarding any suspected citizen without proper review by the courts. Our own constitutional checks and balances were suspended because of a perceived emergency, and the president could use the latest technologies to violate our most basic privacy rights. The GPS and the Internet moved from military uses to personal civilian ones and then reverted back to government uses and abuses under the guise of national security. I will argue later that just because government agencies provide the conditions for marketplace developments and successes does not give them the right to interfere with individual rights, such as privacy. It is one thing to provide the conditions or institutions, the infrastructure, of a society, and quite another to use particular institutions for control and surveillance.

## Academic Institutions of the Future

Academic institutions from their very conception in the eleventh century had a dual mission: to train young people to use specific skills and to perpetuate the existing political power relations. The first mission has been a moving target, from the duplication of manuscripts all the way to the present concern with computer technology and the production of knowledge in cyberspace, and the second mission shifted from the respect paid to religious authorities to the respect paid to corporate and military authorities whose funding largesse remains on the minds of academics. Academic institutions, as I have argued elsewhere (Sassower 2000), could be a refuge for intellectuals if understood correctly by the general public. By this I mean a way of allowing for the fermentation and exchange of ideas among disinterested members of the academy. This is different from the charge that Paulo Freire (1972), for example, has for pedagogy as an instrument for political transformation through liberation education. Instead, my own concern was to find a way for the academy to be insulated from political pressures and be granted a sanctuary of sorts for the benefit of society as a whole, rather than for the benefit of this or that particular interest, should it be political, military, or financial.

This is not to say that Freire, following to some extent the example of the Italian Marxist Antonio Gramsci, is *misguided* in any sense of the term. Rather, intellectuals who have been vocal about the role of intellectuals in the future, whether as "organic intellectuals," who are the vanguard of the revolutionary forces of their countries (in Gramsci's sense), or as a "new class" that is capable of fighting for changes because "knowledge and knowledge systems are important in shaping social outcomes" (in Gouldner's 1979, 5, sense), have always had a moral injunction for them regardless of their actual or potential political power. The moral high ground, so to speak, is a good starting point insofar as it fosters a certain level of responsibility on those who should know better, who should be able to see the big picture of the political and economic situation and educate others and disrupt accepted norms and provide alternatives to them. But the starting point cannot be the end point; it needs a process and an environment in which to flourish and bring about results. The results, whatever they might be, and the environment of the academy seem at times too detached from the realities of the marketplace, so that many confusions and misunderstandings are in the way. For example, should the knowledge production that takes place in research institutions be for the service of the rest of society or for the exclusive benefit of faculty members and their students? Should that knowledge be produced for specific purposes, as we have seen earlier in the case of the Manhattan Project and the GPS, or should it remain always "basic" and "pure" as means for more practical applications by industry?

These questions were answered in specific ways by some, like Clark Kerr, the former president and chancellor of the University of California, Berkeley, in historical terms. It is as if each period of history has its own vision and image of what intellectuals' role in society ought to be and how academic institutions, universities and colleges, should bring about their fruition. Kerr builds his argument about the "multiversity" on Machlup's ideas, which we covered earlier in the chapter (Kerr 1995, 66), insofar as he appreciates the magnitude and future potential of the knowledge industry within the economy. And in following this line of thinking, Kerr is open to the idea that the university has become an instrument for the marketplace not only in training qualified people for the workforce—a notion already expressed by Adam Smith more than two hundred years ago—but also in terms of the specific research needed by the military and industry. The university, then, is not an incidental part of the culture or a monastery-like institution for higher contemplation, but instead is an essential component of the development and advancement of the economy and society (192–194). It is fascinating to note in this context that the social need to invest in institutions of higher learning must be pleaded for by academic leaders because of funding pressures from other sectors, such as prisons (196–197). As much as the university system is still crucial for relatively inexpensive research, using as it does, the army of unemployed research assistants and graduate students, there are still pressures on its budgets and an ongoing culture of distrust from the public at large (the American phenomenon of anti-intellectualism) and from policymakers who believe that learning is not as important as doing. And, of course, advances in communication technologies are progressively undermining the need for classrooms and lecture halls as we have traditionally known them.

The fact that the Internet has changed our knowledge-gathering apparatus and techniques is obvious, whether one uses Wikipedia (an open-source and free encyclopedia) or any other Web site that has a database, but what is not obvious is how this has affected our knowledge production, distribution, and consumption. Just because we have more access to knowledge available to us for free does not necessarily mean that we know more or that our knowledge terrain has necessary been enriched or increased. Can one trust what one finds on the Internet? What qualifies as trustworthy knowledge? What filters and criteria are set in place to ensure the credibility of the data on the Internet? Technological advances have made a difference in our culture not only in terms of access to knowledge (through the Internet), but also in terms of the production of knowledge (universities are not the only sites for such production). Moreover, the distribution mechanisms of old, such as academic institutions, turn out to be serving only one-quarter of their clients (students) as full-time residential students. Adult learners who are no longer financially dependent on their parents, who have responsibilities outside the learning environment, and who are identifying themselves in terms other than being students (and in many cases are older than traditional postsecondary education students) make up three-quarters of those who are in the knowledge-acquisition mode (Council for Adult and Experiential Learning 1999). Some of these adult learners still join, on a part-time basis, academic institutions, but some are taking courses here and there on the Internet or join professional groups that offer online courses for enrichment or for the purpose of switching jobs and acquiring a new skill-set.

The fact that more public universities depend on funding outside traditional sources (state allocation and research grants) has meant that they cater to a broader audience of potential clients and, because of that, have become more sensitive to economic needs and technological changes. What emerges in this stage of pedagogical transformation is neither the complicity alluded to by Kerr of the university being the servant of the military-industrial complex nor the complacency of liberal and classical education of the ancients (learning as a calling and vocation). Instead, we come to see a more integrated, and, of course, clumsy at times, process of providing knowledge-acquisition and processing skills that are needed by society at large as opposed to this or that particular interest group. As this process becomes more elaborate and sophisticated it pushes the entire economy from manufacturing and agriculture to service and knowledge industries. As a country we produce and export patents and intellectual property, scientific research, higher education, advertising, images and films, music and news, networks and databases, and this production overall takes more and more of our resources in terms of capital and human investments so that we can distinguish ourselves from other countries where manual labor is cheaper and where natural resources are more abundant.

The way this figures into the general argument of this book is the extent to which the marketplace needs broader social, political, and legal support: If the marketplace is indeed about knowledge and information, about data collecting and processing, and about the ways in which innovations can effectively transform and improve our culture, then we ought to worry, as a society, about improving the conditions under which this marketplace can thrive. Once again, this is not a vision of obliterating the marketplace and replacing it with a socialist or Orwellian centralized planning agency (which in turn can be translated into a utopian or dystopian narrative). Instead, this is a vision and a recommendation for changing the conditions under which the markets for knowledge can be more efficient and allow for greater freedom and justice. The university system plays a crucial role in bringing this vision one step closer to completion, however imperfect this completion will necessarily remain (see Karabell 1998). But the role the university system plays is not limited to what Kerr imagined it in the provision of research and technologies and skilled labor into the marketplace. It seems to me that the academic or university system has a broader mission even within this framework. It goes without saying that the university system ought to train critical and analytical people who will then become more informed and more engaged citizens in society. But what also goes on in the university, and what is unique to it despite its medieval genealogy (Schachner 1938), is the fact that the university provides a microcosm of the society in which it operates, because it is a relatively small community where competition for power and prestige, for funds and careers, presage what is happening and what will be happening in the general community at large.

If this is the case, then a dose of political reality needs to be part of the discussion about the role and future of the university system. So, it might be odd that the kind of imploration regarding the role of the academy ends up being proposed simultaneously by the so-called right and left of the political spectrum. Perhaps the main reason for this is the deep conviction that the academy, the university system, the educational national apparatus we have been speaking of is part and parcel of society and as such is influenced by its political, ideological, social, and economic factors and conditions. The notion that academic institutions are outside the mainstream of the culture or that they remain insulated from its influences is no longer tenable in the twenty-first century. The information age is propped by the academy and finds its own genealogy linked to it in a mutually beneficial and reciprocal way. In his *The Knowledge Factory*, Stanley Aronowitz reminds us that "nearly ten percent of the adult population under age sixty-five is enrolled in vocational, technical, or liberal arts college[s] and millions of others have already earned postsecondary credentials" (Aronowitz 2000, 3). But this stunning statistical data are always contextualized in terms of the relationship between the knowledge factory and the workforce, between how knowledge is produced by the academy and its usefulness to the military-industrial complex, so that, in Aronowitz's words, "garden variety social scientists" are "the intellectual servants of power" (4). Kerr's vision, then, has become the dominant view of the importance of the university system in producing useful knowledge for the marketplace and the state, from industrial and military applications to domestic and international policies (Aronowitz, 30–45). In describing the current state of affairs of higher education in the United States, Aronowitz laments the lack of critical and even creative thinking and writing in the academy, a place that has become nothing more than a factory for the preparation of a trained workforce almost in the mold envisioned by Smith some two hundred years ago. What about the transformative power of learning? What about the potential for change and the incorporation of new, at times subversive, ideas that counter the mainstream ideology of capitalist power relations?

It seems that the view from the left remains grim, for there seems to be no way out of the financial indebtedness of the academy to corporate America, in the form of grants and subsidies, research funding, and the establishment of academic and policy centers. As Peter McLaren claims, "As schools continue to be financed more and more by corporations that function as service industries for transnational capitalism, and as bourgeois think-tank profiteerism prevails in guiding educational policy and practice, the U.S. population faces a challenging educational reality" (Castells et al. 1999, 15). McLaren's concern is not solely with the influence of corporate America, but also with the misguided notion that in the information age more and better-paying jobs will be created and that this would lead to a global democratization of the workplace. Instead, he claims, there is greater devastation in the global economy, because this new age of communication and information technologies helps concentrate knowledge and wealth in fewer and fewer hands and thereby increase global unemployment, misery, and injustice (16ff.). The concentration of economic power translates, as far as Manuel Castells is concerned, into political power that is codified culturally. Unlike the postindustrial revolutions of the twentieth century, the current information age is one that will dramatically change not only social and power relations, but the very structures through which knowledge and information have been produced and distributed. The fact that this is both a global issue and a pervasive feature of all knowledge production will eventually transform the way we see ourselves in relation to others (40–47). Whereas education seems to have been the rallying cry for decreased inequalities, as a form of democratization not only in the workplace but in society in general, there are those, like Ramon Flecha, who suggest that the education process itself can cause unforeseen future inequalities (Castells et al., 65ff.).

What the leftist critics have managed to explain is that the promises of the information age, regarding the shift from manual and menial labor to cognitive and intellectual labor, might fall short if not attended to in the social and political arenas. One cannot rely on the marketplace alone to ensure greater equality and justice among the population simply because we are already at the dawn of the twenty-first century. Instead, we must find ways to improve on what we have already accomplished and ensure that democratic institutions are preserved through academic and cultural institutions rather than diminish in power and prominence in the face of a growing economy and a stronger international marketplace. Pedagogical practices can be of help, according to Henry Giroux, a leading educational reformer who strikes an optimistic note in the midst of the doom and gloom expressed by his fellow-academics. For him, the transformation from modernist to postmodern pedagogy is one that appreciates the demise of notions of certainty and progress, rationality and universalism, as inadequate to handle the cultural diversity and ethnic pluralism of the postmodern world. Academic institutions, and by extension, other financial and political and cultural institutions, remain modernist and as such too rigid to handle the fluidity required in the information age, where knowledge is produced everywhere and anywhere and not only within the confines of research universities (Castells et al., 93ff.). This would mean, for example, a greater openness to critical ideas and a more receptive forum for incorporating different concepts and values that have been previously deemed inappropriate or uninteresting. The Internet can play a role in ensuring some level of public access and critical openness. By this I do not mean more access to databases, which, as Wikipedia has shown, can be open to public scrutiny and contribution (open-source work), but a way to enhance the democratization of knowledge consumption. It is true that some search engines, like Google, can be skewed in some ways because of the auctions that allow some names or concepts or companies to buy their way to the top of any list, but this alone does not make the entire enterprise suspect or worthless. With a little training, the elderly, for example, have become better advocates of their own health management (Campbell and Wabby 2003), and thus are less anxious about using computers to seek information through Web sites, such as ElderCareOnline. Likewise, young people are more likely to find opportunities that were unavailable to them in previous generations regarding data sources and interpersonal communication (and this is not limited to YouTube, but extends to entertainment venues and materials).

Another way of thinking of the university system, one that has educated more than one-third of the population, is that in the chain of production, distribution, and consumption of knowledge, it encompasses all of these three steps or these three links in the chain and extends them beyond its own confines. New research and technologies emanate from the university, the university through its regular curriculum and through all of its additional forms of education—adult learning, extended studies, study abroad, foreign student exchange, K–12 teacher training and accreditation, online courses, local television programming, and continuing education of professional organizations—distributes knowledge, and finally it is one of the most intense consumers of knowledge through its faculty, graduate and undergraduate students, and all the peripheral community-service programs it fosters. In short, the university system, broadly conceived, plays multiple roles in enhancing the knowledge industries. If we are looking for ways in which the community can support its marketplace so that mutual and reciprocal benefits are more likely to be present, the university system provides a convenient place to focus on such support. With little funding, a campus can become the center for intellectual and cultural and technologically interesting activities that the entire community can support.

Though the focus so far has been on knowledge production, distribution, and consumption, one should remember to include the activities the community should support and that will improve the community, such things like dances and concerts, art fairs and theater, sporting events and public debates. Just as we learn to appreciate the dictum of "on the shoulders of giants" as a way to express respect for the knowledge of the past that allows us in the present to look farther into the future, so can we appreciate the group effort it takes to put on a play, a concert, or even a sporting event, in a manner already acknowledged by Machlup's taxonomy of knowledge. In all of these fields and subdisciplines, it is clear to all participants that the collective effort of many provides for the condition of success for every individual, may she or he be a scientist, engineer, football player, or actor. The idea that one emerges on the set or the stage fully formed without the help of many others is a folly we all admit to. So, in this spirit, the academy can become an exemplar of what the future has in store for us, despite its hierarchy and power structure, its insecurities and rigid rules, because it is also a community of scholars, some more senior and mature, and others in the making. As a sign that this is not only wishful thinking, there is a growing literature on mentoring in the academy because of and not despite the different roles of professors and students or senior and junior professors (see Johnson 2007). All we need in order to make this community a role model for the marketplace and society as a whole is to keep it open, in the Popperian sense of the Open Society (1966), and always critical and self-critical. These two conditions will ensure that the academy does not become self-righteous and insulated from its surroundings, and that it will remain self-correcting when new ideas and suggestions implore it to change and transform, grow and respond to a larger audience than it has traditionally responded to. When it does so, even if it does accept grants and funding from political powers or the marketplace, it will remain independent and critical, without bowing its head to the authorities, without losing its integrity.

In order not to conclude this chapter on a high note that will be dismissed by those concerned with the financial realities of the academy (and those of the economy in general), we could say that even when marketplace efficiency restricts the unbridled expenditure of the academy (its inherent waste of buying books and providing facilities), this alone does not undermine the potential for insisting on maintaining integrity on campus, whether of academic research or budgeting. Every exchange within the community of scholars and students must be driven by a deep commitment to retain one's integrity and improve the overall conditions of the community. And this commitment, as we have seen in the previous chapter, has been set in motion by Adam Smith in his model of our moral sentiments and how they should be regarded socially as well as individually. Moreover, as we are seeing now in the financial crises of 2008, this commitment can be easily met when we provide regulatory mechanisms by which not only integrity, but also efficiency, can be clearly documented and accounted for. As the academy has learned over the years, the pragmatic price of accountability is worth paying for academic freedom and responsible spending.

# CHAPTER 3

# Individualism and the Community
## *From Competition to Cooperation*

Whereas the first chapter illustrated the extent to which individual activity in the marketplace is conditioned by the larger framework supplied by the state, the second chapter focused on the particular nature of the marketplace in the information age. Both chapters remind us that the classical capitalist model has never really materialized or been implemented over the past two centuries, but rather only some variant of that model, a truncated model that has worked fairly well insofar as it has adapted to changing technical and social circumstances, from industrialization to urbanization. Adam Smith's vision of the division of labor is by now commonplace not only in factories (or what has been called Fordism after the assembly-lines at Ford Motor company), but also in virtual offices that use the Internet as a means of cheap communication. Likewise, Smith's concern with efficient markets as conduits of information exchange, including the pricing of goods and services (or what some call market supply and demand), has borne its own fruits in domestic and international markets. But these insights, attributed to Smith and to the classical economists of his era and further developed some hundred years later by neoclassical economists by means of more sophisticated mathematical tools, were couched in a deep intellectual appreciation of the moral foundation that could bring about and nourish such market behavior. The marketplace, in short, was not and could not be divorced from the larger social, political, moral, and legal frameworks that supported its formation and protected its smooth functioning, and, therefore, required a pragmatic approach to solving its inherent problems.

This point about the larger context of market behavior is worth belaboring because it also helps us appreciate the folly of appealing to *homo economicus*, the rational economic man, who is supposed to be the prototype for market behavior, one whose choices are exclusively driven by rational assessment of risks and opportunities, by self-interest and the consequences of any decision or choice. As we saw in the previous two chapters, contemporary behavioral economists acknowledge this folly and have collected impressive data from numerous experiments (admittedly primarily run with students on university campuses) to show the extent to which humans are more often than not irrational in their choices and decision-making processes. Put differently, one is tempted to revisit the history of ideas so as to find all the instances in which thinkers have debated the balance between human cognition and emotions, between one's rational faculties and one's feelings: Can we control our emotions? Should we? I will have more to say about this topic in the next chapter. At this juncture, I would like to extend our discussion of the conditions under which individual success can be fostered and must be appreciated.

The standard view of contemporary economists and businesspeople regarding human emotions or, more accurately, human nature, is that humans are driven by fear and greed. I heard that much from no other than Robert Rubin, the former treasury secretary in the Clinton Administration, and a major figure in the investment banking industries in his various positions and roles in financial giants, including Goldman Sachs and Citicorp. What are the implications of this view of human nature? Does this mean that we can gauge and judge human behavior in these terms? Moreover, does fear motivate people to behave in particular ways, just as greed does? Is the fear in question here the kind that terrifies us and paralyzes us, or the kind that pushes us to do irrational things we later regret? Is the greed the kind that motivates or induces us to step on each other's toes to climb higher on a ladder of financial rewards, or the benign one that encourages us to help others in the hope that this help will be reciprocated or will have some personal benefits attached to it? I raise these questions here not simply as theoretical constructs, but in light of the calamities suffered during the 2008–2009 financial crises. Fear and greed, whether in the mortgage industry or elsewhere on Wall Street, have indeed pushed the economy into a new abyss, one that will take a long time to exit. I also raise these questions in light of a great many experiments undertaken in the 1970s and 1980s that attempted to gauge the levels of greed and fear in individuals. Admittedly most of the subjects of these experiments were students (e.g., Thaler 1992, 16ff.). In this sense, then, I also wish to examine the financial reasons for cooperating both domestically and internationally, moving our thinking and perception to wider horizons that are intimately connected to the behavior of the marketplace, might it be one of goods and services or of ideas and relationships. But instead of undertaking a full-fledged examination of the entire marketplace, I will limit my focus to venture capital firms that in some ways incorporate more vividly the ideals of the capitalist marketplace.

## Venture Capitalists and Angels: From Greed to Philanthropy

It should be noted from the outset of this section that what has been viewed as a marginal source of financing will become the major source of financing in the near future, as commercial banks and traditional investment banks will become more and more regulated, and, therefore, will be less and less adventurous in financing innovation and creativity. As the 2008 financial crises remind us, even those with capital are less likely to invest in traditional financial instruments because of the inherent instability of these instruments and the potential for loss. My prediction is that even those in the comfortable, but slowly disappearing middle class will find themselves seeking out investment opportunities as means of savings for their retirement. These opportunities will more likely come through small, local venture companies whose direct involvement with their clients on both sides—the investors and the adventurers—could bring about a certain level of security and comfort that banks no longer can provide. Some, of course, will be the large-scale, more traditional venture capital firms whose history I recount here. But even they, as Jon Gertner (2008) suggests, are bound to walk a fine line between caring about green technologies of the future and profits, especially because their investments (and those of others like them) already account for close to 20 percent of the investments of the private sector.

One of the few historically informed books on venture capital and its American formation in the past century is by Spencer Ante (2008). Following the career of one French-born professor from Harvard Business School, Ante contextualizes the great transformation of the American business landscape in these terms:

> In the second half of the twentieth century, the United States experienced a historic transformation, in which a society dominated by large corporations such as Standard Oil, U.S. Steel, and General Motors shifted to a nation driven by venture-backed start-ups such as Digital Equipment Corporation, Intel Corporation, Microsoft, Starbucks, and many others.... A recent study by the National Venture Capital Association found that U.S. venture-backed

companies between 1970 and 2005 accounted for ten million jobs and nearly 17 percent of the nation's gross domestic product. (xix)

In addition to providing a comprehensive biographical account of Georges Doriot, the founder of the American research and development company that was underwriting some of the first venture-backed companies on the East Coast, Ante explains how difficult it was to convince wealthy Americans to invest in risky new ventures, especially in the new computer-driven terrain whose technology was unfamiliar to aging wealthy investors. Ante recounts, step-by-step, every trial and tribulation that Doriot underwent in order to support and eventually be vindicated with his investment in Digital Equipment under the leadership of Ken Olsen in the 1960s. He concludes by saying that "in nine years, ARD's $70,000 investment had skyrocketed in value by a factor of five hundred, validating Doriot's model and proving the shortsightedness of SEC inspectors" (196). This investment "was the venture capital industry's first home run, single-handedly proving that venture capitalists could generate enormous wealth by backing the leader of a hot new business" (197).

When we think of venture capital, we commonly think of the original Silicon Valley phenomenon and the West Coast, where the proliferation of computer companies has been in the news. But, as Ante reminds us, the industry was "pioneered by ARD and a few other Northeastern firms in the three decades following World War II" (227). Their prominence was due in part to the combination of MIT as the premier engineering university and Harvard as the premier business and management university in the United States. The Boston area became the locus of numerous research centers that were heavily funded by the Department of Defense, and, because of that, drew a large number of researchers that eventually went on their own, like Ken Olsen of Digital. In addition to the growing prominence of the University of California system, the California Institute of Technology and the relatively new Stanford University provided a nexus of creative centers of excellence that were nurtured, among others, by Stanford's provost Frederick Terman, according to Ante (227–228). Attracting capital to such a concentration of scientific and engineering talent was relatively easy after seeing the success of the Boston area. Ante mentions some of the pioneers on the West Coast, such as Draper, Gaither & Anderson, founded in 1958, and Davis & Rock, capitalized in 1961 with $5 million. To compare these ventures with ARD, Ante records that "in their first year, Davis & Rock put up $280,000 to help start Scientific Data Systems, a computer maker that Xerox bought in 1969 for $950 million" (231). Perhaps because Ante is so invested in the career narrative of his hero, Georges Doriot, he keeps on comparing the kind of work he has pioneered with the later improvements of others:

> West coast venture firms will happily take credit for inventing many of the key attributes of the venture business. But that's not the entire story. Kleiner, Perkins, for example, is often credited with being the first venture firm to practice hands-on management, first to organize portfolio companies to create a sort of keiretsu (a set of companies with interlocking business relationships), and also first to implement corporate governance measures such as distributing audited quarterly and annual reports. In truth, ARD had pioneered and been using these practices for more than two decades before any other west coast firm. (232–233)

Yet, Ante admits that the incubation of firms "from scratch" as a way to nurture new and tentative talent was a much more common West Coast practice, so that the potential for success was watched over, step-by-step, from the very inception of an idea (234). Ante mentions the eventual success of Apple and Genentech as exemplars of what the West Coast ended up doing in relation to what the East Coast was doing. But the major changes in the venture capital business, as far as Ante is concerned, had more to do with the easing of regulations and the permission for pension funds to participate in venture capital investments. Instead of being bound by the 1974 "prudent man" rule of the Employment Retirement Income Security Act of the U.S. Labor Department that would not permit risky investments in venture firms, by 1979 a new rule allowed pension fund managers to consider the investment risk in venture firms to be part of a wider diversified portfolio that would allow taking such risks. This change in regulatory provision "opened the floodgates to venture capital." According to Ante, "in 1978, 23 venture funds managed about $500 million of capital. By 1983, there were 230 firms overseeing $11 billion. Almost one-third of that new money came from pension funds, up from 15 percent in 1978" (250).

As I have been arguing all along, the market for venture capital funds could not have grown as much and as quickly without government intervention. It is not as if government agencies themselves invested in venture firms, the way the Department of Defense funded many projects on university campuses and in the private sector. Rather, a combination of tax legislation that slashed capital gains taxes in 1978 from 49.5 percent to 28 percent, and eventually in the 1990s to 15 percent, plus a regulatory allowance for pension funds investment in risky venture firms brought about the financial bonanza of venture capital. Greed alone would not have sufficed. This greed had to become more benevolent, more socially and morally acceptable by the legal and political authorities, so as to be prominently displayed as a form of generous subsidy for budding new talent and creativity. It is fascinating to note that legislative and regulatory bodies follow the "prudent man" rule as a way to mitigate risk-benefit assessments or perhaps as a way to be able to stand up to the scrutiny of the "average citizens," however poorly such a category is defined. The market for venture firms might remain on the fringes of most financial and economic activity in the United States, but on another level it stands at the heart of what the capitalist model is all about: coming up with new ideas and products, taking risks, and enlarging the market itself. Entrepreneurship is how capitalism defines or characterizes its leaders and its hard-core adherents. Because of this capitalist spirit, many urban legends have sprouted over the years. Similar to the myth of the lone genius or the starving artist who lives alone in a quest for creativity and who is appreciated only posthumously, the myth of the heroic entrepreneur who is despondent while pursuing a dream and vindicated when riches are forthcoming makes up much of the financial and economic lore and culture of postcapitalist society.

But, as we see in the case of venture capital firms, firms whose leaders are innovators and risk-takers, who think outside the box, so to speak, who perceive a need and supply it to the greater benefit of the public at large, these individual heroes and heroines can succeed only with the help of other firms and investors, and that help in turn is financially supported (in the tax code) and legally protected (in terms of intellectual property rights). Unlike standard, large corporations that raise funds through the offering of (stock market traded) shares to the public or finance their expansion through their profits from ongoing sales, venture firms lure investors with the promise of future benefits. The categories of venture investors is commonly divided into three kinds: first, venture capitalists who have been traditionally institutional investors, such as pension funds, insurance companies, endowment funds, and foundations; second, what have become more recently known as angel investors who are wealthy individuals; and third, family and friends or self-financed endeavors. According to Anand Rajaraman, these three different categories of investors evaluate their investment strategies differently, not only because of the amounts involved in each case, but also because of the particular relationship each has to the venture firm and its founders. Yet, there are three major categories of evaluation that remain the same across the different assessment process: market, team, and technology. Obviously, in the case of your own investment in your ideas or the help you might get from family and friends, the requirements are a bit more lax: They all believe in you and want to help your fledgling company in a "bootstrap mode" until such a time when you could go to an angel investor or even a venture capital firm to pitch your idea. There is a hierarchy here: It is easier to convince yourself, your family, and your friends than a complete stranger who has no stake in your success aside from a monetary one.

Rajaraman suggests that angel investors are willing to accept an unproven market for your product, but both the team and angel must have some inclination or belief that the market potential is there, and that its existence could be proven to a venture capitalist. The team, as far as angels are concerned, must include someone the angel has known from a previous experience, either business-related or personal. The factor of personal trust is essential. Likewise, the technology must be in an area where the angel has some expertise or where he or she believes that it has a promise, given what is already known. Overall, the angel will be more involved in the process of completing a prototype or model that will then be pitched more rigorously and effectively to a venture capital firm. At this level, venture capital firms are looking for huge potential returns on their investments, so that the potential market need for the product must be enormous. One must remember that venture capital funds operate with an overall calculated risk model: They assume that only one in ten investments will be fruitful, so that this one success will not only be profitable by itself but will also repay all the other, failed investments. Some call it diversification, some call it risk management, and still others call it calculated gambling. You should remember that venture capitalists (more so than angels) refuse to play casino-like gambling games, because they know the house will win no matter what; instead, what might be understood as their speculations on what idea or project might beat the odds are expected to prevail and make profits. And finally, the way venture capitalists evaluate technology is more remote from the way angels do, because they lack the expertise in all the areas in which they invest. Because of this, they expect the technology to be a breakthrough and hence extremely valuable, or they see it as unique and therefore not easily replicated by competitors (what some call barriers to entry into that particular market) (Rajaraman 2008).

As we have seen historically, there are two main strategies used by venture investors to cash out on their investments, what is called an exit strategy: a buyout by a larger firm or an initial public offering. Truthfully, most ventures fail, and angels and venture capital firms alike lose all their investments: There is usually nothing left to sell or recoup, because most of the investment is spent on intangible assets, such as human capital and not on real estate acquisition or inventory. Most of the money goes into paying the salaries of the inventors or toward a prototype that might never operate properly or that no one might ever want to buy. In cases where a larger firm buys out the venture firm, the investors sell their shares and receive a multiple of their original investment. But in order to evaluate this return on investment properly, one needs to add the time factor: How long has it taken for this to happen? Let us assume an initial investment of $1 million made to start a company on January 1, 2000. And let us assume that on December 31, 2007, the company was bought for $2 million. On the face of it it seems a fantastic return, the doubling of the original investment. But, as economists will remind us, there is an opportunity cost that must be calculated: If the same $1 million were invested elsewhere, what would the return have been? It is this return on investment that must be compared to the actual return of 100 percent over seven years. Let us assume two different compounded annual rates of return, one at 5 percent, which would be equivalent to a government-backed certificate of deposit with almost no risk, and the other at 12 percent, which would be what "hard-money" lenders expect with collateral to cover the amount borrowed. In the first, safe case, the return after seven years would be $1,419,034, whereas in the second, riskier case, the return would be $2,316,047. The difference between the $2 million in the venture capital investment in these two becomes more complex once these two figures are added into one's calculations, not to mention the overall annual inflation rate that makes $1 today worth a little less next year, as its value continuously erodes. Incidentally, as we discussed in the second chapter, regarding the easy access to information and the growth of the knowledge industries, the figures used here were easily calculated through an Internet link without the need to consult experts in the field.

It is because of this that investments in venture capital firms are expected to have returns so much higher than can be expected elsewhere. Why risk 100 percent of one's investment with a risk factor of 90 percent, if instead one could get secured returns of anywhere between 5 and 12 percent annually? The upside must be so much greater to warrant such investments, unless, of course, we are dealing with family, friends, and angels whose main purpose in investing is benevolent support rather than a return on investment. Don Dodge, in his blog, provides a six-year analysis of venture investments and illustrates why such investments are actually not such a good idea. According to him, in 2001 venture capitalists invested $32.1 billion in 3,416 companies, whereas angels invested $30 billion in more than 50,000 companies (obviously the amount invested per company is much smaller for angels). He compares this total investment of $52 billion with returns of $16.8 billion in mergers and acquisitions by other firms and $3.5 billion in initial public offerings, for a total of $19.8 billion in the two exit strategies. If one were to calculate this return for this year (knowing full well that it takes 3–7 years for exit strategies to materialize) it would be about 32 percent. Not bad, but this number does not include the return of the investment itself, so that the actual total exit number should have been close to $72 billion to do well. If we were to follow his numbers (based on the Center for Venture Research) for the averages between 2001 and 2006, we would get a total of $145.4 billion invested by venture capitalists, $135.4 billion by angels, and exit strategies of $80.5 billion for the total of mergers and acquisitions during this period, and $28.4 billion of total initial public offerings. He concludes by saying that investments have averaged $40 billion per year, and exits have averaged $18 billion. In short, venture capital investment is not a great business to be in (Dodge 2007).

So, why be a venture capitalist or an angel? Why take such enormous risks with very little promise of a great return or any return at all? Chronic gamblers and speculators have a ready answer: It is an addiction they cannot kick. They love the thrill of the risks associated with uncertainty, in an almost self-destructive way. But what about rational investors, or investors who believe that they, and only they, can find the Black Swan, as Nassim Taleb, the intellectual maverick and practitioner of the trading floors, calls it: an event that is an outlier with extreme impact and that is poorly explained after its occurrence, namely, a unique and unexpected case that is so far outside the parameters of a normal statistical distribution of risk as modeled by a bell curve as to be unpredictable. If that is what you are after, he says, then you should reach for the very extreme situations where the potential upside is enormously large, instead of hedging your bets on the semirisky stakes that you believe you can beat. More specifically, Taleb suggests that one's investment strategy should be to put close to 90 percent of one's capital in very safe, low-rate earnings instruments, like Treasury Notes, and the other 10 percent in extremely speculative bets, "as leveraged as possible (like options), preferably venture capital-style portfolios," to which he adds that even venture capital funds do not make enough bets, but rather follow a narrative of investments that make sense to them. "If venture capital firms are profitable, it is not because of the stories they have in their heads, but because they are exposed to unplanned events" (Taleb 2007, 205). Taleb is worth listening to not only because of his brilliant analysis of some misguided usages of statistical and probabilistic tools, but because he has been a practitioner who lucratively bucked the trend of trying to guess the outcome of unpredictable events. He admits that the future cannot be predictable either in principle or in practice, and suggests that therefore one should refrain from pretending to be able to do so. Instead, one should acknowledge the inherent and fundamental uncertainty and unpredictability of the future, and prepare, as best one can, for unexpected events to occur (hence, to invest in wild cards, in Black Swans, so to speak) so that the loss is minimal, but the gain is potentially enormous.

I have to confess that I have been engaged in venture capitalist practices in the past fifteen years in a variety of roles. Each case provides a different model of what in fact happens outside the standard confines of the financial institutions that help grease the wheels of the marketplace. All of them might seem to be small and under-the-radar cases, but as the literature on the subject makes clear, they are becoming more and more the new standard of postcapitalism, a model of the marketplace that relies much more on personal relationships and the impartial spectator to govern good behavior rather that the detachment of the invisible hand.

In the first case, I raised about $1 million from family and friends to open a brewery, restaurant, and gallery in an old warehouse. In addition to putting up whatever funds I had, I had to plead for $50,000 without any clear idea how I would repay my investors. As one of my investors reminded me, I had no exit strategy. As time went by and no great profits were forthcoming (but we still had a good business model), I took out loans and repaid my investors, one by one, with a 20 percent rate of return after two years. This model worked because I ran the company and was personally involved in every facet of the business. Like other entrepreneurs in this situation, I did not compensate myself for my work (no salary and benefits) and considered my labor sweat equity, as some call it. After ten years I sold the business to a great chef. I financed the sale over ten years, so that the new owner basically was using me now as his angel to finance his business. It remains a mystery to this day how to assess the rate of return of the original venture: Should one include the annual compensation of the owner and all the benefits? Should one include the original investment minus the amount that was repaid with interest to all the other investors? Depending on which method of calculating one uses, the results will vary widely. This, of course, is different from a straightforward calculation an investor makes who does not operate the venture. One of the things missing from the literature on venture firms are the personal rewards that the founder enjoys along the way, from pride and emotional satisfaction to a salary and health and car insurance and all the other deductions permitted by law (and that cannot be used without having a company).

The second experience I want to briefly examine lies outside the framework of venture firms, because it has to do with a commercial real estate investment as opposed to computer technologies or other knowledge industries (but could be seen in this context as venture-like investment). A commercial broker approached me and my partners to purchase a 25,000-square-foot building on a major road in our city. The price was $1.2 million, and the annual rent would be $144,000. The seller was the renter, and the lease was for ten years. This seemed like a safe investment. What we did not know at the time was the financial condition of the seller/renter. We did not realize that they proposed this arrangement because they needed these funds to continue their operation. Sure enough, within one year the company was bankrupt, and we had an empty building to lease. To some extent we, the landlords, were the angels who gave money to the company for its future operations and expansion plans; in fact, we were their partners who received in return not shares of the company but its real estate, the building. Though adversarial in some sense, landlord and tenant are in fact partners who need to know each other, help each other through rough spots, and ensure a mutually beneficial financial arrangement that will last as long as possible. Ever since that experience some ten years ago, I have treated my tenants as partners and have on more than one occasion provided gradually increasing lease rates so as to indirectly finance their first steps, their new ventures. No, we did not receive shares in exchange, and no, we did not scrutinize their business plans (trust me, most of them would not know how to structure them anyway), but yes, we assumed a certain role of an angel, looking over them and nourishing them, giving them moral and psychological support rather than acting toward them as adversaries. What I have discovered as well is how lonely it is for a company with one to three employees to operate and to become successful. Indeed, the Internet allows you to open your own limited liability company on your own and fairly cheaply, but what then? Who is there to advise you, counsel you, and ensure you avoid some basic pitfalls and mistakes that others have made in your position?

The third set of cases I experienced more recently had to do with more traditional forms of angel investing in venture firms. In one case my partner personally knew a bright and promising graduate student who embarked on a new software/Internet venture with tools not commonly then in use. This personal relationship in addition to some personal expertise of one of the investors convinced us to invest. Seven years later we are still wondering what might happen to this company that has changed its name and location more than once, has been able to collect fees along the way, and was able to raise some venture capital funds from the likes of Sequoia. Is survival enough? By now, as you can imagine, our $150,000 is worth very little; we could have earned more than $105,000 at 10 percent annually had we invested it elsewhere. Is there an upside? How long should one wait? Our shares have been diluted with every new round of funding, so that these questions become theoretical, because we, as small shareholders can neither sell our shares to anyone else (they are not publicly traded) nor force the company to close (and take tax deductions for our losses); in fact, we are marooned on a desolate island with no rescue ship on the horizon.

Another case in the third category relates to someone who knew me from my restaurant and who succeeded in an earlier venture and was able to sell his company to a major software firm (all names and details are confidential). He came to us and showed us a presentation about a scrolling and digital sign, and despite his "mad scientist" look, his demeanor was sweet and convincing, and the technology he was promoting took advantage of current knowledge and pushed it to a new level of sophistication (in terms of connectivity and ease of end user control). My partner and I were so impressed by how his technology would empower end users to control their printing cycles (quick turnaround on design and proof instead of a lengthy period between initial design conception, design execution, and approval after proofing the design) and costs and the ways in which advertising campaigns could be easily launched in multiple locations that we gave him $100,000 within two weeks. A prototype was almost complete in China, and the software was being developed in India for this interactive information and logistics system. Time went by and within six months another $100,000 was needed. After putting up more money and seeing that no sales were imminent, and that the finished product was far from being completed, we realized that in addition to an "idiot-proof" technology that would be accessible and easily operational, a business model had to be developed, which demonstrated how everyone who participated (especially the end user who would be buying these signs for around $15,000 per unit) would make money. My partner and I became more and more involved, and the more involved we became, the more we realized that the business model was unworkable: We could not sell the signs, no matter how excited every potential buyer was at first. The Chinese model had to be redesigned from scratch, and the Indian software company quadrupled its budget for completion. Within fifteen months we closed the company and offered the prototype to anyone who was willing to store it. Were we duped? Were we willing gamblers? Or were we simply angels who gave some genius guy a chance to create and invent, to dream and imagine a better way to handle signage? The image of angels is the most appealing, with their white wings and benevolent disposition.

As I write, more opportunities knock on our door, perhaps because by now this door is recognized as an entryway to untold sums of money to be invested in venture firms. Perhaps by now we have learned from our mistakes, we have done enough deals, and we have lost enough money to appreciate the need to work harder on "due diligence," on getting to know better those we give money to, and have a better idea about all the potential pitfalls before they actually cost us money. Should we stay in the game? Have we become addicted to the thrill of the chase? Or, are we simple businesspeople who have some extra money to spare on these ventures, ventures whose potential for helping the human race might be more appealing than buying another fancy car or a big diamond ring?

Perhaps Nietzsche was right in his analysis of the will to power (1967), where he contends that one of the most intoxicating and powerful emotions humans have is that attending their quest to become more powerful than before and more powerful than others in their community. So, perhaps there is a psychological drive that manifests itself in some in their reach for public office (not to serve but to be admired as a celebrity of sorts) and in some in their incessant reach for business success. The financial rewards are merely an expression of success and not valuable in themselves, because rich people do not sit every day counting dollar bills; but they do like the narratives they tell about their journeys, about their encounters and their adventures. Instead of crossing the Sahara desert, they cross the hallway and write a check for someone who will work very hard to make an idea a financial reality. At best, they are themselves geniuses, but for the most part they are simply lucky, as Taleb correctly says. But luck, too, must be nurtured and have the opportunity to exist. It reminds me of the old Jewish joke about the guy who prays to God every day that he should win the lottery ticket. After weeks of prayer, a voice from the heavens comes down and asks: How can I help you win the lottery if you haven't bought a ticket yet? You see, we need to buy the ticket that allows us entry into lucky-land!

As we discuss in further detail the workings of venture capitalists and angels, as we examine what motivates people to invest and what motivates people to go on their own and try out new ideas and be creative, it becomes more apparent that we need to reexamine the structural settings of the marketplace, whether in its classical or modern configuration, as well as the emotional disposition of all involved. On the one hand, we have some, like Taleb, who claim that the marketplace works for none of the reasons given by the classical economists:

> So I disagree with the followers of Marx and of those of Adam Smith: the
> reason the free markets work is because they allow people to be lucky, thanks
> to aggressive trial and error, not by giving rewards or "incentives" for skill.
> The strategy is, then, to tinker as much as possible and try to collect as many
> Black Swan opportunities as you can. (Taleb 2007, xxi)

This means that it is about market conditions, as we have argued all along,
that allow us all to "tinker" or to get "lucky" as we go about our business.
In this sense, then, Taleb inadvertently does agree with Smith, because according to his model the opportunities are always there for "trial and error,"
for being free to make choices not all of which will result in a profitable
way. But the model must be propped up by a huge legal scaffolding, as I
have said, so that when you fall you only get hurt (as opposed to dying),
and you get another opportunity to try again (using bankruptcy laws, for
example, or borrowing more money from alternative sources).

On the other hand, we have those who wish to revisit Adam Smith's
treatise on human sentiments so as to better understand his later writings
on the workings of the marketplace. We shall return to this theme in the
fourth chapter, where we will examine from different perspectives the
psychological underpinnings that foster the kind of behavior most useful
for the markets. But, as has become evident already at this juncture, there
is a fine line that investors cross when they give their hard-earned money
to venture firms, to individuals who have great ideas and inventions that
have never been tried before. This line has become gray, as we see in the
case of venture capital, when angels and family and friends support someone
they know without a great deal of expectation that they will ever see their
investment back, let alone make a profit from it. Is this kind of investment
really still within the realm of greed? Or has it been transformed to some
sort of philanthropy, one that is sanctioned by the tax code for tax write-
offs? These questions, which I leave open for the time being, recur when
we examine global markets in the next section.

But before we move on, we should note that some, like Nico Stehr
(2008), suggest that the knowledge industries we have discussed so far and
their effect on the accumulation of wealth have allowed consumers in the
affluence of modern capitalism to pay more attention to moral features of
their behavior and choices, and because of this the appearance of "angels,"
for example, or the interest in foreign aid make perfect sense. Moreover,
modes of moral conduct eventually are "inscribed" in products so that
the "moral content of commodities" is becoming more transparent in the
marketplace (Stehr 2008, ix). The social and moral evolution of markets,
then, is a process that can be found in affluent capitalist societies or in what

We do not yet have a firm answer as to which of the possible explanations for East/West synchrony is the most important. Recent discoveries about comets (Blakeslee 2006), climate (Chew 2007; Ruddiman 2005), and work on synchrony (Turchin and Hall 2003; Hall and Turchin 2007) all suggest a satisfactory explanation will most likely combine many different factors and interactions.

Narratives of waves of migration and incursions such as provided by Thompson (2005) correspond fairly well with the growth/decline phases of East and West cities and empires. But the only quantitative indicators we have been able to find for Central Asia suffer from flaws that make it difficult to affirm or deny the role of trade fluctuations (see Chase-Dunn et al. 2006).

In order to test the explanations for East/West city and empire synchrony we need quantitative data over the relevant time period and in the relevant regions for settlement and empire sizes, climate change, epidemic diseases, migrations, trade, and warfare. The trade route data are useful in providing lists of Central Asian settlements to be studied. Our future work will focus on the largest of these and will assemble estimates of settlement sizes and network structures.

It may well be, as our preliminary findings suggest, that the East-West correlation is weakened by consideration of Central Asian empire fluctuations. If we return to Barfield's narrative discussions (1989), however, and keep in mind discussions of the nature of Central Asian confederations (see especially Kradin 2002; see also Kradin, Bondarenko, and Barfield 2003; Hall 2005), another interpretation of those data is possible.

When steppe confederacies weaken, due to decline in China, pastoralists may turn to the Central Asia states, statelets, and city-states both to supply agricultural and craft goods and to dispose of surplus animals and animal products. If so, then Central Asian empires would, in fact, expand as East Asian empires declined. When China, and East Asian empires in general, strengthened, pastoralists, via the outer frontier strategy, would likely have returned to associations with those empires, withdrawing or abating relations with Central Asian empires, states, or city-states for more robust suppliers.

Now, if this is the case, then two issues are clarified. First, the synchronizing mechanisms we suggest above are indeed responsible for East-West correlations. Second, this would give some insight into why South Asia dances to a different tune. These kinds of connections are far weaker across the mountain barriers. South Asian states are not viable alternatives to either East or Central Asian states as suppliers of agricultural and craft goods.

Finally, we need to develop more robust accounts for how all the factors listed above—climate change, epidemic diseases, migrations, trade, and warfare—shaped these processes. All of these factors shaped the degree of urbanization, the volume and velocity of trade, and relative dependence on pastoral versus agrarian resources. Central Asian pastoralists, as we and many others cited above have noted, were extremely flexible and adaptable and adjusted their ways of making a living rapidly to changing circumstances.

We also need to employ analyses with different coding schemes to discover how sensitive our findings are to coding decisions. As with the original East-West synchrony discovery, correlations that are robust with respect to coding and data issues suggest much more confidence in the overall findings. Findings that fluctuate with data and coding decisions would indicate that there are factors and processes that are not sufficiently theorized nor sufficiently precisely and accurately measured. This, in turn would suggest a need to reexamine the narrative histories to discover the relevant factors and processes. But, it is ever so with empirical research on historical processes.

Regardless of the specific details of further research, we are confident that the vital role of Central Asia and Central Asians in the development of all of Afroeurasia will remain important and yield further insights into the processes of world historical evolution.

# Note

1. This chapter is one of the products of a National Science Foundation–sponsored project on "Measuring and modeling cycles of state formation, decline and upward sweeps since the Bronze Age": http://irows.ucr.edu/research/citemp/citemp.html, SES-057720. An earlier version was presented at the Society for Cross-Cultural Research, February 21–24, 2007 San Antonio, Texas.

# References

Barfield, Thomas J. 1989. *The Perilous Frontier: Nomadic Empires and China.* Cambridge, MA.: Blackwell.
_____. 1991. "Inner Asia and Cycles of Power in China's Imperial Dynastic History." Pp. 153–182 in Gary Seaman and Daniel Markes (eds.), *Rulers from the Steppe: State Formation on the Eurasian Periphery.* Los Angeles, CA: Ethnographic Press, Center for Visual Anthropology, University of Southern California.
Beckwith, Christopher I. 1991. "The Impact of the Horse and Silk Trade on the Economies of T'ang China and the Uighur Empire." *Journal of the Economic and Social History of the Orient* 34:2:183–198.
Blakeslee, Sandra. 2006. "Ancient Crash, Epic Wave." *New York Times,* November 14, 2006, Science Section.
Chase-Dunn, Christopher, Alexis Alvarez, and Daniel Pasciuti. 2005a. "Power and Size: Urbanization and Empire Formation in World-systems." Pp. 92–113 in C. Chase-Dunn and E. N. Anderson (eds.), *The Historical Evolution of World-Systems.* New York: Palgrave
———. 2005b. "World-systems in the Biogeosphere: Three Thousand Years of Urbanization, Empire Formation, and Climate Change." Pp. 311–332 in Paul S.

Ciccantell, David A. Smith, and Gay Seidman (eds.), *Nature, Raw Materials, and Political Economy*. Research in Rural Sociology and Development, vol. 10. London: Elsevier.

Chase-Dunn, Christopher, and Salvatore Babones. 2006. *Global Social Change: Comparative and Historical Perspectives*. Baltimore: Johns Hopkins University Press.

Chase-Dunn, Christopher, and Thomas D. Hall. 1997. *Rise and Demise: Comparing World-Systems*. Boulder, CO: Westview.

Chase-Dunn, Christopher, Thomas D. Hall, Richard Niemeyer, Alexis Alvarez, Hiroko Inoue, Kirk Lawrence, Anders Carlson, Benjamin Fierro, Matthew Kanashiro, Hala Sheikh-Mohamed, and Laura Young. 2006 "Middlemen and Marcher States in Central Asia and East/West Growth/Decline Phases." IROWS Working Paper no. 30. Available at http://www.irows.ucr.edu/papers/irows30/irows30.htm

Chase-Dunn, C., and E. Susan Manning. 2002. "City Systems and World-systems: Four Millennia of City Growth and Decline." *Cross-Cultural Research* 36:4:379–398. Available at http://irows.ucr.edu/research/citemp/ccr02/ccr02.htm

Chew, Sing C. 2001. *World Ecological Degradation: Accumulation, Urbanization, and Deforestation 3000 B.C.–A. D. 2000*. Walnut Creek, CA: Altamira Press.

———. 2007. *The Recurring Dark Ages: Ecological Stress, Climate Changes, and System Transformation*. Lanham, MD: Altamira Press.

Christian, David 1994 "Inner Eurasia as a Unit of World History." *Journal of World History* 5:2:173–211.

———. 2000. "Silk Roads or Steppe Roads? The Silk Roads in World History." *Journal of World History* 11:1:1–26.

Cribb, Roger. 1991. *Nomads in Archaeology*. Cambridge: Cambridge University Press.

Di Cosmo, Nicola. 2002. *Ancient China and Its Enemies: The Rise of the Nomadic Power in East Asian History*. Cambridge: Cambridge University Press.

Frank, Andre Gunder. 1992. *The Centrality of Central Asia*. Comparative Asian Studies no. 8. Amsterdam: VU University Press for Center for Asian Studies Amsterdam (CASA).

Guang-da, Zhang. 1996. "The City-states of the Tarim Basin." Pp. 281–302 in B. A. Livitsky, Zhang Guang-da, and R. Shabini Samghabadi (eds.), *History of the Civilizations in Central Asia*, vol. 3. Paris: UNESCO.

Hall, Thomas D. 2005. "Mongols in World-System History." *Social Evolution & History* 4:2 (September):89–118.

Hall, Thomas D., and Peter Turchin. 2007. "Lessons from Population Ecology for World-Systems Analyses of Long-Distance Synchrony." Pp. 74–90 in Alf Hornborg and Carole L. Crumley (eds.), *The World System and the Earth System: Global Socioenvironmental Change and Sustainability Since the Neolithic*. Walnut Creek, CA: Left Coast Books.

Korjenkov, Andrey, Karl Baipakov, Claudia Change, Yury Peshkov, and Tamara Saavelieva. 2003. "Traces of Ancient Earthquakes in Medieval Cities Along the Silk Road, Northern Tien Shan and Dzhungaria." *Turkish Journal of Earth Sciences* 12:241–261.

Kradin, Nikolay N. 2002. "Nomadism, Evolution, and World-Systems: Pastoral Societies in Theories of Historical Development." *Journal of World-Systems Research* (Fall):368–388. Available at: http://jwsr.ucr.edu/index.php.

Kradin, Nikolay N., Dmitri M. Bondarenko, and Thomas J. Barfield, eds. 2003.

*Nomadic Pathways in Social Evolution.* The Civilization Dimension Series, vol. 5. Moscow: Russian Academy of Sciences: Center for Civilizational and Regional Studies.

Lattimore, Owen. 1940. *Inner Asian Frontiers of China.* New York: American Geographical Society.

Liu, Xinru, and Lynda Norene Shaffer. 2007. *Connections Across Eurasia: Transportation, Communications, and Cultural Exchange on the Silk Roads.* New York: McGraw-Hill.

Mair, Victor H., ed. 2006. *Contact and Exchange in the Ancient World.* Honolulu: University of Hawai'i Press.

McNeill, William H. 1976. *Plagues and People.* Garden City, NJ: Anchor Books.

Rosen, Staffen. 1999 "The Sino-Swedish Expedition to Yar-tonguz in 1994." Pp. 59–72 in Mirja Juntunen and Birgit N. Schlyter (eds.), *Return to the Silk Routes: Current Scandinavian Research in Central Asia.* London: Kegan Paul.

Ruddiman, William F. 2005. "How Did Humans First Alter Global Climate?" *Scientific American,* March, pp. 46–53.

Sherratt, Andrew. 2006. "The Trans-Eurasian Exchange: The Prehistory of Chinese Relations with the West." Pp. 30–61 in Victor H. Mair (ed.), *Contact and Exchange in the Ancient World.* Honolulu: University of Hawai'i Press.

Sinor, D., and S. G. Klyashtorny. 1996. "The Turk Empire." Pp. 327–348 in B. A. Livotsky, Zhang Guang-da, and R. Shabani Samgjabado (eds.), *History of Civilizations of Central Asia,* vol. 3, *A.D. 250 to 750.* Paris: UNESCO.

Sorenson, John L,. and Carl L. Johannessen. 2006. "Biological Evidence for Pre-Columbian Transoceanic Voyages." Pp. 238–297 in Victor H. Mair, *Contact and Exchange in the Ancient World.* Honolulu: University of Hawai'i Press.

Taagepera, Rein. 1978 "Size and Duration of Empires: Systematics of Size." *Social Science Research* 7:108–127.

_____. 1997. "Expansion and Contraction Patterns of Large Polities: Context for Russia." *International Studies Quarterly* 41:475–504.

Teggart, Frederick J. 1939. *Rome and China: A Study of Correlations in Historical Events.* Berkeley: University of California Press.

Thompson, William R. 2005. "Eurasian C-wave Crises in the First Millennium B.C." Pp. 20–51 in C. Chase-Dunn and E. N. Anderson (eds.), *The Historical Evolution of World-Systems.* New York: Palgrave.

Turchin, Peter. 2007. "Modeling Periodic Waves of Integration in the Afroeurasian World-System." Unpublished paper (9th draft).

Turchin, Peter, and Thomas D. Hall. 2003. "Spatial Synchrony Among and Within World-Systems: Insights from Theoretical Ecology." *Journal of World-Systems Research* 9:1(Winter):37–64. Available at: http://jwsr.ucr.edu/index.php.

# PART TWO

Asian Struggles

---

# DICTATORSHIP AND DEVELOPMENT IN CHINA

## THEIR IMPACT ON THE WORKERS OF THE WORLD

Robert K. Schaeffer

## Introduction

Since 1978, the dictatorship in China, assisted by governments and global institutions in the core, has adopted policies that have enabled it to acquire a global,
comparative advantage in low-wage labor. This development has disadvantaged
workers in the core, the semiperiphery, the periphery, and in China itself. This
chapter examines the role of dictatorship in the development of China.

Since 1978, the Communist Party dictatorship in China has adopted
developmentalist policies that have helped it secure a global, comparative advantage in low-wage labor and promote rapid industrialization and development.
The policies that made industrialization and development possible in China
were not based on the "free-market" strategies associated with the Washington
Consensus, or what Chris Chase-Dunn has called "ideological globalization"
(Arrighi 2007: 185). They were instead based on the party's control of labor,
technology, capital, monetary policy, and the state. Core states and private
investors have helped the party consolidate power and pursue its develop-

mentalist agenda by permitting China to reenter the interstate system and the world economy without requiring China to adopt the structural adjustment, privatization, and free-market policies required of other indebted or "reentry" states in the period of widespread democratization. Core states and global economic institutions have made an exception for China because, they argue, its reentry will enable firms in core states to capture Chinese markets; political and economic integration will eventually, inevitably promote democratization in China; and the import of low-wage goods from China will make it possible to maintain consumption levels in the core without increasing the wages of workers in the core.

But the industrial developmentalism associated with the rise of China has had adverse consequences for workers in the periphery, in the semiperiphery, in the core, and in China itself. To appreciate these developments, it is important first to analyze the developmentalist policies adopted by the regime in China.

## Industrialization and Development?

After it took power in 1949, the Chinese Communist Party adopted policies designed to promote industrialization and development. During the first thirty years, from 1949 to 1978, the regime's industrialization policies did not result in appreciable development. But during the thirty years since 1978, industrialization in China resulted in significant economic development. As Arrighi (2007: 185) has argued, "industrialization" is not necessarily synonymous with "development," which he has defined as closing the income gap that separates the semiperiphery and the periphery from the core. If this is true, then why did industrialization in China fail to promote development during the first thirty years of communist rule but succeed during the next thirty years?

During the first thirty years, China, like many other states in the periphery and semiperiphery, promoted rapid industrialization. But because China did not have access to foreign investment, foreign aid, or foreign military assistance (except for a brief period of Soviet foreign and military aid during the Korean War), the import-substitutionist industrialization it practiced was more mercantilist-autarkic than most. The regime's effort to force the pace of industrialization during the Great Leap Forward in the late 1950s was a conspicuous failure. It disrupted agriculture, led to widespread hunger and acute famine in some regions, and contributed to the death of between 14 and 16 million people (Cross 1988: 101). During the 1960s, the regime continued to promote industrialization, though at a slower pace, and collectivized agriculture, which increased grain production from 195 million metric tons in 1957 to 304 million metric tons in 1978, a significant achievement that allowed China to feed the population, which grew from 574 to 962 million in this period, and to improve diets slightly (Shen 2004: 50).

At some cost, Chinese policies resulted in substantial industrialization. As Arrighi (2007: 190) has noted, China's percentage of GDP in manufacturing as a percentage of First World manufacturing doubled in this period, from 81.8 percent in 1960 to 165.8 percent in 1980. But Chinese industrialization in this period did not result in any real development. According to Arrighi (2007: 191), China's GNP per capita, as a percentage of First World GNP per capita, actually fell slightly, from 0.9 in 1960 to 0.8 in 1980.

Although agricultural development and industrialization in China did not result in much real development in this period, the party's mercantilist policies delayed China's reentry into the world economy until the late 1970s. This was important because it meant that China did not adopt the debt-financed development strategies common to other peripheral and semiperipheral states in the 1970s. This enabled it to avoid the ruinous structural adjustment programs imposed on most debtor states during the debt crisis of the 1980s (Schaeffer 1997: 226–245). As James Galbraith (2004) has written, "both China and India steered free of western banks in the 1970s and spared themselves the debt crisis." It turned out that Chinese mercantilism, which deferred its reentry into the capitalist world economy until the late 1970s, protected it from a ruinous development strategy. So even though industrialization in China did not contribute to significant economic development in the first period, it nonetheless created a manufacturing and agricultural infrastructure that could be reformed in the second period. "Without that foundation," one economist (Meisner 1999: 247) has argued, "the post-Mao reforms [of the late 1970s] would have had little to reform."

Although agroindustrial change in China did not result in appreciable development in the period between 1949 and 1978, domestic reform and foreign assistance in the period after 1978 resulted in rapid agricultural and industrial growth and substantial development.

When Deng Xiaoping took power in 1978, he instituted several "reforms"—which he described as "crossing the river by groping for stepping stones"—while at the same time maintaining "controls" over important parts of the economy and political life. Although the "reforms" have received considerable attention, less attention has been paid to the role of "controls" in Chinese development.

Deng introduced three important reforms. First, the regime abandoned policies that had encouraged population growth and introduced a strict, one-child policy, which was enforced by close surveillance of child-bearing households, widespread sterilization and abortion, and a system of economic penalties for noncompliance. These steps dramatically slowed the pace of population growth.

Second, the regime abandoned its collective approach to agriculture and leased public land to farm households, giving them an incentive to make independent production decisions and reap their benefits. The government increased the prices paid to farmers for produce delivered to the state and allowed farmers to sell food in excess of their quotas on the market for even higher prices. These reforms increased agricultural production from 305 million metric tons in 1978 to 407 million metric tons by 1984 (Selden 1983: 19).

Third, the regime borrowed money to invest in industry, permitted foreign investors to build factories to manufacture goods for export, devalued the currency to make these goods cheap in overseas markets, and allowed Chinese entrepreneurs to set up businesses that could produce goods for the domestic market. Using foreign loans totaling $40 billion during the first decade of reform and foreign investment amounting to $28 billion, the regime expanded and modernized its manufacturing base (Segal 1992: 183). The rapid growth of Chinese exports, which grew from $9.7 billion in 1978 to $52 billion in 1989, enabled the regime to repay foreign loans and avoid the debt crises common to other peripheral and semiperipheral states in this period (Shirk 1993: 48).

But even though the regime altered its approach to population, agriculture, and foreign capital, it maintained its control of technology (using technological transfer or theft to secure foreign technology for technologically deficient domestic industries), capital, monetary policy (keeping the yuan unconvertible and undervalued), and labor. The regime's control of labor was a key component of the regime's developmental project.

In China, the dictatorship has long used policies designed to control labor supplies and suppress wages. The government's residential permit system (*hukou*), which designated where people could live and work, was established in 1955 to control and allocate the labor supply (Chan 2004: 229–230; Solinger 1999). It was designed primarily to prevent workers in rural areas from moving to urban areas. During the 1980s, as the government and foreign investors expanded industry in urban areas, the demand for labor increased (Guthrie 2006: 209–213). The regime allowed rural workers to migrate to the cities to meet demand, but kept the *hukou* system intact, so that migrant workers were treated like illegal immigrants in their own country. Migrant workers could not lay claim to the legal protection provided workers with residential permits and work assignments, could not claim the minimum wage, could not obtain food rations or any of the health and pensions benefits associated with legal employment, could not, until recently, send their children to school, and could be arrested and "deported" to the countryside if they complained about working conditions, petitioned the government for redress, or demanded higher wages (Yardley 2004a; Gilboy and Heginbotham 2004: 257; Eckholm 2004).

The regime's labor-control policy, which allowed massive migration to occur but kept it illegal, created a huge reserve army of labor, now estimated at between 90 and 114 million workers, and a bifurcated labor force (Yardley 2004b; Gilboy and Higenbotham 2004: 260). Urban workers with residency and work permits are allowed to work for foreign investors and domestic entrepreneurs in the export-manufacturing sector, for low wages. Illegal migrant workers are not permitted to work for foreign investors, and they labor instead for Chinese employers for even lower, less-than-legal wages. This policy keeps labor supplies plentiful and keeps down wages, both because it makes labor plentiful and because the large illegal labor force suppresses the wages of legal workers, just as it does in the United States.

But although the government's policies, which combined "reforms" and "controls," produced significant development in the 1980s, they also created problems, primarily inflation, which is a discriminatory economic process. Rising food prices associated with agricultural reform, and rising rents associated with rural-to-urban migration, increased prices for urban workers, both legal and illegal, who could not raise their wages to keep pace. Inflation in China reached double-digit rates in 1985 and rose 28 percent in 1989 (Naughton 1989: 270; Kristof 1989).

When students rallied at Tiananmen Square in the spring of 1989, they were joined by urban workers who were disadvantaged by inflation and economic reform, creating a *minjung* or student-worker movement that challenged the Communist Party's control of the state (Schaeffer 2005: 196–197). The destruction of the student-labor coalition in Tiananmen Square enabled the party to reassert its control over labor, which meant that labor costs and political demands could be contained. The reassertion of dictatorship in China came at a time when other peripheral and semiperipheral countries in Asia and around the world were democratizing, leaving China as one of the world's few remaining dictatorships. At this juncture, foreign investment in China surged, emptying out of semiperipheral states in Asia and then from other peripheral, semiperipheral, and core states around the world. In the decade after Tiananmen Square, foreign investors poured $339 billion into China, and by 2000 directed one-half of all foreign direct investment into the country (Zheng 2004: 4, 6; Pottinger and Kyne 2004). It was this dual development—the party's reassertion of control over labor and the fortuitous demise of labor-controlling dictatorships around the world—that enabled China to secure a global comparative advantage in low- and lower-wage labor in the years after Tiananmen Square.

It is also important to recognize that the regime's developmentalist policies were not alone responsible for its success. Core states, primarily the United States, played a key role in assisting Chinese development and making its policies efficacious.

## The United States and Chinese Development

U.S. officials invited and facilitated China's reentry into the interstate system and the capitalist world economy without requiring the regime to adopt political reforms or the kind of free-market, Washington Consensus policies imposed on other indebted (countries in Latin America and Africa) or reentry (countries in Eastern Europe and the former Soviet Union) states during the period of global democratization.

The United States facilitated the admission of the regime into the United Nations, secured it a permanent seat on the Security Council, and recognized its sovereignty over Taiwan, which was thrown out of the United Nations, without demanding any political reforms or concessions on its part. Contrast this to the treatment of apartheid regimes in Rhodesia and South Africa, or communist regimes in Cuba, North Vietnam, and North Korea during this period. After Tiananmen Square, U.S. officials decided not to punish the regime for slaughtering 2,600 people and arresting thousands more, but instead allowed private investors to transfer technology and invest heavily in the regime. In the late 1990s, the United States helped China gain admission to the World Trade Organization despite widespread evidence of on-going labor and human rights violations, patent and technology theft and piracy, government subsidies in manufacturing and illegal dumping and, perhaps most important, without relinquishing control of its monetary policy, which keeps the yuan unconvertible and undervalued.

It is remarkable that core states did not use reentry as an opportunity to impose structural adjustment on China, as they did for almost every other indebted, democratizing, and reentry state. But why did the United States and other core states make an "exception" for China?

Initially, President Richard Nixon invited China to reenter the interstate system to undermine the Soviet Union and end Chinese support for North Vietnam during the war in Vietnam. For Chinese leaders, abandoning their North Vietnamese allies was a small price to pay for U.S. recognition and for the U.S. decision to abandon Taiwan, a long-time U.S. ally.

Later, U.S. officials welcomed reform in China because they believed it would enable U.S. firms to capture markets in China, a dream that dates back more than a century (Shenkar 2006: 103). The prospect of opening the Chinese market, with one billion consumers, to U.S. agricultural and industrial goods has provided a key rationale for not demanding reforms or concessions from the regime. The irony is that U.S. policymakers and investors have been slow to realize that the regime has taken steps to prevent the capture of China's domestic market by foreigners. They have done so by allowing domestic firms and state-run enterprises to employ lower-wage "illegal" migrant workers so they can undercut labor costs in foreign-run firms, by providing domestic firms with below-market interest rates on loans so they can obtain capital more cheaply than foreign firms, by creating excess capacity and driving down prices and profit margins so foreign firms cannot compete in domestic markets, by transferring foreign technology to domestic firms or allowing them simply to steal technology so that foreign firms lose their technological advantages, by discouraging domestic retailers from displaying or selling foreign-made goods, and, an important point, by keeping the currency undervalued so that domestic firms have a price advantage over more expensive foreign imports (Lardy 2002: 89; Gottschang 1992: 271). Moreover, in recent years, "tastes in China are also changing to the detriment of American companies ... not because of anti-Americanism but because of Chinese nationalism," one businessman in China observed (Bradsher 2005b: C4). As a result of these policies, it has been very difficult for foreign firms to capture the markets they expected to conquer when China "opened" its doors to foreigners (Rhoads and Hutzler 2004).

U.S. officials and economists have also argued that China need not adopt serious political reforms as a condition for reentry because participation in the capitalist world economy would eventually and inevitably lead to democratization in China. "While democratic reform may not in all cases be an inevitable outcome of economic reform, it is, at this point, an inevitability in China," one economist wrote in 2006 (Guthrie 2006: 303).

Optimism about the inevitability of democratization in China has been undeterred by the facts. The early period of reform, and the student-worker movement it engendered, led to the violent suppression of the prodemocracy movement by the regime and the consolidation of its power, with massive support from foreign investors. In the nearly twenty years since Tiananmen Square, the Communist Party has grown stronger, not weaker (Kahn 2007). The party can now plausibly claim that economic growth and development in this period was due to its sound economic policies and astute leadership, rather than admitting that it was dictatorship, supported by foreign capital, and the widespread collapse of dictatorships elsewhere that made it possible for it to deliver its legal and illegal workforce to domestic and foreign capitalists at the lowest possible prices.

An analysis of democratization in other peripheral and semiperipheral states since 1978 suggests that dictatorships fell not because they promoted economic growth, but because they experienced economic crisis (Schaeffer 1997). Given this pattern of democratization, it is difficult to see why China would democratize in the absence of any significant economic crisis.

Of course, workers in urban areas and peasants in rural areas have protested the regime's policies and practices in the years since Tiananmen Square (Perry and Goldman 2007). One might make the argument that widespread grassroots protest might, eventually, contribute to democratization in China. But if one looks at grassroots movements in other countries, grassroots political protest is usually effective only where its power is decentralized. In the United States, the civil rights, environmental antitoxics, and antinuclear power movements were effective, in large part, because they confronted local authority, not the power of central government authorities (Schaeffer 1999: 201–203). In the Chinese context, it is difficult to imagine that local grassroots groups can accomplish what a broad-based coalition in Tiananmen Square could not achieve—a decisive weakening of central power authority and a devolution of power to wider political constituencies or successors. Indeed, Elizabeth Perry and Merle Goldman (2007: 2) have warned that "China's current grassroots political reforms could actually help forestall rather than facilitate the advance of formal democracy at the national level."

In recent years, U.S. policymakers have argued that it is not necessary to demand political or economic concessions from China because Chinese exports have made it possible to maintain or increase levels of consumption in the core without increasing wages because low-priced manufactured goods reduce the cost of consumer goods for U.S. workers. This rationale is what might be called the Wal-Mart strategy. The problem with this rationale is that outsourcing jobs to China results in job loss in the United States, which weakens consumer demand in the United States.

These different political and economic considerations persuaded policymakers in the United States and in other core countries to make an exception for China and allow it to reenter the interstate system and the capitalist world economy without adopting either "democratization" or "structural adjustment" as a price for its admission. This seems shortsighted and unfair to all the other countries that were required to pay a high price for participation. It also suggests that core states exempted China because it did *not* democratize. The pattern of investment flows suggests that investment surged into China at a time when dictatorship was being consolidated in China but was being abandoned elsewhere, a development that might be described as capital flight from democratizing states. This should not be surprising, given the fact that Wallerstein has argued that the capitalist world economy has always combined "free" and "coerced" forms of labor and "democratic" and "despotic" forms of government in the same, unitary world-system.

## The Workers of the World

The developmentalist policies adopted by the regime in China and promoted by core states have had an adverse impact on workers in the periphery, the semiperiphery, and the core and in China itself.

### *The Periphery*

Many countries in the periphery have large supplies of poor workers who earn about what Chinese workers earn, sometimes even less. India, for example, has a huge supply of low-wage labor, many of whom speak English. But except for a small sector of English-speaking service jobs, which employ about two million people, India has been unable to attract much foreign investment. Between 1990 and 2000, India received only $4 billion in foreign investment, despite the introduction of market-reform policies and the availability of a huge supply of low-wage labor, whereas China received eighty-five times as much investment (Rai 2004).

Investors in the core prefer China not simply because it has low-wage workers but also because the dictatorship promises to keep wages low. In democratic peripheral countries such as India, workers can migrate freely, change jobs, and organize collectively to demand higher wages and better benefits and working conditions. That is exactly what they have done in the English-speaking outsourcing and technology service sector: "Entry level salaries in the software industry [in India] have been rising by an average of 10 to 15 percent in recent years" (Sengupta 2006: A6).

Because wages can and do rise more easily in democratic peripheral states than they can in a dictatorship, foreign investors have preferred to employ low-wage workers in China. The expansion of foreign investment in China has allowed it to expand the production of industrial and agricultural goods that are also made by other peripheral states and to capture market shares at their expense. In the case of textiles, the expansion of Chinese textile exports has come at the expense of "the developing and especially the least-developed economies that will be hard pressed to find alternative venues for growth and employment" (Shekar 2006: 105).

The expanded production of tea in China has likewise caused "alarm in other developing countries that depend on growing tea, like India, Sri Lanka, Indonesia, Bangladesh, Kenya, Malawi, and Zimbabwe" because Chinese supplies will lower prices and capture markets and displace millions of people who depend on this crop for their livelihood. In Sri Lanka, for example, tea production, which is one of the world's most labor-intensive crops, helps feed nearly one-tenth of the population (Bradsher 2005c: A1).

Many of the peripheral states in Asia—India, Bangladesh, Sri Lanka, Indonesia, Malaysia, Thailand—are at least nominal democracies (though there have been recent military coups in Bangladesh and Thailand). When they compete with China for foreign investment and export markets, they are at a disadvantage because they are democratic. But there are other peripheral states in Asia and Africa that are also dictatorships, like China, which means they can offer low-wage workers on terms much like those in China. The problem for them is that dictatorships in these states earlier tried to use debt to promote development and, when it failed, were forced to adopt structural adjustment policies. As a result, government spending fell and their infrastructure substantially deteriorated. The poor quality of infrastructure in these dictatorships is a deterrent to investors and raises the real cost of producing goods, low wages notwithstanding.

## The Semiperiphery

States in the semiperiphery have also lost manufacturing industries and jobs to China in recent years. During the 1970s and 1980s, one-party states such as

South Korea, Taiwan, and Mexico built up export manufacturing industries, generically *maquiladoras,* to supply goods to core countries, principally the United States. But in the late 1980s, regimes in South Korea and Taiwan slowly began to democratize, holding elections and opening them to participation by opposition parties, as Mexico did a decade later. When they did, foreign and domestic investors, who expected democratization to lift the decades-long ceiling on wages, moved their manufacturing industries to China, where the government's suppression of worker protest at Tiananmen Square imposed a new ceiling on wages in China. In South Korea and Taiwan, the capital flight from democratizing semiperipheral state to consolidating dictatorship in China was first apparent in industries that produced footware, toys, games, and sporting goods. In 1987, when the democratization process began, the United States imported 60 percent of these goods from South Korea and Taiwan, and only 5 percent from China. But by 1991, two years after Tiananmen Square, imports from South Korea and Taiwan had fallen to 30 percent, whereas import from China had risen to 30 percent, and by 1999, the United States imported 90 percent of these goods from China and only 5 percent from South Korea and Taiwan (Lardy 2002: 52). A similar shift affected personal computers in the late 1990s. During the 1990s, "tens of thousands of firms in Taiwan shifted operations across the strait to the mainland," largely because they were "lured by Chinese wages that [were] a fifth of those in Taiwan" (Bradsher 2005a: W1). Business in Taiwan invested $100 billion in China during the 1990s. As a result, economic growth in Taiwan slowed from 6 percent annual growth in GDP in 1990 to 0 percent in 2001, and unemployment tripled (Dean 2004; Bradsher 2005a).

The same process occurred in Mexico. During the 1990s, "Mexico lost nearly half a million manufacturing jobs and 500 maquiladora manufactures" to China, where workers earned one-quarter of the wages paid to Mexican workers (Fishman 2004: 50). Mexico lost another 287,000 jobs, mostly in telephone equipment, household appliances, and electric assemblies between 2000 and 2003, as part of "an exodus of factories ... to China" (Malkin 2002: W1; Shenkar 2006: 111). This latter shift occurred during a period of "democratization" in Mexico, when the Institutional Revolutionary Party (PRI) lost control of the presidency to an opposition party.

## The Core

Between 2000 and 2006, the United States lost more than three million jobs, or one-sixth of its manufacturing jobs, as a result of automation and outsourcing, primarily to China (Greenhouse 2007; Shenkar 2006: 133). A similar process is also underway in Japan, where domestic firms are "relocating plants to China" (Barboza 2006).

The low wages that dictatorship in China can provide are an important reason why businesses in the core outsource jobs to China. But exchange rates also play an important role. The regime in China keeps the yuan pegged to the dollar at a rate that makes its exports cheaper than they would if exchange rates were set by market forces. The regime has been able to deflect U.S. demands to appreciate the yuan by threatening to sell its large stock of U.S. treasuries—worth $1 trillion in 2007 (Yardley and Barboza 2007). If it did, U.S. officials would have to raise interest rates to cover its huge budget deficits, a move that would trigger a recession and increase unemployment in the United States. Faced with this prospect, U.S. policymakers would rather let U.S. businesses outsource jobs to China and blame it on "globalization" than raise interest rates, cause a recession, and take the blame for growing unemployment in the United States.

For Japan, the appreciation of the yen against the dollar-yuan (the yuan is fixed in relation to the dollar) has meant that imports from China have become even cheaper, which has encouraged Japanese business to manufacture and import goods from China.

## China

The developmentalist policies adopted by the regime and sanctioned by states in the core have had adverse economic and political consequences for workers in China. In economic terms, the regime's labor-control policy discriminates against rural migrant workers, who receive lower pay than their "legal" brethren and who often have their wages garnished or withheld by their employers to hold them in place. They receive none of the public economic benefits—housing, health care, pensions—that legal urban workers receive (French 2007). To accommodate the growth of cities and provide land for housing and industrial construction, the government has seized land from rural farmers, displacing 70 million farmers during the 1990s (Yardley 2004a). For legal, urban workers, the huge army of migrant labor has suppressed wages and raised urban rents (Barboza 2005).

The government's expansionary policies, fueled by massive amounts of foreign investment, have kept inflation rates high, from 6 to 10 percent annually, which discriminates against both rural and urban workers who cannot increase their wages at the same rate. The regime has virtually abandoned its once-universal health care system, which reduced infant mortality from 200 per 1,000 live births to 34 and increased life expectancy from 35 to 68 years between 1952 and 1982 (French 2006). By 2006, 80 percent of the population was uninsured and ill treated (French 2006).

Although China has made economic gains, measured in per capita income, most workers have not gained. As one group of economists has noted, "One of the world's most egalitarian societies in the 1970s, China in the 1990s became one of the most unequal countries in the region and among developing countries generally. This retreat from equality has thus been unusually rapid"

(Riskin, Remwei and Shi 2001: 3). The regime defends growing inequality by arguing, like Kuznets, that it is a temporary phenomenon. "Let some get rich first," officials argued in the early days of reform (Riskin, Remwei, and Li 2001: 18). More recently, they have argued that inequality would lead, in a series of stages, to eventual equality: "Prosperity to some, to most, then to all" (Knight and Song 2001: 120). But thirty years into the reformist project, inequality is still increasing and the first stage has now become a permanent condition.

Chinese developmentalism has also disadvantaged workers in political terms. It has enabled the regime to consolidate domestic political power and enhance its stature within the interstate system. For Chinese workers, this means that the regime can deny migrants their rights as citizens; deprive legal and illegal workers of human rights; and subject them to an arbitrary legal system that practices widespread torture, according to the UN Commission on Human Rights, and annually imposes the death penalty on 10,000 people (Kahn 2005b). Although Chinese workers have a constitutional right to petition the government for redress, petitioners are "as likely to be harassed, kidnapped, jailed or tortured as they are to have their complaints adjudicated by a higher authority" (Kahn 2005a: A12).

The inability of workers to engage in a meaningful political process has meant that the regime has been able to consolidated its political power and, significantly, expand its economic power by creating a new bourgeoisie, which comprises largely Communist Party cadre. This class transformation, much like those described by Wallerstein during the English and French "revolutions," where the aristocracy became bourgeoisie, has made it possible for the elite to capture most of the benefits associated with industrialization and development in China.

# References

Arrighi, Giovanni. 2007. "Globalization and Uneven Development." In *Frontiers of Globalization Research: Theoretical and Methodological Approaches,* ed. Ino Rossi, pp. 185–202. New York: Springer-Science.

Barboza, David. 2005. "China Builds Its Dreams, and Some Fear a Bubble." *New York Times,* October 18.

———. 2006. "Some Assembly Needed: China as Asia Factory." *New York Times,* February 9.

Bradsher, Keith. 2005a. "After an Exodus of Jobs, a Recovery in Taiwan." *New York Times,* March 19.

———. 2005b. "Made in U.S., Shunned in China." *New York Times,* November 18.

———. 2005c. "Read the Tea Leaves: China Will Be Top Exporter." *New York Times,* October 11.

Chan, Kam Wing. 2004. "Internal Migration." In *Changing China: A Geographical Appraisal,* ed. Chiao-min Hseih and Max Lu, pp. 229–242. Boulder, Colo.: Westview.

# 7

# CHINA, ASIA, AND LABOR STANDARDS AFTER THE 2005 MULTI-FIBER ARRANGEMENT

### Robert J. S. Ross

## Introduction: South-South

In the early part of this decade, Ross and Chan (2002) and Chan and Ross (2003) argued that much of the competition for the markets in manufactured goods of the global North was South-South—competition for market share among peripheral and semiperipheral economies. This chapter examines the effects of the dramatic 2005 change in the rules of the world textile and apparel trade to assess the Chan and Ross and other predictions about the end of quantitative national ceilings—the Multi-fiber Arrangement (MFA)—on clothing exports to rich country markets.

The MFA expired on January 1, 2005. It had provided for quotas—quantitative country by country (and item by item) ceilings on exports of textiles and clothing from lower-income countries to the EU and the United States. The quotas that are broadly referred to as the MFA refer to the original 1974 exception and supplement to the Uruguay round of General Agreement on Tariffs and Trade (GATT) negotiations. When the World Trade Organization was formed, the MFA was moved into the WTO agreement and retermed the Agreement on Textiles and Clothing (ATC). According to the ATC (universally referred to as MFA), the national quotas of exports to the United States and to the EU were to grow, item by item, at a steady rate each year, and as well, rising numbers of all items were to be quota-free. By January 2005 all textile and clothing items were to be released from quota constraints (World Trade Organization 2007).

As the end of the MFA drew near in 2004, observers of the world textile and apparel trade feared that a dramatic surge of Chinese exports would accelerate a labor standards "race to the bottom" of unprecedented dimensions. (Appelbaum 2004, 2005; Chan and Ross 2003; Clean Clothes Campaign 2004a, 2004b; Foo and Bas 2003) Using the Mexico versus China competition for the U.S. apparel market as their model, Chan and Ross (among many others) forecast that the existing "race to the bottom" in labor standards would be accelerated because of China's combination of rural labor surplus and a dictatorial labor regime that suppressed labor costs.

## A Strange Protectionism: The MFA

There is no small irony in the reversal of the global discourse on the MFA/ATC. A trade agreement that had been characterized by developing country governments, neoliberal economists, and progrowth nongovernmental organizations (NGOs) as "protectionist" and a sign of core nation raw power had now, paradoxically, become the symbol of a regime of positive globalization. (See, e.g., Oxfam 2004; Hudgins 1985; Raghavan n.d.; Yearman and Gluckman 2005) If it was protectionist, it was unusually ineffective. In the course of a generation the United States (and less so the EU) voluntarily gave up one of its largest industries. In the United States apparel employment fell by 842,000 from 1974 to 2002; according to a somewhat different classification of U.S. industries, from 1990 to 2006 apparel jobs fell from more than 900,000 to just under 240,000. Whichever time series one chooses, the United States lost more than one million jobs in combined textile and apparel production after 1974, about 65 percent of the combined industries.[1] If that was protectionism, it was but a slender reed.

Throughout the Cold War period—and after—the United States used apparel production and then MFA quota as an anti-Communist and counterrevolutionary alliance-making tool (cf. Rosen 2002) in the Cold War and in the Central American civil wars.[2] In the process, EU and U.S. quota distributions made the provisioning of textiles and apparel to the world export market the most globalized industry in the world.

As the end of the quota regime approached in January 2005, the global discourse about the MFA changed from one that emphasized its protectionist and rent-seeking structure to a discourse in which the MFA/ATC was understood as having spawned a true globalization of the textile and clothing industries. As each country with an expanding clothing or textile industry reached the limits of its quota, apparel brands and retailers in the older industrial countries of the global North sought suppliers in yet other low wage/low cost regions. By the eve of quota termination, as of 2004, eighty-nine different countries exported at least $10 million in clothing to the United States (calculated from Office of Textile and Apparel [OTEXA] 2007). Small countries (and their advocates) and those whose costs of production were higher than China's worried—at length—that they would lose market share to China or even be eliminated entirely from the U.S. and EU clothing supply chain.[3]

## A High Stakes Game Even Though the Rag Trade Is Cheap

The stakes involved in quota elimination were high on many dimensions. There were about 20 million jobs in the global textile and clothing complex in 2005, and at least 7.5 million of these were clothing workers. (Rosen 2005:7) Drawn into the global supply chain by the scanning functions of the big brands' managers, numerous low-income countries saw this venerable industry as the start of hoped-for industrialization. Heavy reliance on textile and clothing exports was the poignant result for many. Table 7.1 is a list (compiled by the United Nations Conference on Trade and Development [UNCTAD]) of the twenty countries most dependent on textiles and clothing as a fraction of their total exports in 2003.

In the run-up to the expiration of the MFA there were numerous projections of the effect of the end of the quotas. One projection from the American Textile Manufacturers Institute predicted that China would obtain about 75 percent of the U.S. clothing and textile market (American Textile Manufacturers Institute 2003, 2004). A somewhat more refined study, presenting a broadly accepted view of the structure of the global apparel trade, was commissioned by UNCTAD and put forward by Appelbaum (2004) and Appelbaum, Bonacich, and Quan (2005). This body of work predicted, indeed, that China would loom large in the emerging structure of world apparel trade. But the Appelbaum study also proposed underlying structural trends: (1) concentration of national sourcing as the end of quotas "released" investors to move toward a smaller number of low-cost platforms; (2) increasing power of retailers with "price-making" power in an oligopolistic market; and (3) some remaining advantages of geographic proximity, for example, for Mexico. At the time that Chan and Ross were writing—the early 2000s—China and Mexico held roughly equal shares of the U.S. import market—about 15 percent each. Because of the North American Free Trade Agreement (NAFTA) treaty, there was no quantitative ceiling on Mexico's apparel exports to the United States but there was a ceiling on Chinese exports.

During the first few months of 2005, with no quotas, the surge of apparel imports from China to the United States was as least as large as expected—blowing the proverbial barn doors off their metaphoric hinges. In response the

Table 7.1   Exporters That Are Highly Dependent on Exports of Apparel and
Textiles, 2003 (percentage share of total merchandise exports)

| Economy | Apparel | Textiles | Total |
|---|---|---|---|
| Cambodia[a] | 84.3 | 1.08 | 5.3 |
| Haiti[b] | 82.2 | 1.98 | 4.1 |
| Bangladesh | 75.9 | 7.3 | 83.3 |
| China, Macao SAR | 71.0 | 11.7 | 82.8 |
| Pakistan | 22.9 | 47.5 | 70.3 |
| Lesotho[b] | 65.3 | 5.0 | 70.3 |
| Mauritius | 52.9 | 4.1 | 57.1 |
| Sri Lanka | 51.7 | 3.3 | 55.0 |
| Tokelaua | 13.0 | 40.5 | 53.4 |
| Nepal | 34.6 | 16.4 | 51.0 |
| Dominican Republic[b] | 41.5 | 1.7 | 43.3 |
| Lao People's Democratic Republic[b] | 41.6 | 0.2 | 41.8 |
| Tunisia | 37.0 | 3.7 | 40.7 |
| Albania | 34.3 | 0.3 | 34.6 |
| Morocco | 32.4 | 1.5 | 33.9 |
| FYR Macedonia | 30.0 | 3.1 | 33.1 |
| Madagascar | 31.1 | 1.4 | 32.5 |
| Turkey | 21.1 | 11.1 | 32.2 |
| Maldives | 32.0 | 0.0 | 32.0 |
| Fiji | 26.8 | 1.2 | 28.0 |

*Source:* United Nations Conference on Trade and Development 2005.
[a]As of mid-2005 a senior Cambodian official put the clothing fraction of total exports at 93 percent (Siphana 2005: 2).
[b]Includes estimates by the UNCTAD secretariat.

United States and the EU resorted to clauses in China's WTO accession agreements that gave them the right to restrain Chinese imports (to allow orderly market adjustments) through the end of 2008. These partial restraints were implemented but the actions did not restrain all categories Chinese exports of clothing and in the meantime all other countries' quotas expired.

As a result of the MFA expiration, even though China's exports were still partially restrained, the world apparel market was in a previously unparalleled largely "free" state. An examination of the resulting structure of clothing imports to the United States allows an examination both of previous predictions and, as well, of underlying structures.[4]

## Chinese Surge and Domination

In the first instance, the Chinese (PRC) share of apparel imports to the United States by dollar value jumped from $8.93 billion in 2004 to $18.5 billion in

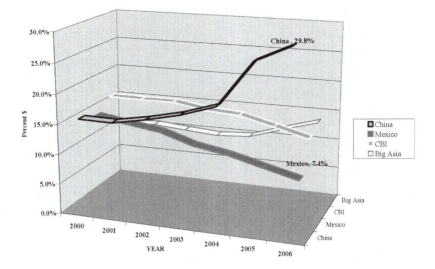

Figure 7.1    Shares of U.S. Apparel Imports

2006. The total Chinese (PRC and Hong Kong) proportion of the value of clothing imports to the United States went from 15.7 percent in 2000 to 29.8 percent in 2006 (Office of Textile and Apparel [OTEXA] 2007). In almost direct proportion, Mexico's market share of imports dropped from 14.7 percent to 8.8 percent in dollar value of exports to the United States in this period. Mexico's market share loss was an absolute (not inflation corrected) loss of $1.3 billion in exports of clothing. The closest competitor to Mexico for U.S. market share in 2006 was Indonesia, whose share grew to 5.1 percent of the value of the U.S. clothing import market. Indonesia was part of a group of "Big Asia" clothing exporters that increased drastically its U.S. import share: Indonesia, India, Bangladesh, and Vietnam collectively went from around 10 percent to 13.6 percent of the import market from 2000 to 2006. See Figure 7.1.

In sum, the predictions that Chinese producers would overwhelm their competitors for the U.S. market proved true—and they gained total market share even during the period when certain categories of their imports were put under "standby restraints." Whether Chinese clothing exports will reach 75 percent of U.S. apparel imports, or 50 percent of world exports—as some predicted—remains to be seen.

## Concentration

The post-MFA projections of the world apparel trade envisioned a market where the concentrated buyers—the retailers and brands of the global North—would focus their orders on a more limited number of national locations of suppliers. (Appelbaum 2004 inter alia) When national quotas were abolished, the logic of both a factor cost minimizing analysis and internal transaction costs dictated that orders would flow toward fewer contractor factories that could fulfill, for example, the (full package) needs of the brands while also meeting their rigorous low-cost requirements. The predictions were that fewer national locations would meet these requirements than were used under the artificially dispersed regime of the MFA.

Although part of 2005 and all of 2006 were under partial restraints on Chinese imports, other countries were not so restrained. A global analysis of the restructuring of import shares is thus a moderately fair test of the concentration thesis. As it turns out, it is moderately accurate.

One convenient metric for the concentration thesis involves using national sources of imported clothing as analogues to firms in a market. In that case we can examine a four-firm concentration ratio as a test of the concentration thesis. In 2004, the last year before the expiration of all MFA quotas, the top four national suppliers to the U.S. import market (counting the PRC and Hong Kong as one entity) accounted for 38 percent of all U.S. apparel imports by value. In 2006 the top four accounted for just under 47 percent—an increase in concentration of 22 percent. Such a rapid increase in an analogue national market of firms would be almost without precedent. The top ten national sources of U.S. clothing imports in 2004 accounted for 57 percent of the market; in 2006, they accounted for 66 percent (Office of Textile and Apparel [OTEXA] 2007).[5] In 2004, 89 countries exported at least $10 million of clothing to the United States. In 2006, 78 countries exported at least $10 million of clothing to the United States. Alternatively, in 2004, 24 countries had at least a 1 percent share of the U.S. import market ($648 million); this was unchanged in 2006.

About the concentration thesis, the evidence appears to support the following conclusions. First, there has been concentration of national sources of imported clothing. Second, there are still many (small) suppliers who have not been crowded out by the big Asian exporters, and fully two dozen (the same number as in 2004) who reach the 2006 2 percent threshold—$716 million.

China indeed dominated the newly (almost) deregulated world clothing market with absolute dollar gains compared to Mexico's losses and Indonesia's moderate gains. Overall the changes when disaggregated also have regional and labor standards stories within them.

## Regional Shift

The shift from higher-cost providers to lower-cost providers creates a strongly regional picture of the changes. As Figure 7.1 showed, the Central American and Caribbean exporters covered under the Caribbean Basin Initiative (CBI) umbrella lost significant market share to the large Asian producers—Indonesia, India, Bangladesh, and Vietnam.[6]

The cluster of smaller Central American and Western Hemisphere countries (with three exceptions) lost market share, whereas all of the low-wage Asian exporters gained, and the middle-income and higher-income Asian countries (Malaysia, Taiwan, and South Korea) lost market share. Restraints were replaced on Chinese exports only in the latter half of 2005—so for most of that year the Chinese exporters rapidly gained share in relation to all competitors. Yet, in the global chess game, Bangladesh, where officials and business spokespersons feared they would lose to the Chinese, gained even more from other—perhaps Western Hemisphere—competitors. Bangladeshi exports to the United States increased by about 20 percent from 2004 to 2005 and then another 23 percent from 2005 to 2006. For the Bangladeshi economy this was no small matter; clothing composed almost a 78 percent share of its 2005 merchandise exports (Heron 2007). Figure 7.2 shows that in the Western Hemisphere, the only exporting nations who gained share from 2004 to 2006 were Nicaragua, Haiti, and Peru. Nicaragua increased its clothing exports to the United States by 48 percent between 2004 and 2006; Haiti increased its exports by 39 percent. The other distinction shared by these two countries is that they are two of the three lowest per capita income economies in the Western Hemisphere and have correspondingly low wages.[7] The CBI nations as a whole declined $1.1 billions in current dollar exports of clothing to the United States in the 2004—2006 period—almost 12 percent. This is reflected in the ranking of the top twenty importers to the United States, as shown in Table 7.2. Comparing the top twenty

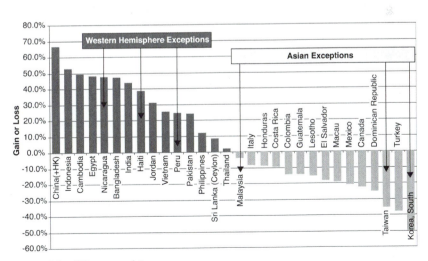

Figure 7.2   Winners and Losers

Table 7.2   Top Twenty Importing Countries, 2004 and 2006

| 2006 Rank | (Losers in Italics) | 2004 Rank | |
|---|---|---|---|
| 1 | China(+HK) | 1 | China(+HK) |
| 2 | Mexico | 2 | Mexico |
| 3 | Indonesia | 3 | Honduras |
| 4 | Vietnam | 4 | Vietnam |
| 5 | India | 5 | Indonesia |
| 6 | Bangladesh | 6 | India |
| 7 | *Honduras* | 7 | Dominican Republic |
| 8 | Cambodia | 8 | Bangladesh |
| 9 | Philippines | 9 | Guatemala |
| 10 | Thailand | 10 | Korea, South |
| 11 | Sri Lanka (Ceylon) | 11 | Thailand |
| 12 | *Guatemala* | 12 | Philippines |
| 13 | *Dominican Republic* | 13 | El Salvador |
| 14 | Pakistan | 14 | Sri Lanka (Ceylon) |
| 15 | *El Salvador* | 15 | Taiwan |
| 16 | Italy | 16 | Canada |
| 17 | Jordan | 17 | Macau |
| 18 | *Canada* | 18 | Cambodia |
| 19 | *Macau* | 19 | Italy |
| 20 | *Taiwan* | 20 | Turkey |
| Cumulative Share | 86.10% | | 81.00% |
| Number of Top Ten in Western Hemisphere | 2 | 4 | |

between 2004 and 2006, all of the national suppliers who lost share were in the Western Hemisphere except for Macao and Taiwan; of the top ten, four were in the Western Hemisphere in 2004 and only two in 2006.

## *The Proximity Hypothesis*

CBI and Mexican losses provide a partial test of one important theory about the structure of the global apparel market in relation to current retail practices. That theory concerns the importance of proximity in an age of lean retailing. The new information technology of the retail-manufacturing relationship, according to one influential and massively funded study of the U.S. apparel textile complex, offered an opportunity to American manufacturers to reap "new competitive advantages."(Abernathy, Dunlap Hammond and Weil 1999: 1) This conclusion was based on technological relationships that begin with the real-time information about the status of inventory that managers obtain from bar code scanners at checkout counters. The scanner reports the specifics (color, size, etc.) of garments sold, by the hour, day, week, month, season or year. A manager can thus discern the level of inventory on hand in stores and warehouses and know to a day or so when to reorder and which styles and variants are succeeding. This information retrieval capacity allows shrinkage in the amount of inventory on hand (thus conserving capital) and it reduces the reorder cycle from months to weeks. The Abernathy group thought (and they continue to hope against the data—see Mukherjee 2005 and Weil 2006) that the shortened reorder cycle would give American or Central American suppliers supply chain advantages for the U.S. market.

In the eight brief years since Abernathy et al. mailed in their manuscript (1998–2001) the American apparel industry has lost 400,000 jobs (639,000 to 238,000)—63 percent of the industry. (Calculated from U.S. Department of Labor, Bureau of Labor Statistics 2007) Having deserted the U.S. proximity hypothesis (Mukherjee 2005) the Harvard Center for Textile and Apparel Research (re)placed its hope on North and Central American proximity. Mexico's fading grasp on the jeans market seems a weak prop for the theory.

The increasing perfection of Asia to North America logistics has made China and India much closer than they once were relative to Mexico or the Caribbean. Western Hemisphere suppliers are hanging on by thin threads of turn-around time and cheap labor. The former is, it turns out, thinning all the time; and the existence of even ostensibly democratic regimes in the Western Hemisphere would seem to be in some tension with long run viability in the race to the bottom.

## Is There a Race to the Bottom?

Despite the restraints on the Chinese import stream through the end of 2008, it appears that predictions of Chinese domination of the textile and clothing markets are well sustained. Supplier consolidation has occurred but not yet to the largest extent imagined by the pre-2005 projections. Regional shift has occurred as anticipated, favoring low-wage Asian suppliers, including Bangladesh, India, Pakistan, Cambodia, and even Vietnam (which is still constrained by certain quotas because it is not yet in the WTO). Lurking behind much concern about the end of the ATC was the broad question of labor standards.

Systematic data about labor conditions are extremely difficult to attain, especially since actual industrial practices are much worse than even inadequate national laws. In China, for example, there is a small consultancy industry that teaches factory managers how to keep multiple sets of books, including one to show to U.S. corporation social auditors to convince them they are following Chinese labor law. (Roberts and Engardio 2006) The corporate oriented Fair Labor Association and the more independent auditor Verité, in addition to a *Business Week* investigation, found that in China, and in most export factories elsewhere, majorities of firms fail to pay national minimum wages or overtime (for the United States, see Ross 2004) Therefore only notional use could be made—even in principle—of official wage statistics. Anecdotes about poor conditions or abusive treatment, although abundant in the textile and clothing businesses, do not allow a fully systematic comparison to shifts in production. There are, however, some ways to discern the pattern in quantitative and relevant qualitative terms.

In the first instance, available data allow an answer to the question of whether the U.S. import stream is becoming cheaper. The answer is yes. In inflation-corrected and in absolute terms, clothing and textiles have been costing importers less over the period 2000–2006—and the release of quota appears to have a relationship to the price decrease. Figure 7.3 uses a standard measure of clothing volume, square meter equivalents, to measure the inflation-corrected cost of clothing imports to the United States from 2000 to 2006.[8] It shows declining cost in each year and a very sharp decline from 2001 to 2002 and from 2004 to 2005. The first sharp decline—7.3 percent—was one in which large numbers of clothing items were released from MFA quotas as part of the ten-year gradual reduction in the total amount of clothing subject to quota. The second decline—7.1 percent—took place during the year in which China's imports were unrestrained from January through May (Office of Textile and Apparel [OTEXA] 2007).

There is additional inferential evidence that at least part of the source of the price declines is attributable to shifts in supplier locations. It seems fair to estimate that clothing workers' earnings, when compared cross-nationally, would be highly correlated to the levels of living and compensation in their respective nations. That is, it is likely that national differences in clothing and

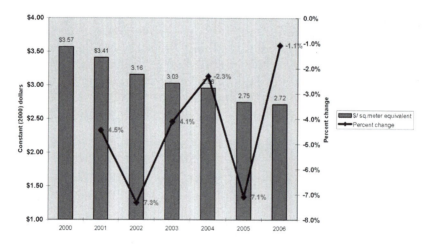

Figure 7.3   Dockside Cost/Square Meter Equivalent

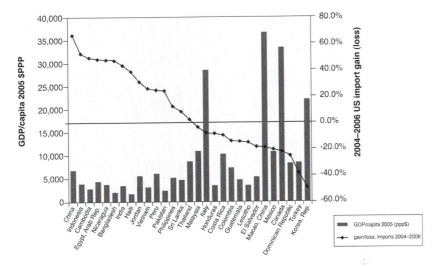

Figure 7.4 GDP/Capita and Percent Change in U.S. Apparel Imports

textile workers' wages bear a roughly similar relation to the economies in which they find themselves in many different countries. For example, in nations with very large rural labor surpluses and very low incomes, we would expect that although clothing factory workers would have higher levels of cash income than rural workers, they would have lower levels of wages than those in more capital intensive industries. Over a large number of nations we would then expect there to be a very high correlation between garment wages (and conditions) and overall levels of GDP/capita. If clothing sourcing, freed of quota restraint, were highly influenced by labor costs, then we would expect a nontrivial (negative) relationship between source shifting and GDP/capita. Figure 7.4 shows that lower GDP/capita (2005) is clearly related to higher gains in the U.S. import markets. The correlation is about −0.51.

Sharply declining prices of clothing imports implies either shifting sourcing decisions—which did occur—or declining cost of production including compensation to workers. In any case it may or may not result in lower retail prices. Over the last two decades the rapid replacement of domestic with imported sources of clothing has certainly resulted in lower retail clothing prices. Figure 7.5 shows that the Consumer Price Index for All Urban Consumers (CPI-U) increased almost ten times (9.6) as fast as the cost of apparel since 1987. The 2004–2006 period did not, however, show as sharp a decline at the retail level as it did at dockside. From 2004 to 2006, the retail cost of clothing declined a bit more than one-third as much as the dockside cost (−0.75 percent retail v. −2.1 percent FOB). The implication is that source shifting in the post-MFA world was a source of new profits for clothing retailers.[9]

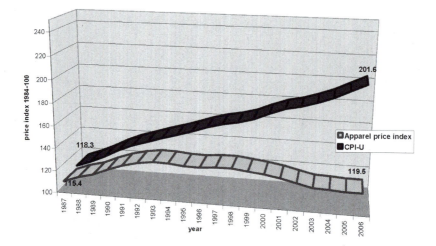

Figure 7.5    Apparel Price v. Consumer Price Index

Apart from the evidence of source shifting to lower-income countries and of lowered measured prices of imports to the brands and retailers, there is also qualitative evidence that buyers continued their generation-long evasion and suppression of unions and their reluctance to pay for worker improvements in pay or conditions.

The viewing-with-alarm pre-2005 documents about labor standards and the release from MFA quotas are numerous and commonplace. They tend to use the word "challenge"—as in the "challenge to maintain labor standards" or the "challenge to compete" in other industry-specific ways with Chinese or Indian competition. Without quantitative evidence for *heightened incidence* of worker abuse, there is nevertheless qualitative evidence of continued choice by buyers and producers to move employment away from more organized or conscious workers and toward places where workers are the most vulnerable. Here are some are some other types of indicators that the race-to-the bottom in labor standards is alive and well:

The Bangladesh Export Promotion Bureau web site, as of May 6, 2007, claimed under the heading "Production Oriented Labor Laws" that "Law forbids formation of any labor union in EPZs."[10] It noted the minimum (monthly) wages for apprentices/trainee as U.S. $22.00, but this appears to be the prevailing garment wage. ("Bangladesh EPZ" 2007; National Labor Committee 2006a). Although Bangladesh has long been a target of Western campaigners against child labor, the U.S.- based National Labor Committee (2006a) found 200–300 child laborers at a large factory producing for, among others, Hanes underwear and Puma. Bangladesh has gained market share in the post-MFA period.

After a more than a decade of struggle, most recently in cooperation with the United Students Against Sweatshops solidarity campaigns in 1998 and 2003, the BJ&B cap factory in Alta Gracia, Dominican Republic, owned by the Yupoong Company, a Korean multinational that is among the world's largest producers of sport caps, closed its unionized factory in December 2006 (Ross 2006). It left a few hundred workers without their legally entitled severance payments. Yupoong opened a Bangladesh factory in 2000 and has gradually moved employment out of its Dominican factory since then.

After a long struggle at the Kukdong/Mexmode factory in Mexico in 2003, workers gained a union contract, wage gains, and pledges for decent food and water. By 2005 they were unable to collect their contracted wage gain, and employment levels at the factory were drastically reduced (Ross 2006).

Despite a U.S.-Jordan trade agreement notable for its explicit inclusion of labor rights (White House 2000), Jordan-based factories aiming for duty-free no-quota access to the U.S. market used involuntary servitude among thousands of Bangladeshi workers in a number of factories (National Labor Committee 2006b). Despite Jordanian government intervention to address the worst abuses, human trafficking, forced overtime, 15-hour shifts, persistent minimum wage violations, and passport confiscations by employers continue to be used to exploit thousands of workers from Bangladesh and Sri Lanka as well as Jordanians (National Labor Committee 2007).

Cambodia is, as is Jordan, a signatory to a bilateral trade agreement with the United States that linked highly favorable clothing import quota to Cambodia's agreement to enforce core International Labor Organization (ILO) labor standards in its garment industry. This 1999 agreement includes ILO monitoring of labor conditions at factories. The international consensus is that this regime of labor law and monitoring did improve conditions in Cambodian garment factories (see, e.g., Marston 2007 and Siphana 2005; but see Wells-Dang 2002 for skepticism on the matter). The impending end of the MFA regime threatened to erode Cambodia's advantage in gaining access to the large U.S. market. Many analysts argued, though, that legal wages and other conditions were so low and permissive in Cambodia that even after the end of quotas Cambodia would actually gain market share as brand name buyers sought to share its good labor standards reputation. The warning flag was put up in 2004 when the leader of a Cambodian garment workers union was murdered as were at least two other union activists. Then Chey Mony, the brother of Chea Vichea, the slain leader, was "detained" and forced into exile. One inference: employers—with some official connivance—are seeing to it that official policies in favor of the right of association and of minimum labor standards will not push the costs of production beyond what they consider the threat of the China price ("Action: Justice Still Needed in Chea Vichea Murder Case" 2007).

Marston (2007) observes the removal of MFA quotas and the "race-to-the-bottom" problem in Cambodia this way:

[A] growing culture of fear, linked to the end of the quota system, has been used to ensure that garment workers remain docile in the face of new challenges. According to Alonzo Suson, Director of the American Center for International Labor Solidarity (ACILS), a non-profit organization with links to the AFL-CIO union federation in the United States, "The end of the MFA was used to put workers in line. [They're told] "Do more work, be conservative, don't ask for much, and don't rock the boat."

Although increasing international competition is a valid concern, it appears that it is often exaggerated and used as a threat to remind workers of the precariousness of their employment and to keep them from demanding better wages or improved working conditions.

## Discussion: South-South

The end of the MFA regime continued but did not accelerate U.S. job loss in the apparel industry. Far from protecting the apparel industry, the MFA provided a long inevitable glideway to extinction. Enmeshed in a supply network where the global labor reserve can be mobilized for pennies an hour, remaining U.S. apparel workers are at serious risk of sweatshop conditions themselves (Ross 2004). The basic shifts in apparel sourcing brought about by the end of the MFA have heightened the South-South competition among suppliers in low-income peripheral economies, however. In particular, the lower wages, and either lax labor law enforcement or outright repression, or both, have given Asian suppliers advantages over Western Hemisphere suppliers in the competition for the U.S. market.

Since the MFA expired there has been a more or less predicted shift in world apparel export production. This shift included a large component of higher wage to lower wage motion that in turn entailed relative gains to Asian sources and losses for Western Hemisphere producers. The cost of clothing also continues to decline. This is the result of source shifting and possibly also a product of deterioration in workers' conditions.

As things now stand, the world's working class in labor-intensive manufacturing has at its center the Asian and in particular the Indian and Chinese working classes. Richard Freeman has pointed out that the entry of China, India, and the former Soviet bloc has doubled the global labor pool, bringing about 1.47 billion workers into the competitive mix. In the process, Freeman estimates the capital to labor ratio has been cut by 55–60 percent (Freeman 2005). It is here, in Asia, that what is now called the "China price" the lowest dependable product price for a commodity—will be determined.[11]

In the meantime, the 87,000 officially counted protests in China in 2005 (there may have been many more) exceeded the 74,000 of 2004 (Lum 2006).

All around the world, much depends on whether that number rises and what the Chinese government will do about it.

# Notes

1. See the U.S. Department of Labor Current Employment Survey SIC (Standard Industrial Classification) statistical series compared to the NAICS (North American Industry Classification System) series at www.bls.gov.

2. This suggests the summary slogan: beating Communists with brassieres (in the interests of etiquette, we might pass over it; in the interests of entertainment, we will not).

3. A Google search for the words *Multifibre Arrangement* and *2005* produced 75,000 hits on April 28, 2007.

4. U.S. imports of clothing were about 28 percent of the world total in 2005; Among the twenty-five EU members of that period imports were about 44 percent. Extracted from the WTO trade database: http://stat.wto.org/StatisticalProgram/WSDBViewDataPrintableVersion.aspx?Language=E&TOPIC=MT&SUBTOPIC=CO&PAGEINDEX=1&ROWSCNT=30&STARTYEAR=2001&ENDYEAR=2005&MSTR_QUERY_TYPE=PRINT . This investigation is focused on the U.S. data.

5. Compare these concentration ratios to the 2002 Economic Census, which shows transportation equipment: top 8: 52 percent; apparel: top 8: 21.3 percent(United States Census 2002)

6. CBI includes twenty-four Central American and Caribbean countries: Antigua, Aruba, the Bahamas, Barbados, Belize, British Virgin Islands, Costa Rica, Dominica, Dominican Republic, El Salvador, Grenada, Guatemala, Guyana, Haiti, Honduras, Jamaica, Montserrat, Netherlands Antilles, Nicaragua, Panama, St. Kitts and Nevis, St. Lucia, St. Vincent and the Grenadines, and Trinidad and Tobago.

7. Honduras is comparable to Nicaragua in GDP/capita when using purchasing power parity (PPP) dollars.

8. The Office of Textile and Apparel (OTEXA) (2007) database reports clothing imports by SME (square meter equivalents) and by dollar value. It thus permits simple division: dollars/SME.

9. Although retail clothing prices went down 0.75 percent, the CPI-U went up 6.7 percent—a difference of 7.5 percent

10. In fact the U.S. State Department *Human Rights Report* notes that a new law allows Workers' Associations, but these may not have affiliation with unions outside the Export Processing Zones.

11. The China price is not only about labor costs, for the Chinese market is among the least regulated markets, and thus it has the smallest time lost in permitting and other such matters.

# References

"Action: Justice Still Needed in Chea Vichea Murder Case." 2007. Labour Behind the Label. Available at http://www.labourbehindthelabel.org/content/view/157/115/1/0/. Accessed May 9, 2007.

American Textile Manufacturers Institute (ATMI). 2003. *The China Threat to World Textile and Apparel Trade*. Washington, D.C. Available at http://www.ncto.org/quota/china.pdf. Accessed April 30, 2007.

————. 2004 *Update Number 3: The China Threat to World Textile and Apparel Trade*. Available athttp://www.ncto.org/newsroom/china0904.pdf. Accessed April 30, 2007.

Appelbaum, Richard. 2004. *Assessing the Impact of the Phasing-out of the Agreement on Textiles and Clothing on Apparel Exports on the Least Developed and Developing Countries*. Center for Global Studies, University of California, Santa Barbara, Year 2004 Paper 05. Available at http://repositories.cdlib.org/isber/cgs/05. Accessed December 12, 2006.

Appelbaum, Richard P., Edna Bonacich, and Katie Quan. 2005. "The End of Apparel Quotas: A Faster Race to the Bottom?" Center for Global Studies. Paper 2. February 5. Availalble at http://repositories.cdlib.org/isber/cgs/2. Accessed March 1, 2009.

————. 2005. *The End of Apparel Quotas: A Faster Race to the Bottom?* Global and International Studies Program, University of California, Santa Barbara. Year 2005 Paper 35. Available at http://repositories.cdlib.org/gis/35. Accessed December 12, 2006.

"Bangladesh EPZ." 2005. Export Promotion Bureau, Bangladesh Ministry of Commerce. Available at http://www.epb.gov.bd/bangladesh_epz.html. Accessed May 7, 2007.

Chan, Anita, and Robert J. S. Ross 2003. "Racing to the Bottom: International Trade Without a Social Clause." *Third World Quarterly* 24, no. 6: 1011–1028.

Clean Clothes Campaign. 2004a. The Phase-out of the Multifiber Arrangement, SOMO Bulletin on Issues in Garments and Textiles no. 5, April. Available at http://www. cleanclothes.org/publications/04–04-somo.htm. Accessed December 12, 2006.

————. 2004b. Trade and Investment Agreements, SOMO Bulletin on Issues in Garments and Textiles no. 4, February. Available at http://www.cleanclothes.org/publications/04–02-somo.htm. Accessed December 12, 2006.

Foo, Lora Jo, and Nikki Fortunato Bas. 2003. "Free Trade's Looming Threat to the World's Garment Workers," Sweatshop Watch Working Paper, October 30. Available at http://www.sweatshopwatch.org/global/index.html. Accessed December 12, 2006.

Freeman, Richard. 2005. "China, India, and the Doubling of the Global Labor Force: Who Pays the Price of Globalization." *The Globalist*. June 3. Available at http://hussonet.free.fr/freeman5.pdf. Accessed May 7, 2007.

Heron, Tony. 2007. "Small States and The Politics of Multilateral Trade Liberalisation." Paper prepared for the Small State Capacity Building Workshop, University of Birmingham, UK, April 4–5, 2007. Available at www.polsis.bham.ac.uk/research/Heron.pdf. Accessed April 19, 2007.

Hudgins, Edward L. 1985. "Why Limiting Textile Imports Would Hurt Americans." Heritage Foundation, Backgrounder no. 458. Available at http://www.heritage.org/Research/TradeandForeignAid/upload/87488_1.pdf. Accessed April 27, 2007.

Lum, Thomas. 2006. *CRS Report for Congress: Social Unrest in China*. Order Code RL33416. Congressional Research Service. Available at http://www.fas.org/sgp/crs/row/RL33416.pdf. Accessed May 7, 2007.

Marston, Ama. 2007. *Labor Monitoring in Cambodia's Garment Industry: Lessons for Africa*. Realizing Rights; the Ethical Global Initiative. Available at http://www.reports-and-materials.org/Marston-Labor-Monitoring-Cambodia–1-May–2007.pdf .Accessed May 9, 2007.

Mukherjee, Andy. 2005. "Latin American Flow Means Few Jobs in U.S. Saved by Anti-Asian Embargo." *Los Angeles Business Journal.* Available at http://findarticles.com/p/articles/mi_m5072/is_1_27/ai_n8709334. Accessed June 6, 2007.

National Labor Committee. 2006a. *Train Wreck for Corporate Monitoring at the Harvest Rich Factory in Bangladesh.* Available at http://www.nlcnet.org/article.php?id=195. Accessed May 7, 2007.

———. 2006b. *U.S.-Jordan Free Trade Agreement Descends into Human Trafficking and Involuntary Servitude.* Available at http://www.nlcnet.org/article.php?id=10. Accessed May 7, 2007.

———. 2007. "U.S.-Jordan Free Trade Agreement: Progress on Worker Rights, but Much Remains To Be Done." March 30. Available at http://www.nlcnet.org/article.php?id=241. Accessed March 1, 2009.

Office of Textile and Apparel (OTEXA). 2007. "U.S. Imports of Textiles and Apparel" Database. International Trade Administration, United States Department of Commerce. Available at http://otexa.ita.doc.gov/scripts/tqads1.exe/catpage. Accessed March 1, 2009.

Oxfam. 2004. *Stitched Up: How Rich-country Protectionism in Textiles and Clothing Trade Prevents Poverty Alleviation.* Briefing paper 60. Available at http://www.oxfam.org.uk/what_we_do/issues/trade/bp60_textiles.htm. Accessed April 27, 2007.

Raghavan, Chakravarthi. N.d. "Barking Up the Wrong Tree: Trade and Social Clause Links." Third World Forum. Available at http://www.twnside.org.sg/title/tree-ch.htm. Accessed April 27, 2007.

Roberts, Dexter, and Pete Engardio. 2006. "Secrets, Lies, and Sweatshops." *Business Week,* November 27. Available at http://www.businessweek.com/magazine/content/06_48/b4011001.htm. Accessed May 1, 2007.

Rosen, Ellen Israel. 2002. *Making Sweatshops: The Globalization of the U.S. Apparel Industry.* Berkeley: University of California Press.

Rosen, Howard. 2005. Labor Market Adjustment to the Multi-Fiber Arrangement Removal. MFA Forum. Available at http://www.mfa-forum.net/downloads/mfa-forum_labour_market_adjustment.pdf. Accessed on March 1, 2009

Ross, Robert J. S. 2004. *Slaves to Fashion: Poverty and Abuse in the New Sweatshops.* Ann Arbor: University of Michigan Press.

———. 2006. "A Tale of Two Factories: Successful Resistance to Sweatshops and the Limits of Firefighting." *Labor Studies Journal* 30, no. 4 (Winter): 1–21.

Ross, Robert J. S., and Anita Chan. 2002. "From North-South to South-South: The True Face of Global Competition." *Foreign Affairs* 81, no. 5: 8–13.

Siphana, Sok. 2005. "Labour Standards, Social Labels, and Company Standards: Example of Cambodia." Paper prepared for Economic and Social Commission for Asia and the Pacific conference, "Weaving the Fabric of Regional Cooperation for a Competitive Garment Sector," June 1–2, 2005, Beijing, China. Available at http://www.unescap.org/tid/mtg/tradenv_s5.pdf. Accessed May 6, 2007.

United Nations Conference on Trade and Development. 2005. *TNCs and the Removal of Textiles and Clothing Quotas.* New York: United Nations.

United States Census Bureau. 2002. *Economic Census. Manufacturing-Subject Series. Concentration Ratios.* Available at http://www.census.gov/prod/ec02/ec0231sr1.pdf. Accessed April 19, 2007.

Weil, David. 2006. "Lean Retailing and Supply Chain Restructuring: Implications for Private and Public Governance." Paper prepared for conference "Observing Trade: Revealing International Trade Networks," Princeton Institute for International and Regional Studies, Princeton University. Available at http://www.princeton.edu/~ina/gkg/confs/weil.pdf. Accessed June 6, 2007.

Wells-Dang, Andrew. 2002. "Linking Textiles to Labor Standards: Prospects for Cambodia and Vietnam." Policy Report, Foreign Policy in Focus. Available at http://www.fpif.org/pdf/reports/PRtxt-labor.pdf. Accessed May 9, 2007.

White House. 2000. "United States and Jordan Sign Historic Free Trade Agreement." Press release. Available at: http://clinton4.nara.gov/WH/new/html/Tue_Oct_24_163554_2000.html. Accessed May 7, 2007.

World Trade Organization (WT0). 2007. "Textiles Monitoring Body (TMB): The Agreement on Textiles and Clothing." Available at http://www.wto.org/english/tratop_e/texti_e/texintro_e.htm. Accessed on May 2, 2007.

Yearman, Keith, and Amy Gluckman. 2005. "Falling Off a Cliff." *Dollars and Sense.* September/October. Available at http://www.dollarsandsense.org/archives/2005/0905yearman.html. Accessed 27 April 2007.

# 8

# AQUACULTURE COMMODITY CHAINS AND THREATS TO FOOD SECURITY AND SURVIVAL OF ASIAN FISHING HOUSEHOLDS

## Wilma A. Dunaway and M. Cecilia Macabuac

Because commercial aquaculture has been touted to be one of the most important solutions to world hunger, the World Bank and the International Monetary Fund stimulated the expansion of the "Blue Revolution" throughout Asia, Africa, and Latin America in the 1980s and 1990s. Although shrimp comprises less than 1 percent of global fisheries output, it is the most valuable seafood product in international trade. Consequently, prawn farming has proliferated in poor countries since 1975 (Barraclough and Finger-Stich 1996). Despite increased commercial outputs, less fish and seafood is now available to peripheral populations, and malnutrition and hunger are on the rise in those countries engaged in export aquaculture (Yoshinori 1987). After 1975, the Philippines expanded its commercial aquaculture until it rose to be one of the world's most important shrimp exporters. Since 1989, however, the Philippines has been a *food extractive enclave* in the bust stage of export-oriented aquaculture and commercial fishing. This study analyzes the impacts of that boom-to-bust process on subsistence fishing households and describes the inequitable strategies through which women have struggled to cope with economic and ecological crisis.

## Target Area and Methods of Research

To support its export production agendas in agriculture, fishing, timbering, and mining, the Philippine government targeted the island of Mindanao (see Map 8.1) for extensive exploitation of natural resources in the late 1980s. Eleven provinces were targeted for rapid development of prawn farms, and the government privatized mangroves and offered tax abatements to entice investments from multinational corporations. Rapid expansion of prawn farming put new massive strains on the resources that had historically supported subsistence fishers. Before commercial aquaculture, 770,000 small-scale fishers were critical to the national food supply because they produced two-fifths of the country's fish output. These subsistence producers fish within 3 miles of coasts and sell most of their catches for local consumption. After expansion of shrimp ponds, the total annual output of these small fishers dropped by 80 percent, endangering local food security (JEP ATRE 2004).

We selected for our study the Panguil Bay area of northern Mindanao, which was targeted for rapid aquaculture development. Between 1982 and 1991,

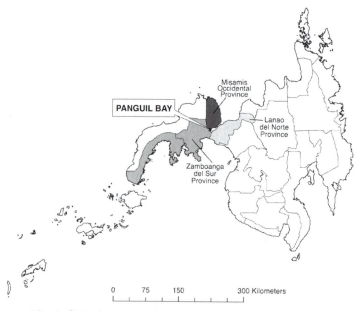

Map 8.1   Island of Mindanao, the Philippines

shrimp ponds expanded 18 percent annually, tripling the area utilized by export aquaculture in just a decade (Naawan School of Fisheries 1991). Surrounding the bay are seventy-six communities that support more than 450,000 people (Loquias 1990–1991), including nearly 10,000 households that engage in small-scale fishing, prawn farming, or seaweed cultivation (Israel et al. 2003). The typical Panguil Bay fisher is a thirty-nine-year-old male who has helped to support a household of five through seasonal fishing for 30 years (JEP ATRE 2004). More than 70 percent of Panguil Bay adults have 6 years or less of elementary education, and a majority of women are illiterate or nearly so (Israel et al. 2003). Thus, Panguil Bay households are typical of the conditions that face a majority of Filipino artisanal fishing families. Even though this area was assessed by the government to be the richest shallow water fishing ground in Mindanao, it is now a fishery in severe crisis, and it exhibits one of the highest poverty and unemployment rates in the country. Well before 1990, export shrimp farming had reached the bust stage in Panguil Bay, and most of the corporate ponds had ceased operations or decreased production. Presently in these coastal villages, a day's catch fetches an average income of less than $1 a day, situating these families among the world's poorest (Asian Development Bank 2005: 60–61).

With the help of local NGOs and fishery officials, we selected three communities that permitted case studies of the impacts of three forms of aquacultural production on subsistence fishing. Located in the town of Kapatagan, the Lapinig community was involved in aquaculture as early as 1957 and now has corporate fishponds that employ intensive harvest techniques. Located in Tangub City, the Silanga community experienced a shrimp boom in the 1970s but now has only small-scale fishponds. Located in Ozamis City, the San Roque community specializes in seaweed gardening. Over a one-year period in 2005 and 2006, numerous interviews and focus groups were conducted with fishery, local government, and NGO officials. Focus groups were conducted in each of the villages to permit subsistence fishing women to identify problems facing their families. To pinpoint household transformations, inequalities, and survival strategies, we conducted in-depth interviews in the local dialect with husbands and wives in twenty-six subsistence fishing households. In addition, our research has been richly informed by the research of Philippine feminists (e.g., Arnado 2003, Illo and Polo 1990, Israel-Sobritchea 1987, Noralsco 1987, Pineda-Ofreneo 1985) whose household analyses rarely appear in U.S. or European libraries and are largely ignored by Western feminists.

## Impacts of Aquaculture on Subsistence Fishing Households

To maximize profits, capitalists must exploit as many "costless" social and natural conditions as possible. Thus, capitalists shift to society, to the culture, to the ecosystem, and to human laborers most of the real costs of commodity production (Dunaway 2001). If households and nature did not absorb so many externalities from commodity chains, the global production process could not endlessly accumulate the capital that is essential to capitalist economic growth (Wallerstein 1999). According to Jacinto (2004: 9), export shrimp farming "is perhaps the most glaring example of social and environmental costs borne by small scale fishers and coastal communities so that consumers in developed countries can meet their increasing demand for cheap and affordable shrimp." Consequently, aquaculture commodity chains externalize to households and to nature most of the costs of production. As the food resources of Panguil Bay and the Philippines have been more deeply integrated into the global food commodity chains (McMichael 1994), export aquaculture has externalized four costs to subsistence fishing households: (1) loss of access to ecological resources, (2) deterioration of local livelihoods, (3) loss of food security, and (4) loss of social services.

## Loss of Access to Ecological Resources

The country's intensive aquaculture has caused loss of biodiversity, salinization of agricultural lands and drinking water, destruction of coral reefs, and massive mangrove deforestation (*Philippines Environmental Monitor* 2000). The export prices of prawn and seaweed "do not reflect the true costs of producing fishery products as long as externalities are not made to 'show up' in the value chain. With social and environmental costs missing from the equation, what is actually expensive and wasteful become apparently cheap" (Jacinto 2004: 17). Every acre of an industrial shrimp farm destroys 200 acres of productive ecosystem. Shrimp ponds degrade the ecosystem so extensively that fish catches are lowered too far to provide a livelihood, forcing household members to migrate in search of employment. In addition to degrading the ecosystem, commercial aquaculture development has required the elimination of common property rights and the reallocation of mangroves to monopolistic use of pond operators. "Mangrove forested areas in the Philippines have been steadily transformed from a common property resource, of multiple use and benefit to a large number of people, to a private good, of single use for shrimp ponds, whose benefits are narrowly channeled to the benefit of a select few" (Nickerson 1999: 279). The national government issued long-term leases assigning prawn pond owners sole control over mangroves and waterways. This land reform delegitimated traditional access of subsistence households to these forests and transformed fishers into unwelcome squatters around shrimp ponds (Primavera 1997). To make matters worse, the Philippine government does not provide safe public water systems in the areas where shrimp farms have expanded, so aquaculture pollutants threaten the water available for household use. Little wonder that diarrhea is a major cause of death around Panguil Bay. Forced to rely on rivers and canals for bathing and laundry, a large proportion of bay residents are infected with incurable, life-threatening *schistosomiasis* (World Health Organization 2000).

Filipino fishing women have been more negatively affected than men by these ecological changes. Female resource gatherers who have traditionally relied on mangroves, coastal waters, and rivers for subsistence and for livelihood must internalize the external costs associated with the elimination of community property rights. In addition to losing significant food resources and craft materials, women must now also work harder to secure fuel wood or charcoal for household cooking. Now that commercial prawn ponds have appropriated most of the waterways and mangroves, women have been pushed out of fishing and out of many of their traditional artisan crafts into marginal activities, such shell gathering or craft piecework on a putting-out basis. Males work in boats, whereas women are more directly exposed to diseases, pollutants, and parasites because they wade into water on a consistent daily basis to gather oysters, catch small fishes and crustaceans, or do laundry. In addition, environmental threats to water safety require females to assume increased caregiving responsibility for sickened family members.

## Deterioration of Local Livelihoods

Despite the rapid expansion of commercial aquaculture and other export agendas, the Philippines presently has the lowest economic growth rate in Southeast Asia, and its foreign direct investment has declined to less than one-fifth of its 2002 level (Escobar 2004). Despite market-oriented economic reforms, the Philippine export structure is now less diversified and less industrialized than it was in 1980 (Lim and Montes 2002). More than half the GNP is now earmarked for external debt repayment (IBON Foundation 2005). The transformation of small-scale fishing and seaweed gathering into export-oriented aquaculture can be traced to structural adjustment policies imposed on the Philippines. During the decades that shrimp aquaculture has boomed and busted in the Philippines, the economic conditions facing families have steadily worsened. Devaluation of Philippine currency resulted in a 72 percent drop in the value of the peso. Subsequently, prices inflated at an average rate of 9.7 percent yearly while consumer prices rose as much as 27 percent in some years (Casino 2004: 1–2). Unemployment is rising owing to the loss of jobs after trade liberalization, and household incomes have steadily declined since 1995. Wealth and income have been increasingly concentrated into a few hands, and the Philippines now has a higher incidence of poverty than its Asian neighbors. Nearly half of all Filipino families struggle to survive on less than fifty-seven cents a day per person while the incomes of two-thirds fall below one dollar a day per person (Schelzig 2005). Little wonder that most Philippine citizens are convinced that their livelihoods have worsened, that the national economy is in crisis, and that there is widespread government corruption (IBON Foundation 2004).

In addition to these macrostructural trends, export-oriented aquaculture has externalized hidden costs to fishing households. Shrimp farming is grounded in short-term economic motives. In most instances, the prawn pond has a productive lifespan of only five to ten years. Abandoned after that, the dead resource can no longer be utilized for agriculture or resource-gathering activities (Naylor 2003: 886). On the one hand, export-oriented aquaculture has not generated long-term economic growth. On the other hand, the highest incidence of poverty occurs in those Philippine regions where prawn farming has expanded most rapidly (Jacinto 2004). Since shrimp farms require few workers, they have not generated new employment opportunities to offset the job losses their construction has caused. In fact, export-oriented shrimp cultivation has been a "rape and run industry" that decimates fifteen jobs for each it creates and destroys five to ten dollars of ecological and economic capital for every dollar earned through exports (Shiva 2000: 15). Most of the profits in the Philippine shrimp commodity chain accrue to multinational corporations, Philippine agribusinesses concentrated in Manila, and middlemen traders. Rural prawn ponds generate only a few below-subsistence jobs in their local communities, and urban shrimp processors pay low wages to their female labor forces. In fact, most fishing households derive no income from aquaculture, and the vast majority of fishers cannot afford to start a small aquaculture pond (Irz et al. 2004). While providing little income to local people, shrimp farms eliminate the ecological access that is required to support the fishing, agriculture, livestock raising, and handicrafts through which subsistence households earned a livelihood.

## Loss of Food Security

Peripheral countries that specialize in export-oriented aquaculture have grown less and less food self-sufficient since the 1980s. Since 1993, Philippine seafood output has not kept pace with population needs, and there has been an annual shortfall of 600,000 metric tons. All over the country, household fish catches have declined to less than 1 kilo per day, reflecting the depletion of coastal resources (Aguilar 2002). Panguil Bay fishing households increasingly must compete in five ways with agroindustrial aquaculture for dwindling animal protein. First, massive outputs of prawn, fish, and seaweed are exported to rich countries. Second, two-thirds of the species swimming in rich-nation aquariums derives from the Philippines and Indonesia, and many of these endangered species once comprised part of the local food chain of fishing households. Third, massive levels of food fish and shellfish are fed to export prawn and fish. Because shrimp feeds contain about 30 percent fishmeal and 30 percent fish oil, intensive shrimp farming actually results in a net loss of fish protein (Naylor 2003: 883–884). One kilo of farmed shrimp must be fed 5 kilos of wild fish that would otherwise be available for the local food chain. While shrimp are being fattened for export through their consumption of natural protein, one-third or more of Philippine households suffer malnutrition, the highest incidence among small fisher families (Philippine Food and Nutrition Institute 2005). As one Philippine fisher puts it, "the shrimp live better than we do. They have electricity, but we don't. The shrimp have clean water, but we don't. The shrimp have lots of food, but we are hungry" (Environmental Justice Foundation 2003: 1). Fourth, massive levels of food fish are destroyed and wasted by shrimp producers. Every time a prawn farm opens its gates for seawater exchange or to flush out wastes, it destroys fish and shellfish that could be consumed in local food chains. When prawn farmers apply toxins, such as tea-seed, to eliminate "unwanted" fish that stray into the pond, they once again waste valuable nutrients and biodiversity (Primavera 1997). As a result of all these factors, the quantity and quality of protein resources in Panguil Bay waters have declined dramatically (*Philippines Environmental Monitor* 2000). At present, the average daily catch is only about 16 percent of the average daily catch in 1970 (Adan 2000).

Fifth, shrimp aquaculture threatens food security through loss of rice lands to prawn pond expansion or to salinization (Primavera 1997). While exporting high levels of sea-foods, the Philippines has become so dependent on grain imports that the country's agricultural sector now registers an annual trade deficit (IBON Foundation 2005). Since the expansion of export-oriented aquaculture has diminished the Philippines' rice production (Primavera 1997), the country now imports a higher percentage of rice for consumption even as domestic consumer prices have steadily risen (Cabanilla 1997). With far fewer fish to sell, many families cannot afford rice, so they substitute cornmeal that can be purchased at about 60 percent of the cost of rice.[1] Since the mid-1980s, the diet of Philippine fishing households has been increasingly limited to a few vegetables, small amounts of fish, and cornmeal or rice (when it can be afforded), with protein missing from many meals and on many days (Philippine Food and Nutrition Institute 2005, Pineda-Ofreno 1985). One fisher wife rationalized why she buys 1 kilo of corn per meal when money is short. When food rations are inadequate, "corn is preferred over rice," she explained in a field interview, "because it makes us feel fuller."

The substitution of corn for rice is a hidden externalized health cost for fishing households. Rice contains small amounts of fat, dietary fiber, calcium, phosphorous, potassium, sodium, Vitamin $B_1$, Vitamin $B_2$, and niacin, in addition to 11 percent of the average daily requirement of protein. In sharp contrast, diets high in corn cause the body not to absorb iron efficiently, including the high iron levels in fish. In a country in which iron deficiency anemia is problematic, cornmeal like that which is increasingly consumed by poor Philippine households has "practically no food value" and actually can cause health problems. In addition to providing unhealthy levels of sugar and empty carbohydrates, high consumption of corn and fish with few supplementary vegetables and fruits will lead to deficiencies in calcium, Vitamin A, phosphorus, copper, niacin, amino acids, Vitamin K, Omega$_3$ fatty acids, boron, and magnesium (International Rice Research Institute 2003). Although Panguil Bay fisher wives market their husbands' dwindling fish catches in local markets at low prices, they must in turn take that low income and purchase expensive food imports. Income from small fish sales cannot cover the cost of imported rice and salt that have been heavily centralized under the control of a few wholesalers and retailers (Szanton 1972). As one fishing wife observed:

> Now we spend less and less on foods and buy only necessities.... Household expenses usually exceed the family's income.... We rarely have fish.... Meat is rarely served.... When they wake up in the morning, the children open all our pots and often find them empty. There are days when we do not earn even a single centavo (Illo and Pineda-Ofreneo 2002: 152).

In fact, workers in *food extractive enclaves,* such as Panguil Bay and the Philippines, are the hungriest, most malnourished people in the world; these are the agricultural and fishing households that cultivate and process food for the rest of the world. At the end of the twentieth century, the richest fifth of the world consumed nearly half of all meat and fish, the poorest fifth only 5 percent (Shiva 2000). Protein-energy malnutrition, iron deficiency anemia, iodine deficiency, and Vitamin A deficiencies are typical of the countries that export high levels of shrimp and fish (World Health Organization 2001). At least one-third of the Filipino population is now chronically malnourished. In a country that produces iron-rich fish for export, per capita food consumption has declined dramatically. Because most Filipino diets lack adequate levels of fruits, green vegetables, fats and oils, cereals, poultry, and meats, deficiencies of iron, iodine, calcium and Vitamin A are common (Philippine Food and Nutrition Institute 2005). In 2003, nearly one-third of the families in Northern Mindanao lacked sufficient income to provide food for their households, and nutritional deficiencies are a major cause of death in this area (Philippine National Statistical Coordination Board. 2003). More than one-third of Northern Mindanao children are underweight and underheight. Two of every five Northern Mindanao children are stunted, and another 8 percent suffer from *miasma* (wasting). Iron deficiency anemia occurs in 20 percent of Northern Mindanao children and about one-third of pregnant and lactating women. Because they are iodine deficient, one-third of Northern Mindanao residents are at risk of goiter or impaired cognitive and motor development. Iodine is a very crucial nutrient during pregnancy, since deficiencies can cause brain damage in the fetus, low birth weight, premature labor, and increased prenatal or infant mortality. Two-fifths of Northern Mindanao children and one-quarter of the pregnant women are Vitamin A deficient, placing them at risk of blindness (Philippine Food and Nutrition Institute 2005). Despite the nutritional risks, the Philippine Food and Nutrition Institute now threatens the food security of infants by recommending a cheaper baby formula that contains a half cup of corn and a half cup of soy (Philippine Food and Nutrition Institute 2005).

## Loss of Social Services

In the wake of structural adjustment agreements to shift public funds into economic growth agendas, the Philippine government has made cuts in three public services that have hit fishing households especially hard. First, health care delivery has been privatized and decentralized to the local level, leaving rural communities with inadequate medical personnel. Fishers suffer a higher mortality rate than any other occupation in the Philippines, and females in these communities are at higher risk of dying during their child-bearing years than other Filipino females (Philippine Census Bureau. 2004). Two of every five pregnancies is problematic or life-threatening, and the life expectancy of a Northern Mindanao woman is four years less than that of her male counterpart (Philippine National Statistical Coordination Board 2003). Despite their health crises, fishing communities have been left with a shortage of health care personnel. Two factors have been at play to cause a health care crisis in communities such as Panguil Bay. Even though the Philippines trains 2,000 doctors and 10,000 nurses annually, the country exports the vast majority of these new professionals to the United States and the Middle East (DeBrun and Elling 1987). To exacerbate this "brain drain," three-quarters of the country's doctors are concentrated in urban centers. As a result, a majority of rural Filipinos, such as fishing households, must rely on minimally trained nurses, traditional herbalists, and birthing attendants. Most likely, the lack of prenatal and postnatal care accounts for the high incidence of maternal mortality, infant low birth weight, and newborn deaths from blood poisoning of the umbilical cord stump (Philippine Department of Health 2002).

Family planning is the second public service sector that has been eliminated from fishing communities. Rather than point to the country's neoliberal export agenda as the underlying cause of ecological degradation and dwindling natural resources, current public fishery management policy places the blame for food shortages and environmental degradation on "overpopulation" in fishing communities (JEP ATRE 2004). Even though most of the population growth in fishing communities has resulted from the inmigration of displaced agricultural workers, public policy posits "responsible parenthood for sustainable development" to be the solution to food insecurity. While pressuring females to lower birth rates, the Philippine government has gutted family planning services over the last decade.[2] Because of national budget cuts to meet structural adjustment goals and to speed privatization of health care, in early 2005 local centers discontinued their free family planning services. More than half of the wives in fishing households who had relied on free contraceptive methods, such

as Depro-Provera, birth control pills, intrauterine devices (IUDs), tubal ligations, and condoms, are left without affordable family planning mechanisms
(Ardales 1981). Currently, the Philippines government is being funded by a
USAID project aimed at helping the country to privatize its health care system,
by transforming

> from a free contraceptive delivery system to a sustainable and commercial
> delivery model. The program promotes contraceptive products, builds and
> expands the market and harnesses the active participation of the private
> commercial companies to ensure the future of family planning. . . . Efforts are
> concentrated on increasing the usage of oral contraceptive pills and injectable
> contraceptives and expanding the market for these (USAID 2005).

Not only does the USAID program eliminate free services, but it also shifts
the country's family planning strategy away from male condom use and places
full responsibility on women for controlling population growth. In a country
in which few women ever see a doctor before, during, or after a pregnancy,
the NGO associated with this program offers "discounts" on vasectomies and
tubal ligations, surgical procedures that are far out of the economic reach of a
vast majority of the poor fishing couples (USAID 2005).

　　Public schooling is the third service that has been negatively impacted
in rural areas. Even though their children's schooling is often beyond their
economic means, these parents still prioritize it among their basic survival expenses, second only to food. They cannot afford the 40 percent of educational
costs that have been gutted from the Philippines national budget by structural
adjustment policies, however. Even though there are no outright fees for attending the public schools, there are frequent expenses for "school projects"
and "contributions." One mother of three elementary graders explained during a field interview that "there are always required contributions, like to buy
a floormat for the classroom." Since there is no hope of accumulating these
added expenses from fishing, women assume responsibility for generating extra
income to cover children's schooling through nipa thatching, sale of salted fish
or oysters, or production of crafts for the informal sector.

## Household Transformations and Inequalities

In the Philippines, four extrahousehold structural changes have dramatically
compromised fishing household composition and survival options.

1. Local food production systems have been structurally integrated into world
   capitalist commodity chains.

2. National development policies have privatized the commons, eliminated public funding of social services, and privileged a small elite of export-oriented capitalists.
3. Export-oriented extractive industries have depleted and degraded ecological resources.
4. The boom-to-bust cycle of commercial aquaculture has left fishing households with fewer survival options than they had before this economic growth agenda.

In order to overcome the shortfalls that have resulted from loss of ecological resources, elimination of livelihood options, and the externalized costs of export-oriented aquaculture, subsistence fishing households have been forced to restructure themselves.

Judging from the frequency with which they focused on the topic, the widening of women's work represents their most dramatic transformation. The widening and deepening of capitalism engenders dramatic shifts in productive systems and in the transformation of laborer households. Crises and shortages generate revised definitions of the appropriate responsibilities of women within and outside the household.

> These changes, however, do not mean that old forms of the asymmetric sexual division of labor are abolished or replaced by egalitarian ones. They are only redefined according to the requirements of the new production system.... Because of the preservation of the asymmetric division of labor between the sexes in the ongoing processes, these changes do not lead to greater equality between women and men of the pauperized classes, but, rather, to a polarization between them. The social definition of women as housewives plays a vital role in this polarization (Mies 1982: 5).

Although the wife's burden of unpaid household labor remains unchanged, her income-earning and resource-pooling activities outside the household must increase to overcome shortages.

## Widening of Women's Work Portfolio

Panguil Bay women describe a greater intertwining of household-based labors and market labors. For these women who often produce marketable commodities or services in their homes, there is not a line of demarcation between household and market-related labors. In short, fisher wives are both *semidomesticated* and *semiproletarianized* (Mies 1982: 15) because of their widening portfolio of diverse household and extrahousehold labors and of unpaid and income-earning pursuits. Panguil Bay fisher wives reported that their extrahousehold labors have increased since the 1970s, but their husbands have not increased their contributions to unpaid household labor. Females spend hours every day gathering food and fuel resources from the mangroves and the water, processing those resources into edible meals or marketable goods, and cooking without electricity. Traditionally, wives have played several key roles in supporting the fishing work of husbands and older sons, including preparation of provisions for fishing trips, marketing fish, net repairs, securing credit and paying debts related to fishing, and help with boat repairs (Abregana 2000). About one-third of wives assist males directly with fishing (Oracion 2001), but several of the wives have broadened their roles in fishing in nontraditional ways, so that they are now using boats to collect fish from stationary platforms or to fish alone.

In addition to these unpaid labors, women have expanded their *income-earning* and *income-substituting* activities. Globally, the Philippines is unique in the degree to which males dominate the informal sector. Even though they are not as deeply embedded in the informal sector as males, women are still far more likely to earn income from informal sector activities and putting out systems than from waged jobs (United Nations 2000: 122). Women produce and sell crafts, livestock, and dried oysters and fish; operate small stores; and trade in fish in the informal sector. Because of the limited waged and informal sector opportunities, Panguil Bay women routinely engage in *casualized* labor through cottage industries and putting out systems. Traders and regional agents provide inputs from which women produce marketable commodities on a piecework basis, such as roof shingles thatched from nipa trees or wooden jewelry and baskets. Fishing women have double or triple work burdens that combine unpaid household labor with waged labor, informal sector vending, home-based industries, illegal activities, and services (e.g., laundry, herbalist, midwife). "What they cannot buy because they do not have cash, they collect or produce themselves" (Pineda-Ofreneo 1985: 2–3) Because wives are now engaged in new forms of income-earning labor, fewer of them are marketing male fish catches and making daily household purchases. Thus, husbands now exert greater decisionmaking control over daily expenditures. This transformation represents a dramatic shift in power relations within households in which wives have traditionally managed family budgets.

Some Western feminists (e.g., Atkinson and Errington 1990) celebrate "the relative economic equality" of men and women in the Philippines, but Panguil Bay fishing wives do not agree with their idealizations. Philippine society culturally constrains women to prioritize child rearing and household maintenance while simultaneously economically and ecologically limiting their capacities and opportunities to fulfill that role. "If you just count on the earnings of your husband," one fisher wife observed, "it is not enough" (Eder 1999: 114). Despite wives' diverse labor portfolios inside and outside household, their income-earning pursuits remain marginalized, low-paid, and sometimes stigmatized. Moreover, a woman faces the contradictory pressures to remain a "respectable housewife" and to undertake whatever income-earning work is necessary to sustain her household. When our interviewees described themselves as *housewives,* they reconstructed traditional social expectations to encompass with that term whatever efforts they undertook for the benefit of their households. Most women in fishing households must do some form of income-generating or income-substituting labors while managing child care and household maintenance without male assistance. Fisher wives are caught in the contradictory situation of simultaneously meeting household needs and of staying within rigid social conventions about appropriate women's work roles. To overcome this cultural conflict, fishing wives appeal to the Filipino cultural ideal of "sacrificial motherhood." As Afshar and Agarwal (1989: 1) have observed:

> Under the banner of this idealised, heroic nurturance a truly womanly woman is enjoined to do anything, to make any sacrifice, for the sake of household welfare, for the sake of her husband, and especially for the sake of her children.... However much the ideal is invoked to justify female passivity and subordination, it can also be invoked to justify activity, particularly to justify the potentially deviant and compromising behaviour involved in working outside the home. Taking up employment is frequently defined, both by working women and their families, as a form of female sacrifice for family well-being.

In the face of this *feminization of responsibility,* fisher wives take on additional income-earning tasks to cover unexpected costs related to children' schooling or health care. As a result of their broadening portfolio of labors, women estimated they are now working three to four hours more per day (about a 20 percent increase since 1980). Panguil Bay fisher wives report that they juggle the contradictory pressures between unpaid household labors and market-related work by reducing personal sleep and leisure.

## Household Subsidization of Export Aquaculture

At the same time that fishing wives are widening their work portfolios to insure household survival, they are also providing hidden subsidies to commercial aquaculture. Integration of subsistence fishers into export commodity chains has not pulled their households out of poverty. Instead, that small group who are drawn into the waged labor force are

> located in household structures in which the work on this new "export-oriented activity" formed only a small part of the lifetime revenues.... In this case, other household activities which bring in revenues in multiple forms can "subsidize" the remuneration for the "export-oriented activity," thereby keeping the labor costs very low (Hopkins and Wallerstein 1987: 777).

At every point in a commodity chain, households subsidize capitalists' low wages in order to sustain the laborers who produce the commodity. Those waged laborers who make contributions to the prawn or seaweed export sectors do not earn a living wage that is sufficient for the reproduction of the household unit. Her husband's aquaculture income was "never enough," one Lapinig housewife explained during an interview. "I have to work in order for the family to survive. I bear the hardship because we could not depend solely on a monthly salary which is actually less than what we need to purchase household essentials." In fact, the hidden inputs of households are preconditions for the productivity of household members who engage in external waged labor required to produce the goods that are traded in the world economy (Dunaway 2001). In reality, *nonwaged* labors generate the bulk of household resources and subsidize the accumulation of profits within the commodity chain (Mies 1986, Salleh 1997).

Peripheral households subsidize commodity chains through low-paid, nonwaged direct inputs (such as harvesting wild fish for prawn feeds) into the production process. Such household-based labor generates market commodities or informal sector inputs into the export production process, but such labor— especially that of women—has typically remained socially invisible and has received below-market prices (Mies 1986). Women and households subsidize the shrimp commodity chain through several forms of invisible labor and hardship. Women make hidden inputs into the shrimp commodity chain at four levels other than waged labor. First, the biological reality of women's lives is sexual and reproductive; thus, mothers make their first subsidy to capitalism through the bearing and raising of successive generations of laborers. Despite its dependency upon this natural female contribution, however, capitalism has externalized laborer reproduction outside the realm of the economic. Second, the household is the site in which women undertake unpaid labor for those members who are waged laborers. By keeping production costs lower, women's hidden inputs subsidize the production process throughout the commodity chain, thereby keeping consumer prices lower and profits higher. A third way in which fishing wives subsidize prawn commodity chains is through their informal sector activities. When they produce low-priced crafts (such as baskets) or provide nonwaged services (such as packing, transport, or trading) that support the export process, they are integrated directly into the commodity chain. Their contributions remain poorly remunerated, however, and socially invisible. There is a fourth more deeply hidden way in which women subsidize the commodity chains in which their households are situated. The subsistence inputs of women and households at one node may subsidize other nodes of the commodity chain. In effect, the commodity chain structures a network in which laborers and consumers at higher nodes exploit households and women at lower nodes. The low wages, malnutrition, and degraded ecosystems of fishing households keep the global prices of shrimp low, permitting the distant consumer to avoid the real costs of production and to pay cheap prices for this luxury food. While the Panguil Bay fisher wife and her children go lacking in essential protein and iron, the Japanese middle-class housewife and her offspring eat an abundance of her hidden sacrifices and neither pay for nor acknowledge them.

## Intrahousehold Inequalities

Fishing women are disadvantaged not only by structural changes outside their families but also by their inequitable households. Unpaid household labor is gender-bifurcated in fishing households. Even though fishing women are responsible for an inequitable share of non-income-generating labor and fishing help to males, fewer than one-third of husbands assist regularly in household work. Since 1985 wives have averaged fifty-one hours weekly of unpaid household labors and assistance with male fishing, whereas husbands have provided only fifteen hours of unpaid household work (Pineda-Ofreneo 1985).

> [W]hen women take on outside economic responsibilities, their supposedly primary responsibility in the household is not diminished.... The amount of time devoted to relatively fixed economic and social responsibilities more than doubled when the demands of housework and family were added to the time spent at paid work. Yet husbands were not inclined to do their share; husbands of employed women reported little more involvement in housework than husbands of unemployed women (Eviota 1986: 203).

Many scholars (e.g., Miraleo 1992) have idealized the degree to which Philippine rural women autonomously control household budgets, but Panguil Bay fishing wives do not agree. "I was supposed to be in charge of the money," one fisher wife complained," but there was no money" (Eder 1999: 113). As Dwyer and Bruce (1988: 235) explain:

> [The wife's] control is largely illusory, for she has no financial autonomy. The pool she manages must cover unavoidable expenditures. In addition, husbands do not withdraw from the scene after delivering their contribution; rather they exercise several mechanisms of control. Most important ... a husband makes sure that "his" money is spent to cover basic family needs as well as his desired level of personal consumption.

Fishing spouses often disagree about how household income and resources should be utilized. On average, most must be allocated for food, water, household tools, and dwelling maintenance, with less than 10 percent available for medical and school expenses. "Even if 92 percent of all Filipino wives hold the purse string," argues Philippine feminist Carolyn Israel-Sobritchea (1987: 91), "there is not much power that goes with it.... While more women in the lower classes keep the money and share with their husbands the right to manage such resources, these powers do not mean much when there is barely enough money to meet household needs."

According to one fisher wife, she and her husband argue more about how money will be spent. "I have to concentrate on basic needs," she explained. "With three kids in school ... there is very little left for other basic needs.... We no longer buy clothes. We recycle old ones.... We have to indoctrinate the children on the value of economizing and prioritizing needs" (Illo and Pineda-Ofreneo 2002: 115). In this context of children going without, women perceive male drinking, smoking, and gambling as unnecessary drains on household resources (Oracion 2001: 9). Panguil Bay wives report that disagreement over the amount of husbands' pocket money is the main cause of quarreling and domestic violence. Some women complained that their husbands utilized as much as one-quarter of household budget for their pocket money. Fishers do not just use money for entertainment and leisure, however, for they must also repair and reinvest in equipment and pay fees associated with their occupation. Consequently, productive expenditures to support the male livelihood that is central to household food and income are often in conflict with household survival needs. In these circumstances, husbands often make independent decisions regarding expenses to cover equipment or fishing loans, leaving it to wives to locate household essentials without an adequate income pool. When women cannot stretch the family budget to cover husbands' demands, they are often the targets of domestic violence, a problem that has continued to escalate throughout the 1990s (Illo and Pineda-Ofreneo 2002).

It is doubtful that we should consider fishing households as "pooling" fully or equitably the income or resources of all members, for males and females secure and control separate funds and often divide financial responsibilities (Eder 1999: 114). Moreover, husbands and wives prioritize spending goals differently, and fishing households commonly exhibit gender-specific expenditures. According to one Panguil Bay wife, women spend "all their earnings on the consumption of the family," but husbands expect to have weekly funds for leisure activities at a level that is not available to their wives. Although men accept responsibility for covering costs of fishing and minimal daily food, women assume responsibility for household and children's expenses.

> At issue is not simply the ways in which women's income is used, but the degree to which men and women differ in taking personal spending money from their earnings. Though the specifics of women's consumption respon-sibilities vary ... , it is quite commonly found that gender ideologies support the notion that men have a right to personal spending money, which they

are perceived to need or deserve, and that women's income is for collective purposes (Dwyer and Bruce 1988: 5–6).

Panguil Bay mothers are aware that children are at greater risk of malnutrition in lean fishing seasons if the women have no independent income. "Cash controlled by women is usually spent by them on family needs, that by men more on personal needs. Not surprisingly, therefore, the daily nutritional shortfalls of children ... are found to be related more closely to the mother's employment than the father's (Agarwal 1988: 89).

In addition to inequalities and power struggles over household budgets, the greater workload of fisher wives has not insured them greater or equal access to crucial needs, such as food or health care. Protein and caloric intake of women is far below that of males (Philippine Food and Nutrition Institute 2005), and women's ailments are ignored until they reach a critical stage (Philippine Department of Health 2002). Lack of access to adequate food is not the only nutritional problem for fishing households, for food is distributed inequitably within households. The most malnourished members of fishing households are mothers, with greater amounts of nutrients going to fathers and teenaged sons (Noralsco 1987). Among our Panguil Bay women interviewees, women reported eating less in order to feed young children. When one pregnant mother's food supply is running low, she loses her appetite, so "the children can eat more."

## Conclusion

In line with world-systems analysts (Smith and Wallerstein 1992; Dunaway 2001), neo-Marxist feminists (Mies 1986) and ecofeminists (Salleh 1997; Mies and Shiva 2001), this study views the household as the basic unit for the material and nonmaterial labors that are essential to reproduce and maintain the work force that is essential to the persistence of the capitalist world economy. Because its members are underpaid in that capitalist system, the household is the unit that makes laborer survival possible through resource pooling and distribution (Smith and Wallerstein 1992; Dunaway 2001). Because full proletarianization into waged workers would increase the cost of production and lower profits, the capitalist world-system has structured a controlling mechanism by which the demands of workers for increased compensation can be restrained. That mechanism is the *semiproletarianized* household that is now the dominant mode worldwide (Wallerstein 1983). In such households, "the wages paid to those members engaging in wage-labor activities can be reduced below the level of household reproduction because the household supplements this income with its other income-generating activities" (Wallerstein 1995: 5–6).

Consequently, it is not through waged labor that women are most inequitably exploited; it is through the *self-exploitation* (intensification of personal labor) of their nonwaged and unpaid coping strategies in *semiproletarianized* households. To provide household basic needs, women juggle an ever-widening work portfolio, in order to have a security net that provides a "hedge against failures in any one component of their survival package" (Illo and Polo 1990: 109–10). As fishing households become more deeply integrated into the global food chain both as exporters and importers, self-exploitation becomes their only alternative. As one fisher observed, "it is solely your body that earns a living.... If you rest, you will have nothing to eat" (Ledesma 1982: 171). In the face of the loss of ecological resources that once supported their livelihoods, poor Philippine fisher households have developed an uneasy and inequitable array of coping strategies that includes

- doing without and eating less
- self-provisioning rather than market purchases
- increased self-exploitation: more fishing, more activity in informal sector, more gathering by women
- new household resource allocation (changes in intrahousehold division of resources)
- expanding or restructuring credit or debts
- increased reliance on family and neighborhood networks
- migration to find work
- removing children from school and putting them to work
- fosterage (shifting children to kin household with more resources)
- more extensive resource exploitation (e.g., dynamite fishing)
- selling or pawning household assets or fishing equipment
- stealing

One Filipino described this ever expanding workload this way:

> A bird wakes up at dawn and immediately flies about looking for food.... The bird spends his days doing this. The next day is the same. Me, too. I wake up and scurry around looking for food and work wherever I can find it ... becoming dizzy trying to keep my family alive. By evening, I'm tired and weak. At dawn, I have to be up again doing the same, like the birds (Kerkvliet 1983: 51).

## Notes

1. At 2005 prices, corn (27 cents per kilo in U.S. dollars) and rice (44 cents per kilo in U.S. dollars) were more expensive in the Philippines than in the United States.

2. One element of the privatization of family planning is the funding of the FriendlyCare Foundation (www.friendlycare.com.ph), whose mission is to "promote responsible parenthood for sustainable development."

# References

Abregana, Betty C. 2000. "Women and Children in Coastal Communities." *SUAKREM Newsletter* 2 (4). Available at http://su.edu.ph/suakcrem/vol2–4.htm.

Adan, E. Y. 2000. "The Impact of Economic Activities on Water Quality and Fish Production in Panguil Bay, Philippines." Ph.D. diss: University of the Philippines–Los Banos.

Afshar, Haleh, and Bina Agarwal, eds. 1989. *Women, Poverty, and Ideology in Asia: Contradictory Pressures, Uneasy Resolutions.* London: Macmillan.

Agarwal, Bina. 1988. *Structures of Patriarchy: State, Community, and Household in Modernising Asia.* London: Zed Books.

Aguilar, G. D. 2002. "Present and Future Role of the College of Fisheries and Ocean Sciences." Working paper, Institute of Marine Fisheries and Oceanology, University of the Philippines in the Visayas.

Ardales, Venancio. 1981. *Time Allocation and Fertility Behavior of Married Women in Fishing Communities of Iloilo, Philippines.* Singapore: Institute of Southeast Asia Studies.

Arnado, M. Janet. 2003. *Mistresses and Maids in the Philippines.* Manila: LaSalle University Press.

Asian Development Bank. 2005. "Poverty in the Philippines: Income, Assets, and Access." Available at www.adb.org.

Atkinson, Jane, and Shelly Errington, eds. 1990. *Power and Difference: Gender in Island Southeast Asia.* Stanford, CA: Stanford University Press.

Barraclough, Solon, and Andrea Finger-Stich. 1996. "Some Ecological and Social Implications of Commercial Shrimp farming in Asia." UNRISD discussion paper, Geneva. Available at www.unrisd.org.

Cabanilla, L. S. 1997. "Achieving Food Security in the Philippines: Some Critical Points to Consider." Working paper no. 97–01, University of the Philippines- Los Banos.

Casino, T. 2004. "Impact of the WTO on the Philippines." Available at www.ibon.org/other/wto-content/teddy.htm.

DeBrun, Suzanne, and Ray Elling. 1987. "Cuba and the Philippines: Contrasting Cases in World-System Analysis." *International Journal of Health Services* 17 (4): 681–701.

Dunaway, Wilma. 2001. "The Double Register of History: Situating the Forgotten Women and Her Household in Capitalist Commodity Chains." *Journal of World-Systems Research* 7 (1): 2–29.

Dwyer, Daisy, and Judith Bruce, eds. 1988. *A Home Divided: Women and Income in the Third World.* Stanford, CA: Stanford University Press.

Eder, James. 1999. *A Generation Later: Household Strategies and Economic Change in the Rural Philippines.* Honolulu: University of Hawaii Press.

Environmental Justice Foundation. 2003. *Smash and Grab: Conflict, Corruption, and Human Rights Abuses in the Shrimp Farming Industry.* London: Environmental Justice Foundation.

Escobar, Arturo. 1994. *Encountering Development: The Making and Unmaking of The Third World.* Princeton, NJ: Princeton University Press.

Escobar, Pepe. 2004. "The Philippines: Disgraceful State, A Five-Part Series." *Asia Times* (October 1, 2, 3, 4, 5).

Eviota, Elizabeth. 1986. "The Articulation of Gender and Class in the Philippines." Pp. 194–206 in *Women's Work: Development and the Division of Labor by Gender*, ed. E. Leacock and H. Safa. South Hadley, MA: Bergin and Garvey.

Hopkins, Terence, and Immanuel Wallerstein. 1987. "Capitalism and the Incorporation of New Zones into the World Economy." *Review* 10 (3/4): 763–780.

IBON Foundation. 2004. "Public Perceptions of Economy and Government." Available at www.ibon.org.

———. 2005. "IBON Feature: WTO at 10: A Decade of Burden for Poor Countries." Available at www.ibon.org.

Illo, Jeanne, and Rosalinda Pineda-Ofreneo. 2002. *Carrying the Burden of the World: Women Reflecting on the Effects of Crisis on Women and Girls*. Quezon City: University of the Philippines.

Illo, Jeanne, and Jaime Polo. 1990. *Fishers, Traders, Farmers, Wives: The Life Stories of Ten Women in a Fishing Village*. Quezon City: Ateneo de Manila University.

International Rice Research Institute. 2003. "Rice Fact Sheet." Available at www.knowledgebank.irri.org.

Israel, D., E. Adan, G. Carnaje, N. Lopez, and J. de Castro. 2003. "Analysis of Long Term Impact of Coastal Resource Management in the Philippines: The Case of Panguil Bay." Working paper, Bureau of Agricultural Research and Philippine Institute of Development Studies.

Irz, X. and J. R. Stevenson, A. Tanoy, P. Villarante, P. Morissens. 2004. "Aquaculture and Poverty—A Case Study of Five Coastal Communities in the Philippines." University of Reading: Department of International Development, Working Paper 4.

Israel-Sobritchea, Carolyn. 1987. "Gender Ideology and the Status of Women in a Rural Economy." Pp. 87–96 in *Essays on Women*, ed. Mary J. Mananzan. Manila: St. Scholastica's College.

Jacinto, E. 2004. "Research Framework on Value Chain Analysis in Small Fisheries." Working paper, Tambuyog Development Center.

JEP ATRE. 2004. "Panguil Bay: Forestry Resource Management Program: Inception Report for the Philippine Bureau of Fisheries and Aquatic Resources, Region 10." Uncirculated document.

Kerkvliet, Benedict. 1983. "Profiles of Agrarian reform in a Nueva Ecija Village." Pp. 43–64 in *Second View from the Paddy*, ed. A. Ledesma, P. Mahil, and V. Miralaco. Quezon City: Ateneo de Manila University.

Ledesma, Antonio. 1982. *Landless Workers and Rice Farmers: Peasant Subclasses Under Agrarian Reform in Two Philippine Villages*. Laguna, Philippines: International Rice Research Institute.

Lim, J. Y., and M. F. Montes. 2002. "Structural Adjustment Program After Structural Adjustment Program, but Why Still No Development in the Philippines?" *Asian Economic Papers* 1 (3): 90–119.

Loquias, Servilla. 1990–1991. "Environmental Issues and Constraints Related to Panguil Bay Coastal Management." *Northwestern Mindanao Research Journal* 15: 41–57.

McMichael, Philip. 1994. *The Global Restructuring of Agro-Food Systems*. Ithaca, NY: Cornell University Press.

Mies, Maria. 1982. "The Dynamics of the Sexual Division of Labor and Integration of Rural Women into the World Market." Pp. 1–28 in *Women and Development: The Sexual Division of Labor in Rural Societies*. New York: Praeger Press.

———. 1986. *Patriarchy and Accumulation on a World Scale: Women in the International Division of Labor.* London: Zed Books.

Mies, Maria, and Vandana Shiva. 2001. *Ecofeminism.* London: Zed Books.

Miraleo, Virginia. 1992. "Female-Headed Households in the Philippines." *Philippine Sociology Review* 40: 46–51.

Naawan School of Fisheries, Mindanao State University. 1991. "Resource and Ecological Assessment of Panguil Bay." Manuscript.

Nash, June. 1994. "Global Integration and Subsistence Insecurity." *American Anthropologist* 96 (1): 7–30.

Naylor, Rosamond. 2003. "Nature's Subsidies to Shrimp and Salmon Farming." *Science Magazine,* 282, 883–888.

Nickerson, Donna. 1999. "Trade-offs of Mangrove Area Development in the Philippines." *Ecological Economics* 28 (2): 279–298.

Noralsco, Cynthia. 1987. "The Woman Problem: Gender, Class, and State Oppression." Pp. 77–86 in *Essays on Women,* ed. Mary J. Mananzan. Manila: St. Scholastica's College.

Oracion, Enrique. 2001. "Filipino Women in Coastal Resources Management: The Need for Social Recognition." SMA Working Paper Series 2001-8, Sociology Department, Silliman University, Philippines.

Philippine Census Bureau. 2004. "Feature for 27 February 2004." Available at www.census.gov.ph.

Philippine Department of Health. 2002. "Philippine Health Statistics." Available at www.doh.gov.ph.

Philippine Food and Nutrition Institute. 2005. "Statistics." Available at www.fnri.dost.gov.ph.

Philippine National Statistical Coordination Board. 2003. "Poverty Statistics." Available at www.nscb.gov.ph.

*Philippines Environmental Monitor.* 2000. Manila: World Bank Group.

Pineda-Ofreneo, Rosalinda. 1985. *Women of the Soil: An Alternative Philippine Report on Rural Women.* Manila: Philippine Women's Research Collective.

Primavera, J. H. 1997. "Socio-Economic Impacts of Shrimp Culture." *Aquaculture Research* 28: 815–827.

Salleh, Ariel. 1997. *Ecofeminism as Politics: Nature, Marx, and the Postmodern.* New York: Zed Books.

Schelzig, K. 2005. "Poverty in the Philippines: Income, Assets, and Access." Asian Development Bank. Available at www.adb.org.

Shiva, Vandana. 2000. *Stolen Harvest: The Hijacking of the Global Food Supply.* Cambridge, MA: South End Press.

Smith, Joan, and Immanuel Wallerstein, eds. 1992. *Creating and Transforming Households: The Constraints of the World-Economy.* Cambridge: Cambridge University Press.

Szanton, Maria C.B. 1972. *A Right to Survive: Subsistence Marketing in a Lowland Philippine Town.* University Park: Pennsylvania State University Press.

United Nations. 2000. *The World's Women: Trends and Statistics.* New York: Oxford University Press.

USAID-Philippines. 2005. "Provision for Wider Family Planning Options." Available at http://philippines.usaidgov/ophn_so3_ir2.dkt.php.

Wallerstein, Immanuel. 1983. *Historical Capitalism.* London: Verso Editions.

———. 1995. "The Modern World System and Evolution." *Journal of World-System Research* 1 (19): 55–68.

———. 1999. "Ecology and Capitalist Cost of Production: No Exit." Pp. 3–12 in *Ecology and the World System,* ed. W. L. Goldfrank, David Goodman, and Andrew Szasz. Westport, CT: Greenwood Press.

World Health Organization. 1997. "Water Pollution Control." Available at www.who.int.

———. 2000. "Water, Sanitation, and Health in Poor Countries." Available at www.who.int/docstore/water_sanitation_health/agride/ch4.htm.

———. 2001. "Nutrition in South-East Asia." Available at www.whosea.org.

Yoshinori, Murai. 1987. "The Life and Times of Shrimp: From Third World Seas to Japanese Tables." *AMPO Japan-Asia Quarterly Review* 18 (4): 2–9.

# UTOPYSTICS AND THE ASIATIC MODES OF LIBERATION

## GURDJIEFFIAN CONTRIBUTIONS TO THE SOCIOLOGICAL IMAGINATIONS OF INNER AND GLOBAL WORLD-SYSTEMS

### Mohammad H. Tamdgidi

Live content, with greed this world desire not.
From the Time's "good and evil" free your lot.
Hold the cup and caress a lover's hair.
Like your days, they, too, will soon be naught.
— Omar Khayyam, circa twelfth century AD

## Introduction

Asian trajectories of mystical traditions significantly challenge the categories and paradigms associated with the world-systems perspective, particularly in the emerging field of utopistics (Wallerstein 1998) and its comparative/integrative variant "utopystics," which advocates cross-cultural explorations in utopia, mysticism, and science (Tamdgidi 2002b, 2006a, 2007b, 2008a, forthcoming [a] and [b]). Provocatively, the inner subjectivist, culturally determined, and

139

enchanted modes of liberation informing Asian mysticisms in their diverse regional forms—such as esoteric fountainheads of Buddhism in East Asia, Hinduism in South Asia, and Islam and generally monotheism in West and Central Asia—subject world-systems analyses' global, politicoeconomic, and scientific/secular frameworks to critical scrutiny. As such, they can provide opportunities for fostering new conversations in favor of infusing the complex geographies of inner experience into the largely global and world-historical geographies of the world-systems perspective.

Marx developed, borrowing from Hegel, his rather derogatory concept of the Asiatic mode of production as one determined by the arid conditions thought to have characterized the landmass spanning West, South, Central, and East Asia, where the need for channeling water to cultivate the land necessitated the building of massive structures that in turn laid the economic basis for the rise of highly centralized states dominated by despots claiming godlike status. Such political and ideological superstructures, in turn, conditioned construction projects that further symbolized the centralized, godlike powers of the despots. Given the materialist, secular, atheist, antireligious, and orientalist frameworks shaping the classical Marxist view of the East and Asia, it was not surprising to note its minimal appreciations for the conceptual and intellectual innovations brought on, in religious form, by the often inaccessible and esoteric mystical traditions emergent from the region—traditions that were themselves often shaped in distinction from the more visibly dominant political, cultural, and economic milieu of the world-systems housing them.

An important attribute of what one may call the "Asiatic modes of liberation" characterizing the mystical traditions in the region has been their ascetic character. From a modernist point of view, such asceticism and world-escaping tendencies may appear backward, outdated, unrealistic, and unworkable as effective strategies for self-, let alone global, transformation—particularly in the context of a modern world-system and a world-systems analysis that perpetually call for dealing with the public issues arising from the everyday running of the capitalist world economy. One may also argue that, despite the escapist forms such ascetic mystical practices may have taken, however, they essentially contained an attribute regarding alternative modes of human liberation that is quite distinct from not only the dominant but even the oppositional and antisystemic, social diagnoses and prognosis found in the West. This has to do with the notion of property ownership that has occupied a central place in the Western and modern discourses on social organization and transformation.

Western discourses on the nature of the good society have often oscillated between arguments for private or collective property ownership; in the mystical traditions, in contrast, the possessive attitude toward things in the world (be they physical things, ideas, feelings, sensations, relations, or processes, etc.) and attachments to them, individual or collective, is the very factor that is problematized as being the source of much of the human suffering. One may choose to interpret this in the narrow sense of its implications in terms of asceticism and world-escaping behavior. But in a different vein, one may regard such a consideration in terms of the awareness of the limits the human propensity to habituation sets on the development and application of human creative powers to understand and transform the inner and broader human social landscapes.

The theoretical and methodological challenges facing such cross-cultural approaches to utopistics and world-systems analysis are intellectually exciting for those interested in developing sociological imaginations of historical world-systems—past, present, and emergent—characterized by simultaneous attention to the dialectics of inner personal and broader global and world-historical forces shaping the trajectories of world-systems. In this chapter I will draw upon G. I. Gurdjieff's (1872?–1949) hybrid teaching of synthesizing elements from diverse Asian mystical traditions in order to advance conceptual frameworks conducive to the understanding of the operational simultaneity of inner and global world-systems and the comparative/integrative pursuit of liberatory strategies in favor of a just global society. I will argue that enriching the world-systems perspective in favor of imaginative sociological approaches that take seriously the personal as well as the world-systemic discourses on and strategies for realistic historical alternatives to the modern world economy necessitate fruitful revisitations of the unit of analysis question in world-systems studies in favor of the adoption of not a singular unit but two-fold, dialectically conceived, micro/macro units of analyses of *inner* and *global* world-systems.

## The Sociological Imagination and World-Systems Analysis

The sociological imagination, according to C. Wright Mills (1959), is characterized by the ability of the mind to relate one's personal troubles to broader public issues. More specifically, it requires its holder to consciously develop and integrate an understanding of one's *inner life* plus what Mills calls his or her "*external career*" (i.e., his or her interactions with others in everyday life) in terms of how they are shaped by the broader "social milieu," consisting of the nature and structure of the *present society* in which he or she lives and the *broader world-historical context* in which the particular and unique features of the present society may best be comprehended comparatively. Mills regards the employment of the sociological imagination as not simply a matter of choice, but a requirement that arises especially from the nature of the culture and society we live in today, and one that must be expected from all sociological endeavors that aim to tackle social problems in a way most conducive to bringing about their effective resolution. The sociology of self-knowledge as proposed and applied in my work (Tamdgidi [1997] 2005, [1999] 2002a, 2002b, 2004/2005, 2007a, forthcoming [a]) has been an effort to further exercise the sociological

142 Mohammad H. Tamdgidi

imagination with a particular emphasis—adopting a nonreductive causal modality of the self-society dialectic—on the exploration of the *investigator's own intra/interpersonal life* in relation to especially the *world-historical* scope of the sociological inquiry.

The world-systems perspective, from its inception, was characterized by several major attributes that have more or less endured throughout the decades and shaped the structures of knowledges produced in the field. These include its holism, its insistence on the primacy of economy, its reluctance to be rigidified into a theory, its Western scientific/secular character seeking to bridge with the knowledge produced in the humanities (hence, its self-characterization as a historical social science), and its concerns for bridging the true and the good, that is, a concern for developing a scholarship that is committed to social change in favor of a just global society.

In his brief but important 2000 essay titled "Where Should Sociologists Be Heading?" Immanuel Wallerstein called for efforts to erase five distinctions whose continuity in world-systems and generally sociological analyses have not borne fruitful results. Namely, he called for erasing the distinction between the studies of the past and of the present (a variant of what he also refers to in terms of the distinction between history and theory, or differently in terms of the distinction between nomothetic and ideographic studies); between studies of the economy, polity, and culture; between studies of the West and the rest; between studies of the true and the good; and between studies in two academic cultures, that is, between the sciences and the humanities.

It is interesting to note that absent from Wallerstein's list of distinctions to be erased was the distinction between the whole and its parts. Nor did he—and these may be variants of the latter—call for erasing the distinction between the macro and the micro, or the global and the personal. This is perhaps due to the fact that the holism of world-systems analysis has been a defining feature of this perspective. In the world-systems perspective, no part of the system can be understood (and thereby effectively transformed) without giving due consideration to the knowledge and transformative requirements of the world-system as a whole.

The problem is, however, that the adoption of such a macro-gravitating conceptual framework characterizing the world-systems analysis does not fit well with the requirements for developing a Millsian sociological imagination. Mills was not oblivious to the need for understanding the nature of the present society as a whole, nor did he fail to point out that the latter needs also to be studied in a world-history context. What Mills required was that the individuals' reflections on public issues at the macro level be undertaken in intimate conceptual conversation with their thoughts on inter/intrapersonal social reality on the micro level.

The positive irony behind Wallerstein's useful advice to sociologists in his 2000 essay is that, if one follows it, one would need to discard many of the a priori determinisms traditionally associated with the world-systems analysis. How can one erase the distinctions between economy, polity, and culture and not also dismantle the analytical primacy of the economy over politics and culture? How can one erase the distinction between the present and the past (and future, if we consider Wallerstein's *Utopistics* [1998]) and not consider how economy, polity, and culture may be differently implicated as primary causal factors across diverse past, present, and emerging world-systems? How can one erase the distinction between theory and history, between nomothetic and ideographic study, and not find a need to conceptualize broadly macro and intimately micro social processes in addition to concrete historical investigations? How can one erase the distinction between the West and the rest, between the true and the good, and between the sciences and the humanities and not pay equal attention to diverse forms of knowledge produced across multiple civilizational traditions, secular and religious alike, that have appeared in history and shaped the diverse regional trajectories of human development?

In the spirit of erasing the distinction between the world-systems analysis and the sociological imagination, in this chapter I aim to apply a mode of analysis informed by what Wallerstein has proposed in terms of the erasure of a variety of distinctions as noted above. If, as Wallerstein has repeatedly stressed, the world-systems perspective is not an already accomplished theory but an evolving and transient conceptual framework open to modification, it can perhaps also benefit from the adoption of imaginative sociological frameworks that would make it more truthful, and effective, in fostering the good in the self and the broader society in favor of utopistic outcomes.

Toward this end, I will draw upon my studies of a particular Asian esoteric tradition associated with the teachings of G. I. Gurdjieff (see Tamdgidi 2002b, 2004, 2006a, forthcoming [b] and more broadly 2005/2006 and 2007a), the twentieth century Transcaucasian mystic philosopher and teacher, as a heuristic device for the development of a microlevel conceptual framework critically complementing the macro conceptual apparatus of the world-systems perspective.

## Gurdjieff's Conceptual Apparatus

Mysticism has traditionally been concerned with seeking direct knowledge or experience of the ultimate hidden meaning or truth of existence. Inspired by the Hermetic principle "As Above, So Below"—and in contrast to its extroversive Western counterpart—Eastern mysticism has generally pursued its aim introversively, through the attainment of personal self-knowledge and transformation in search of "perfect" inner states. Since such ideal inner states have often been associated with or are considered to be derived from the assumed perfect being of god(s), mysticism has frequently been associated with religious doctrines or experiences—even though, strictly speaking, mysticism does not have to be religious or introversive in orientation, such as in the cases of Western pantheistic and nature mysticisms (Bishop 1995).

Gurdjieff's teaching represents an effort at seriously grappling with the problem of habituation as a cardinal factor in human enslavement. Although his conceptual apparatus limits the scope of such a liberatory project to the inner and at most interpersonal dimensions—more or less taking for granted the objective conditions that may be responsible for the fragmented and alienated nature of the inner personal life—one can critically engage with his and similar spiritual traditions in a broader project involving the implications the human propensity to habituation may pose for the perpetuation and reproduction of inner and global world-systems.

George Ivanovitch Gurdjieff (1872?–1949) was an enigmatic Transcaucasian philosopher, mystic, and teacher of esoteric dances, exercises, and movements who has been widely acknowledged for having introduced to the West during the early twentieth century a rational synthesis of Eastern mysticism and, subsequently, for having significantly shaped the ideas and practices of the new religious movements. According to Jacob Needleman, "Gurdjieff gave shape to some of the key elements and directions found in contemporary spirituality" (Needleman 1996: xi). "In the half-century after Gurdjieff's death," writes Needleman,

> Tibetan lamas, Indian gurus, Zen roshis have become increasingly familiar figures in Western culture, and many of them have been struck by the traditional aspects of Gurdjieff's teaching. It is more difficult, however, for the Western scholar, theologian, or seeker to place a figure like Gurdjieff, who seems to fit no formula, wears no robes, recites no mantras, and demands no homage. He seems neither of East nor West. Possibly he is both. (1996: x)

What distinguishes Gurdjieff's ([1933] 1973, 1950, [1963] 1985, 1973, [1981] 1991) mysticism is its hybrid character drawing upon and moving beyond many of the mystical sources of his teaching. As a "seeker of truth," Gurdjieff distinguished three traditional ways of the fakir, the yogi, and the monk in Asian mysticism—ideal-types that may roughly, though not entirely, correspond with certain mystical practices in Islam, Hinduism, and Buddhism—depending on whether the physical, the intellectual, or the emotional center of human organism is one-sidedly exercised in retreat from social life as the initial launching ground for efforts toward the ultimate goal of all-rounded spiritual self perfection (Ouspensky 1949). Suggesting that these three one-sided "ways" to self-perfection are prone to failure since their trainings take longer (thus often unrealizable during a single lifetime) and their one-sidedly developed adepts become often vulnerable to habituating forces upon reentry into social life, Gurdjieff advocated an alternative "Fourth Way" school in mysticism. He characterized this approach as one concerned with the *parallel harmonious development* of the physical, the intellectual, and the emotional centers of the organism to be pursued not in retreat from, but *in the midst of,* everyday life. Such a three-fold task simultaneously taking place in the midst of life was, in his view, essential for awakening the human organism (via the radical attainment of personal self-knowledge) from sleep, mechanicalness, and spiritual imprisonment and for bringing about effective self-transformation in pursuit of harmonious human development in search for the ultimate truth of existence.

Gurdjieff treated the ordinary human "individual" as a multiplicity, fundamentally structured by his or her "three-brained" physical, intellectual, and emotional centers, to which he associates three primary forms of awareness—the instinctive (or unconscious), the waking conscious, and the subconscious.[1] For Gurdjieff the ordinary individual is actually a "legion" of I's acting independently from one another. Conditions of ordinary life prevent the automatic formation of an actual "individual," a master self, and ultimately a "soul," in the human being, making the attainment of these possible only as a result of conscious and intentional efforts on the part of the person him/herself. The journey of self-understanding and change must therefore begin with the conscious labor of self-knowledge. Through self-observation, self-remembering, and external considering of one's interactions with others in or outside school "work," the actual reality and the complex dynamics of one's inner multiplicity, fragmentation, sleep, mechanicalness, and slavery is increasingly revealed to oneself and brought under one's immediate attention. This leads to a deeply felt "shock" to the organism expressed in terms of experiencing the "terror of the situation," that is, of suddenly realizing one's being a machine, a slave, asleep.

Through discovering and then melting down, in the heat of intentional physical, intellectual, and emotional exercises and "sufferings," the chief and subsidiary forms of habituated "buffers" deeply entrenched within and across the three centers, it becomes possible to gradually dealienate and harmonize one's fragmented body, thoughts, and emotions. This—a second intentional shock to the organism—then leads to the more prolonged awakening of the innate sense of objective conscience already in existence but deeply buried in the subconscious. By means of this one can then unite one's inner essence and external personalities into a single, indivisible but consciously and intentionally adaptable, whole guided by a singular master, a truly "individual" "I." The organism, having died to its mechanicalness through experiencing the conscious and intentional shocks of self-knowledge and change, is now exposed to the possibility in time of achieving extraordinary levels of physical health, intellectual productivity, and emotional stability. These higher self-experiences of the organism, according to Gurdjieff, are prerequisites for conscious ascendance in the "cosmic food chain" in the path of fulfillment of duties towards possible understanding of, and union with, God.

According to Gurdjieff, the energies associated with the three inborn and relatively independently functioning centers in the human inner world are not automatically blended into one another by nature but require conscious and intentional effort on the part of the person throughout his or her lifetime to harmoniously develop the organism into an "individual" being. Human evolution and development, according to Gurdjieff, cannot be truly comprehended without an appreciation of the role played by the conscious and intentional human agency.[2] Gurdjieff used the analogy of a passenger's carriage driven by a horse and driver in order to illustrate the three-part architecture of the human organism. In an ideal state, the master "I" represented by the passenger can effectively communicate and direct the actions of the intellectual driver, carriage body, and the emotional horse, by a functioning mediation of the symbolic languages of words (between the passenger and the driver), motion/brake lever (between the driver and the carriage), shafts (between the carriage and the horse), and reins (between the driver and the horse). The ideally developed organism can act in conscious unison, as an indivisible whole, because the forms of consciousness corresponding to the carriage, the driver, and the horse—namely the physical instinctive, the intellectual waking conscious, and the emotional subconscious minds—are able to mutually blend into one another at the will of the master "I" represented by the passenger. In actual conditions found in reality, however, the organism is often alienated and fragmented within to such a degree that the body carriage is drastically out of shape and abused; the driver intellect is in a state of perpetual sleep, drunkenness, and false imagination; and the emotional horse is completely out of control. The supposed master "I" lacks the knowledge and ability to communicate with and guide the centers using their unique languages. Most often, he is simply not there—the organism takes any passerby as its "true self," submitting to it for a short while until the next wandering passenger comes along. The self that promises to get up at 6 a.m., Gurdjieff mused, is often not the self which actually gets up, turns off the alarm, and goes back to sleep. Consequently, depending on the situation of each organism, one or another lopsidedly developed and "fixated" center and its associated selves rob other centers (and their associated selves) of the energy needed for their development, leading to the crystallization of diverse forms of habituated and disharmonious personality types—physical, intellectual, emotional, and a variety of their blends—across human organisms.

The most fundamental challenge Gurdjieff's cosmology and anthropology poses for the sociological thought—including the world-systems analysis *and* that of the Millsian sociological imagination—is the problematization of the singularity of the "individual" considered as a singular acting unit. Gurdjieff turns the notion of "multiple personality disorder" onto its head and in effect tells us that it describes a general human condition responsible for the human propensity to habituation. For Gurdjieff, considering his focus on the microsocial everyday interactions, the working unit of analysis is not the individual, therefore, but the self, or the "I," legions of which occupy, under prevailing conditions, the inner and interpersonal landscapes of the disharmonized and fragmented person in everyday life. Gurdjieff takes the multiplicity of selves as a point of departure of his understanding of the nature of human behavior and troubles, and he regards the existence of individuality, that is, a conscious and intentional unity of diverse selves, to be the ultimate goal of a lifetime's effort rather than a presumed, inborn, and taken-for-granted attribute of the person.

What puts the person to sleep and makes him or her a prisoner of social circumstances, acting like a machine, is the separate functioning of the physical, intellectual, and emotional centers in the organism, which contributes to the presence of unconscious, waking conscious, and subconscious modes of awareness and behavioral patterns in the organism. It is this fragmentation of the organism, and the separate, unevenly developed, functioning of the centers that then set the ground for an inner landscape populated with separately acting and behaving selves.

## Revisiting the Unit of World-Systems Analysis

The most defining concepts of the world-systems perspective are perhaps best expressed in its name, that is, the ideas of the "world" and the "system," implying spatial and temporal considerations to be employed in social analysis. On the one hand, a concretely existing society is to be analyzed spatially in the entirety, encompassing the totality, of social relations organically constituting it. On the other hand, temporally, the enduring and organically fundamental features of those relations are to be identified. The notion of the "world" in "world-system," in other words, does not necessarily imply a globally encompassing social organization, nor should the notion of "system" prevent the recognition of the transient and changing nature of a given society under consideration. The point of a unit of analysis thus considered, therefore, is to always keep the *relational totality* of the *structural features* of a social formation under constant attention and scrutiny when studying any of its respective parts. This interpretation of the "world-system" may be noted in the manner in which Hopkins and Wallerstein (1982) used the concept to identify a variety of social formations in history that were neither necessarily globe-encompassing nor transhistorically enduring. Ancient minisystems, world empires, and world economies have all been considered varieties of world-systems appearing in history.

The value of insisting on the world-system as a singular unit of analysis has therefore been in regard to adopting a holistic methodology that would aid the consideration of each part of the social system in relation to the workings of the system as a whole. In this regard, it is important to note the *relative* nature of what constitutes wholes and parts. For example, the existence and nature of an apple cannot be adequately understood without recourse to its position in the structural system of a tree that constitutes it. In this sense, the apple is considered a part of the tree. An apple, on its own, however, constitutes an organic whole for the parts constituting its own respective inner structure/system. Likewise, what we regarded as a whole previously, that is, the tree, is a whole only unto itself in a relative sense, and actually its existence cannot be adequately explained and understood without the consideration of it as a part of a broader whole, that is, the orchard, the land, the earth's biosphere, and even more broadly the solar system, and so on.

Therefore, it is important to consider that when we use the notion of the "world-system" as a research tool, it can be applied on a variety of spatiotemporal levels without losing its conceptual value. The application of the concept to the study of capitalism, therefore, should be seen as only one such application and should not be limited to it. In fact, failing to regard the capitalist world-system as only a part of broader social or historical wholes constituting it would limit the value of the concept to the point of arriving at misleading conclusions. For instance, if the primacy of economy in a capitalist social formation is overly generalized to an attribute of all human history as a whole (an approach that Marx, in my view wrongly, adopted via his "materialist conception of history"), this would lead to analytical practices and conclusions that ignore the specificity of other types of world-systemic structures in which, variously, politics or culture may predominate or, alternatively, social formations in which the distinction between the three spheres are not institutionalized or rigidly separated, as in ancient civilizational contexts, or as may perhaps be created in emergent or future social formations (cf. Tamdgidi 2006b, 2007b).

Drawing on the example of the apple and the tree, therefore, we could expand the notion of world-systems studies in such a way that would recognize the dialectics of global and inner world-systems. The inner life of the person, in other words, may be regarded as a whole at its own level, which is, from another vantage point a part of the global world-system as a broader whole. Undoubtedly, an adequate understanding of one's inner life cannot be arrived at without an understanding of the larger social world-system of which it is a part—as one would not expect to understand the existence of an apple apart from the tree, the orchard, and so on. It can also be argued, however, that an understanding of the tree as a whole may not yield an adequate understanding of the specific apple now in my hand with all its defects, an understanding of which requires a concrete study of that specific apple. As far as the working of the tree system is concerned, the apple's inner system is in its uniqueness an important part of what makes the tree what it is. I think it is this consideration that led Mills to stress so emphatically that we should practice sociology in both its macro and intimately micro and personal dimensions because the understanding and transformation of one cannot be adequately achieved without the understanding and transformation of the other. After all, how a world-system is conceived and transformed (or not) is always conditioned by the unique biographical circumstances of the person(s) engaging (or not) in such conceptualizations and transformations.

For the purpose of advancing the sociological imagination, and more specifically a sociology of self-knowledge, therefore, this manner of conceptualizing world-systems studies can be very fruitful, for it would expand the notion of the world-system as a unit of analysis into a dialectical consideration of macro- and microsociological twin units of analyses that can accommodate the exploration of nonreductive dialectics of personal troubles and broader public issues.

Moving from spatial to temporal considerations, fusing a simultaneously macro- and microsociological framework into the world-systems analysis must begin with the notion of "system," or more broadly, "structure." When we speak of system or structure, we usually mean to suggest that an enduring, patterned, and repetitive process of social interaction is at work. For instance, the set of concepts "core," "periphery," and "semiperiphery" are used in world-systems analysis to denote structurally enduring systemic zones in the capitalist world-system associated with the presence (or co-presence in the case of semiperiphery) of relatively low-wage and low-skilled labor and weak-state social features (as in the peripheral regions) versus relatively high-wage and high-skilled labor and strong-state social features (as in the core regions). The notion is that the modern world-system continually produces and reproduces a structural pattern of hierarchically organized zones associated with core, peripheral, and semiperipheral characteristics, even though concrete geographical regions constituting the world economy may, in one or another historical time, move up or down the hierarchical ladder.

But what does a patterned, repetitive social interaction *actually* consist of, and why is it treated, or referred to, as systemic or structural? It means that social actors continually, often subconsciously or habitually, engage in behaviors that continually produce and reproduce specific modes of economic, political, and cultural outcomes that maintain the world-systemic status quo. From a microsociological point of view, especially that envisioned in the work of the sociologist Herbert Blumer (1986), social structure is not one standing over and above the concrete conduct of individual social actors but is produced and reproduced *through* the personally conducted social interactions of everyday life at work, home, and street, actual or (nowadays) virtual. To the extent that one, consciously or subconsciously, engages in producing and reproducing patterns of social (economic, political, and cultural) interaction that sustain the perpetuation of the global world-system, one is contributing to its maintenance, and to the extent that one consciously (and perhaps at times unconsciously) disrupts such patterns of world-systemic behavior, one has disrupted the reproduction of the system. At the level of social movements, involving what Blumer calls "joint actions," the continuity of antisystemic and what Tamdgidi (2001) has called "othersystemic" behavior can perhaps lead to the transformation of the system as a whole. In *The Exercise of Influence in Small Groups,* based on his doctoral dissertation, T. K. Hopkins (1964) pointed to this tension and dialectics of the small group of acting participants and the larger social structures when he wrote:

> Any type of social system can tolerate a certain degree of deviance. For each type a characteristic range exists within which the activities of the participants may depart from the norms of the system without occasioning any basic changes in the structure of the system. Departures outside of this range do, however, occasion fundamental structural changes, even, possibly, the dissolution of the particular system. (Hopkins 1964:183)

If we regard the "world-system" not as a state, but as a *process* of "world-systemization," a unity of diverse, consciously and subconsciously/habitually, interacting behaviors (macro- or micro-oriented, economic, political, cultural, physical, intellectual, emotional, and so on), then we can consider personal human behaviors in everyday social interactions in terms of the extent to which they produce and reproduce or, differently, question, resist, and transform what are the constituent, conscious or subconscious, processes of the world-system. Similarly, one can also conceive of human behaviors that actually produce alternative types of social interactions that do not simply aim at resisting and transforming the prevalent "interaction rituals" (Goffman 1982) constituting the world-system, but construct and reconstruct alternative modes of social interaction that may be qualitatively different from those associated with the prevalent world-systemic status quo.

Imperial systems are by their very nature socially stratified systems, and the reproduction of such stratified social structures requires everyday social (personal as well as economic, political, and cultural) interaction rituals that produce and reproduce the stratified imperial social structures. As simplistic as it may seem at first, it may be of interest to consider the extent to which the inner life of the disharmonious person may be characterized, on the micro level, as being hierarchical, similar to the architecture of the hierarchical zones in an imperial world-system. Applying Gurdjieff's ideas, one may similarly identify core, peripheral, and semiperipheral regions in the landscape of multiple selves populating the inner and interpersonal lives of the individual. The consideration of a divided inner life and its population by alienated and stratified selves is not new and original in Gurdjieff, and other scholars have explored this view (cf. Deikman 1982, and Zurcher 1977, for instance). The works of the late cultural theorist Gloria Anzaldúa embody imaginative considerations of the multiplicity of selves in spiritual and self/social transformation (Anzaldúa 1987; see also Keating 2000; Anzaldúa and Keating 2002; Tamdgidi 2006a and forthcoming [a]). George Herbert Mead (1934) also recognized how the existence of multiple personalities can be regarded as a common affair. Even

Marx's reference, in his famous "preface" to *A Contribution to the Critique of Political Economy* ([1859] 1970), to the distinction between what social actors say and do in politics may be reinterpreted in terms of the significance of a divided geography of multiple selfhoods at work complicating the course of human political action. With Gurdjieff, however, this possibility is raised to a paradigmatic trouble afflicting the human race and regarded as a cardinal question to be dealt with in the pursuit of human liberation from inner slavery, mechanicalness, and existential anesthesia.

The consideration sought after here is to associate the continuity of hierarchically organized imperial world-systems with the continuity of hierarchically organized inner world-systems of selves at the personal level. The macro and micro conditions may then be regarded as being twin-born, making the workings of the hierarchical world-system as a whole possible. The distinction between the two spheres, thereby, is erased in such a consideration, since the perpetuation (and, therefore, disruption) of one is dependent upon the perpetuation (and disruption) of the other. It is the inner divisions of centers and the disparate workings of a multitude of alienated selves populating the inner and interpersonal lives of the individuals that allow for the perpetuation of behavioral patterns that un/subconsciously, and at times consciously, reproduce the structural attributes of the world-system that constitutes them in return. Mead's (1934) notion of twinborn-ness of the self and society is quite relevant here, one that Anzaldúa (1987) differently articulates in terms of the simultaneity of self- and world knowledge and transformation (cf. Tamdgidi forthcoming [a] for elaboration of this theme).

Gurdjieff's approach to the study of personal troubles is different from the Millsian in that the former does not take for granted the singularity of the person reflecting on his or her troubles. Besides, in Gurdjieff's view, such states of inner division make the organism vulnerable to habitual behavior that can most effectively be recognized and dealt with through conscious and intentional efforts on the part of the person him/herself. It is one thing to study others' personal troubles and how they are shaped by broader public issues, and another to study one's own.

## Conclusion

The basic point here is that the continued operation of an imperial world-system fundamentally requires habituated behaviors on the part of those participating in and running it. Such a habituated functioning of human behavior is what makes possible the continued operation of the hierarchically organized and stratified world-system that also in turn constitutes, educates, and conditions such behavioral patterns on the part of the participants in the world-system. Disruptions of such automatic processes would effectively involve, to the extent they are undertaken, disruptions in the operation of the world-system hitherto constituting them. But the disruption of a personal behavior on the part of the person first requires becoming aware of the existence of the habitual behavior in the first place, and in particular the extent to which the particular behavior is a product, and in turn reproductive, of the workings of the world-system as a whole. As Gurdjieff put it, for one to set oneself free, one must first realize that one is in prison.

Here is where the significance of a sociological imagination—and of Gurdjieff's contributions in terms of his emphases on the paradigmatic significance of the human inner division and multiplicity, the resulting human propensity to habituation, and the subsequent need for seeking radical personal self-knowledge and change—becomes evident. In Gurdjieff's conceptual framework, the disruption of the person's habitual behavioral pattern does not come by itself without conscious and intentional effort on his or her own part. A teacher can only supply his pupils with leather, Gurdjieff advised; they should make their own shoes. Using the analogy of the carriage, driver, horse, and passenger as described above, Gurdjieff would maintain that the passenger I, the master self—often not even present in the inner world-system owing to long years of the system's malfunctioning—cannot emerge without a conscious and intentional decision and effort on the part of the person to turn his or her own life and organism into an object of his or her observation, autobiographical self-remembering and reexamination, and continual self-reflective study in ever broader contexts.

This conscious and intentional splitting of the self into a subject and an object of study would be the first and a most important step of taking charge of the process, but by no means is it sufficient. The various centers of the organism whose separate habitual functionings make possible the continuation of the habituated and mechanical functioning of the organism and its behaviors have their own languages, and their workings cannot be adequately understood, let along transformed, without specific efforts and exercises—physical, intellectual, and emotional—that would enable the unique behavioral "inner world-system" of the person to be adequately comprehended and transformed in the desired direction. Here is another area in which Gurdjieff's "three-brained" approach to inner world knowledge and transformation becomes distinguished from Mills's merely intellectual approach. To understand and change oneself, it is not sufficient merely to "think" through one's personal troubles; it is necessary to partake in specific physical, intellectual, and emotional exercises that harmoniously develop one's knowledge of oneself and the world across the three physical, intellectual, and emotional dimensions.

Asian mystical traditions, their shortcomings notwithstanding in other regards, diversely provide highly developed and precise meditative techniques for cultivating such continual and many-sided modes of self-observation, self-remembering, external considering, and detachment regarding possessive attitudes to ideas, things, feelings, relations, and processes. Gurdjieff's "Fourth Way" school is notably different, given its aim to move beyond ascetic and world-escaping habits of traditional Asian mysticisms in its effort to cultivate detached attitudes toward social life while living *in its midst* rather than in retreat from it.

Significantly, what needs to be added to Gurdjieff's conceptual apparatus—and this is where he falls short in his teaching—is the effort on the part of the person to also seek an understanding of the extent to which his or her personal life and troubles are shaped by and reproductive of the life of the global world-system on the macro level. Such a two-fold understanding is what Mills characterizes as the sociological imagination, an imagination that the sociology of self-knowledge also seeks to foster by way of its more specific focus on achieving a simultaneity in the investigator's self- and world-historical reflexivity.

Studying Asia through the world-systems perspective is one thing. Another, is to appreciate how historical world-systems, and the world-systems perspective, can be more effectively comprehended and transformed in favor of utopystic outcomes through learning from the ideas and traditions diversely indigenous to the continent.

## Notes

1. According to Gurdjieff these three forms of awareness are present in each of the three centers. In other words, the physical body is said to be constituted primarily of instinctive, but also of consciously, performed and subconsciously learned/habituated behaviors. Likewise, our intellectual activity is regarded as being predominantly conscious, but also accompanied by instinctive and habitually performed dimensions; and so our emotions are considered to involve mainly subconscious, but also conscious and instinctive dimensions.

2. According to Gurdjieff, "In speaking of evolution it is necessary to understand from the outset that no mechanical evolution is possible. The evolution of man is the evolution of his consciousness, and *'consciousness' cannot evolve unconsciously.* The evolution of man is the evolution of his will, and 'will' cannot evolve involuntarily. The evolution of man is the evolution of his power of doing, and 'doing' cannot be the result of things which 'happen.'" (quoted in Ouspensky 1949: 58

## References

Anzaldúa, Gloria E. 1987. *Borderlands/La Frontera: The New Mestiza.* San Francisco: aunt lute books.

Anzaldúa, Gloria E., and AnaLouise Keating (eds.). 2002. *This Bridge We Call Home: Radical Visions for Transformation.* New York: Routledge.

Bishop, Donald H. 1995. *Mysticism and the Mystical Experience: East and West.* London: Susquehanna University Press.

Blumer, Herbert. 1986. *Symbolic Interactionism: Perspectives and Method.* Berkeley: University of California Press.

Deikman, Arthur J. 1982. *The Observing Self: Mysticism and Psychotherapy.* Boston: Beacon Press.

Goffman, Erving. 1982. *Interaction Ritual: Essays on Face-to-Face Behavior.* New York: Pantheon Books.

Gurdjieff, G. I. [1933] 1973. *Herald of Coming Good: First Appeal to Contemporary Humanity.* New York: Samuel Weiser.

———. 1950. *All and Everything: Beelzebub's Tales to His Grandson.* New York: Harcourt, Brace.

———. [1963] 1985. *Meetings with Remarkable Men.* New York: Viking Arkana.

———. 1973. *Views from the Real World: Early Talks of G. I. Gurdjieff.* New York: Arkana/Penguin Books.

———. [1981] 1991. *Life Is Real Only Then, When "I AM."* New York: Viking Arkana/Triangle Editions.

Hopkins, Terence K. 1964. *The Exercise of Influence in Small Groups.* Somerville, NJ: The Bedminister Press.

Hopkins, Terence K., Immanuel Wallerstein, and associates. 1982. *World-Systems Analysis: Theory and Methodology.* Beverly Hills, CA: Sage Publications.

Keating, AnaLouise (ed.). 2000. *Gloria E. Anzaldúa: Interviews/Entrevistas.* New York: Routledge.

Marx, Karl. [1859] 1970. *A Contribution to the Critique of Political Economy.* Ed.and with an introduction by Maurice Dobb. New York: International Publishers.

Mead, George Herbert. 1934. *Mind, Self, and Society.* Chicago: University of Chicago Press.

Mills, C. Wright. 1959. *The Sociological Imagination.* New York: Oxford University Press.

Needleman, Jacob. 1996. "Introduction." Pp. ix-xii in *Gurdjieff: Essays and Reflections on the Man and His Teaching,* ed. Jacob Needleman and George Baker. New York: Continuum.

Ouspensky, P. D. 1949. *In Search of the Miraculous: Fragments of an Unknown Teaching.* New York: Harcourt Brace Jovanovich.

Tamdgidi, Mohammad H., instructor, ed., and contributor. [1997] 2005. *'I' in the World-System: Stories from an Odd Sociology Class. Selected Student Writings, Soc. 280Z: Sociology of Knowledge: Mysticism, Utopia, and Science, Binghamton University, Spring 1997.* Medford, MA: Okcir Press.

———. 2001. "Open the Antisystemic Movements: The Book, the Concept, and the Reality." *Review* 24, no. 2: 299–336.

———. [1999] 2002a. "Ideology and Utopia in Mannheim: Toward the Sociology of Self- Knowledge." *Human Architecture: Journal of the Sociology of Self-Knowledge* 1, no. 1 (Spring): 120–140. [An earlier version of this article was presented to the "History of Sociology" Refereed Roundtable Session at the Ninety-Fourth Annual Meeting of the American Sociological Association, August 6–10, 1999, Chicago.]

———. 2002b. "Mysticism and Utopia: Towards the Sociology of Self-Knowledge and Human Architecture (A Study in Marx, Gurdjieff, and Mannheim)." Ph.D. diss., State University of New York at Binghamton.

———. 2004. "Freire Meets Gurdjieff and Rumi: Toward the Pedagogy of the Oppressed and Oppressive Selves." *The Discourse of Sociological Practice* 6, no. 2 (Fall): 165–185.

———. 2004/2005. "Working Outlines for the Sociology of Self-Knowledge." *Human Architecture: Journal of the Sociology of Self-Knowledge*3, nos. 1 and 2 (Fall/Spring): 123–133.

———. 2005. "Orientalist and Liberating Discourses of East-West Difference: Revisiting Edward Said and the Rubaiyat of Omar Khayyam." *The Discourse of Sociological Practice* 7, nos. 1 and 2 (Spring/ Fall): 187–201.

———. 2005/2006. "Private Sociologies and Burawoy's Sociology Types: Reflections on Newtonian and Quantal Sociological Imaginations." *Human Architecture: Journal of the Sociology of Self-Knowledge*4, nos. 1 and 2 (Fall/Spring): 179–195.

———. 2006a. "Anzaldúa's Sociological Imagination: Comparative Applied Insights into Utopystic and Quantal Sociology." *Human Architecture: Journal of the Sociology of Self-Knowledge*4, Special Issue (Summer): 265–285.

———. 2006b. "Toward a Dialectical Conception of Imperiality: The Transitory (Heuristic) Nature of the Primacy of Analyses of Economies in World-Historical Social Science." *Review* (Journal of the Fernand Braudel Center)24, no. 4: 291–328.

———. 2007a. "Abu Ghraib as a Microcosm: The Strange Face of Empire as a Lived Prison." *Sociological Spectrum* 27: 29–55.

———. 2007b. *Advancing Utopistics: The Three Component Parts and Errors of Marxism.* Boulder, Colo.: Paradigm.

———. 2008a. "From Utopistics to Utopystics: Integrative Reflections on Potential Contributions of Mysticism to World-Systems Analyses and Praxes of Historical Alternatives." Pp. 202–219 in *Islam and the Orientalist World-System,* ed. Khaldoun Samman and Mazhar Al-Zo'by. Boulder, Colo.: Paradigm.

———. 2008b. "Public Sociology and the Sociological Imagination: Revisiting Burawoy's Sociology Types." *Humanity & Society* 32, no. 1: 131–143.

———. Forthcoming (a). "'I Change Myself, I Change the World': Gloria Anzaldúa's Sociological Imagination in *Borderlands/La Frontera: The New Mestiza.*" *Humanity & Society.*

———. Forthcoming (b). *Gurdjieff and Hypnosis: A Hermeneutic Study.* New York: Palgrave Macmillan.

Wallerstein, Immanuel. 1998. *Utopistics: Or, Historical Choices of the Twenty-First Century.* New York: New Press.

———. 2000. "Where Should Sociologists Be Heading?" *Contemporary Sociology* 29, no. 2:306–308.

Zurcher, Louis A., Jr. 1977. *The Mutable Self: A Self-Concept for Social Change.* Beverly Hills, CA: Sage Publications.

# CONTRIBUTORS

**Christopher Chase-Dunn** is Distinguished Professor of Sociology and Director of the Institute for Research on World-Systems at the University of California—Riverside. He is the author of *Rise and Demise: Comparing World-Systems* (with Thomas D. Hall), *The Wintu and Their Neighbors: A Very Small World-System in Northern California* (with Kelly Mann). He is the founder and former editor of the *Journal of World-Systems Research*. Chase-Dunn is currently conducting research on global party formation and antisystem social movements as well as on the growth/decline phases and upward sweeps of cities and empires and future global state formation.

**Wilma A. Dunaway** is Professor in the School of Public and International Affairs at Virginia Tech. She is a specialist in world-system analysis, international political economy, international slavery studies, Native American Studies, and Appalachian Studies. She has won several awards for her four books about Appalachia and about slavery. Her interdisciplinary work has appeared in numerous history and social science journals.

**Thomas D. Hall** holds the Edward Myers Dolan Chair of Anthropology and is University Professor at DePauw University in the Department of Sociology and Anthropology in Greencastle, Indiana. He writes about indigenous peoples; pastoral nomads; ethnicity; world-systems analysis ancient and contemporary; and frontiers. His books include *Social Change in the Southwest, 1350–1880* and with Christopher Chase-Dunn, *Rise and Demise: Comparing World-Systems.* His teaching and research interests include globalization; comparative study of frontiers; and social, economic, political, and cultural changes taking place over thousands of years.

**M. Cecilia Macabuac** is Assistant Professor of Sociology and Director of the Kinaadman Research Center, Xavier University, Philippines.

**Richard Niemeyer** is a graduate student in the department of Sociology at the University of California–Riverside. His research in Political Economy focuses on synthesizing and expanding classical and contemporary theory through the utilization of empirical insights derived from fractal geometry, complex network analysis and dynamical systems.

**Robert J. S. Ross** is Professor and former Chair of Sociology and Director of the International Studies Stream at Clark University where he was elected Faculty Chair of the University 2000–2006. He is an Adjunct Professor of Community Development and Planning. In 2005–2006 he was Chair of the American Sociological Association Section on the Political Economy of the World System. He has taught at Clark University since 1972 and has held visiting appointments at MIT, Michigan and Harvard Universities, and Wheaton College. His books include *Global Capitalism: The New Leviathan* (coauthored) and *Slaves to Fashion: Poverty and Abuse in the New Sweatshops.* His latest work, on labor rights and international trade, is published in *Foreign Affairs, Third World Quarterly, Labor Studies Journal,* and *Dissent* magazine. Ross's work has also appeared in *The Nation, In These Times,* and *Tikkun.* He is an Associate Editor of the *Journal of World-Systems Research.* He has been a consultant to the economic development agency of the city of Boston, the Massachusetts Department of Welfare, and a speechwriter and policy adviser in the Massachusetts State Senate.

**Robert Schaeffer** is Professor of Global Sociology at Kansas State University. He is coauthor with Torry Dickenson of *Fast Forward: Work, Gender, and Protest in a Changing World* and *Transformations: Feminist Pathways to Global Change.*

**Steven Sherman** is a scholar and activist with a doctorate in sociology from Binghamton University. His work has appeared in *Review, Journal of World-Systems Research,* and *Counterpunch.* He maintains the web site www.lefteyeonbooks.org.

**Boris Stremlin** is a comparative macrosociologist with interests in world history, the sociology of knowledge, and geopolitics. His dissertation is on "Constructing a Multiparadigm World History: Civilizations, Ecumenes and World-Systems in the Ancient Near East" at Binghamton University. He taught sociology at Wright State University in Dayton, Ohio. His publications have appeared in *Review* and in the Political Economy of the World-System series.

**Mohammad H. Tamdgidi** teaches sociology and social theory at the University of Massachusetts, Boston. He is the author of *Advancing Utopistics: The Three Component Parts and Errors of Marxism.* He has published in *Review, Sociological Spectrum,* and *Contemporary Sociology,* and his works have appeared in several edited collections. Tamdgidi is the founding editor of *Human Architecture: Journal of the Sociology of Self-Knowledge,* a publication of the Omar Khayyam Center for Integrative Research in Utopia, Mysticism, and Science.

**Ganesh K. Trichur** is Assistant Professor of Political Economy at St. Lawrence University. He has published in *Globalizations* and in the *Journal of World-Systems Research.* His recent publications are on the social effects of Hurricane Katrina (in *Racing the Storm: Implications and Lessons Learned from Katrina* edited by Hillary Potter), on political Islamism and political Hinduism *(Islam and the*

*Orientalist World-System,* edited by Khaldoun Samman and Mazhar Al-Zo'by), and internal migration in China.

**Immanuel Wallerstein** is Director of the Fernand Braudel Center for the Study of Economies, Historical Systems, and Civilizations, Binghamton University, and Senior Research Scholar at Yale University.

# ACKNOWLEDGEMENTS

This volume grew out of the thirty-first meeting of the Political Economy of the World-System (PEWS) Section of the American Sociological Association, 10–11 May 2007, at St. Lawrence University in Canton, New York. I thank St. Lawrence University for offering the space and the financial support to convene the conference in the North Country. Dr. Eve Stoddard (Chair of the PEWS Committee) and Dr. John Collins (Associate Professor) from the Department of Global Studies, were the strongest supporters of the Conference—it was their involvement, encouragement, and help that enabled the Global Studies department to successfully organize the conference. Thanks to Professor Grant Cornwell, Academic Dean of St. Lawrence University, and to Margaret Bass and Liz Regosin, for their support and encouragement. As the chair of the PEWS Committee, Dr. Eve Stoddard provided invaluable direction. Many thanks also to the other members of the PEWS Committee for their involvement in the process—Anne Csete and Erin McCarthy (from the Asian Studies Program), Karl Schonberg, Assis Malaquias, Judith DeGroat, Evelyn Jennings, Florence Molk, Abye Asefa, Elun Gabriel, Donna Alvah, and Vernadette Gonzales. Joyce Sheridan was indispensable for logistical support and Juli Pomainville designed the flyer. Thanks to President Dan Sullivan and Anne Sullivan of St. Lawrence University for warmly welcoming all the participants. Thanks to all the students who attended the conference.

# Political Economy of the World-System Annuals Series

## Immanuel Wallerstein, Series Editor

I.  Kaplan, Barbara Hockey, ed., *Social Change in the Capitalist World Economy.* Political Economy of the World-System Annuals, 01. Beverly Hills/London: Sage Publications, 1978.

II.  Goldfrank, Walter L., ed., *The World-System of Capitalism: Past and Present.* Political Economy of the World-System Annuals, 02. Beverly Hills/London: Sage Publications, 1979.

III.  Hopkins, Terence K. & Immanuel Wallerstein, eds., *Processes of the World-System.* Political Economy of the World-System Annuals, 03. Beverly Hills/London: Sage Publications, 1980.

IV.  Rubinson, Richard, ed., *Dynamics of World Development.* Political Economy of the World-System Annuals, 04. Beverly Hills/London: Sage Publications, 1981.

V.  Friedman, Edward, ed., *Ascent and Decline in the World-System.* Political Economy of the World-System Annuals, 05. Beverly Hills/London/New Delhi: Sage Publications, 1982.

VI.  Bergesen, Albert, ed., *Crises in the World-System.* Political Economy of the World-System Annuals, 06. Beverly Hills/London/New Delhi: Sage Publications, 1983.

VII.  Bergquist, Charles, ed., *Labor in the Capitalist World-Economy.* Political Economy of the World-System Annuals, 07. Beverly Hills/London/New Delhi: Sage Publications, 1984.

VIII.  Evans, Peter, Dietrich Rueschemeyer & Evelyne Huber Stephens, eds., *States versus Markets in the World-System.* Political Economy of the World-System Annuals, 08. Beverly Hills/London/New Delhi: Sage Publications, 1985.

IX.  Tardanico, Richard, ed., *Crises in the Caribbean Basin.* Political Economy of the World-System Annuals, 09. Newbury Park/Beverly Hills/London/New Delhi: Sage Publications, 1987.

X.  Ramirez, Francisco O., ed., *Rethinking the Nineteenth Century: Contradictions and Movements.* Studies in the Political Economy of the World-System, 10. New York/Westport, CT/London: Greenwood Press, 1988.

XI.  Smith, Joan, Jane Collins, Terence K. Hopkins & Akbar Muhammad, eds., *Racism, Sexism, and the World-System.* Studies in the Political Economy of the World-System, 11. New York/Westport, CT/London: Greenwood Press, 1988.

XII.  (a) Boswell, Terry, ed., *Revolution in the World-System.* Studies in the Political Economy of the World-System, 12a. New York/Westport, CT/London: Greenwood Press, 1989.

XII.     (b) Schaeffer, Robert K., ed., *War in the World-System.* Studies in the Political Economy of the World-System, 12b. New York/Westport, CT/London: Greenwood Press, 1989.

XIII.    Martin, William G., ed., *Semiperipheral States in the World-Economy.* Studies in the Political Economy of the World-System, 13. New York/Westport, CT/London: Greenwood Press, 1990.

XIV.     Kasaba, Resat, ed., *Cities in the World-System.* Studies in the Political Economy of the World-System, 14. New York/Westport, CT/London: Greenwood Press, 1991.

XV.      Palat, Ravi Arvind, ed., *Pacific-Asia and the Future of the World-System.* Studies in the Political Economy of the World-System, 15. Westport, CT/London: Greenwood Press, 1993.

XVI.     Gereffi, Gary & Miguel Korzeniewicz, eds., *Commodity Chains and Global Capitalism.* Studies in the Political Economy of the World-System, 16. Westport, CT: Greenwood Press, 1994.

XVII.    McMichael, Philip, eds., *Food and Agrarian Orders in the World-Economy.* Studies in the Political Economy of the World-System, 17. Westport, CT: Greenwood Press, 1995.

XVIII.   Smith, David A. & József Böröcz, eds., *A New World Order? Global Transformations in the Late Twentieth Century.* Studies in the Political Economy of the World-System, 18. Westport, CT: Greenwood Press, 1995.

XIX.     Korzeniewicz, Roberto Patricio & William C. Smith, eds., *Latin America in the World-Economy.* Studies in the Political Economy of the World-System, 19. Westport, CT: Greenwood Press, 1996.

XX.      Ciccantell, Paul S. & Stephen G. Bunker, eds., *Space and Transport in the World-System.* Studies in the Political Economy of the World-System, 20. Westport, CT: Greenwood Press, 1998.

XXI.     Goldfrank, Walter L., David Goodman & Andrew Szasz, eds., *Ecology and the World-System.* Studies in the Political Economy of the World-System, 21. Westport, CT: Greenwood Press, 1999.

XXII.    Derluguian, Georgi & Scott L. Greer, eds., *Questioning Geopolitics.* Studies in the Political Economy of the World-System, 22. Westport, CT: Greenwood Press, 2000.

XXIV.    Grosfoguel, Ramón & Ana Margarita Cervantes-Rodriguez, eds., *The Modern/Colonial/Capitalist World-System in the Twentieth Century: Global Processes, Antisystemic Movements, and the Geopolitics of Knowledge.* Studies in the Political Economy of the World-System, 24. Westport, CT: Greenwood Press, 2002.

XXV.     (a) Dunaway, Wilma A., ed., *Emerging Issues in the 21st Century World-System, Volume I: Crises and Resistance in the 21st Century World-System.* Studies in the Political Economy of the World-System, 25a. Westport, CT: Greenwood Press, 2003.

XXV.     (b) Dunaway, Wilma A., ed., *Emerging Issues in the 21st Century World-System, Volume II: New Theoretical Directions for the 21st Century World-System.* Studies in the Political Economy of the World-System, 25b. Westport, CT: Greenwood Press, 2003.

XXVI.    (a) Reifer, Thomas Ehrlich, ed. *Globalization, Hegemony & Power.* Political Economy of the World-System Annuals, 26a. Boulder, CO: Paradigm Publishers, 2004.

XXVI. (b) Friedman, Jonathan & Christopher Chase-Dunn, eds. *Hegemonic Decline: Present and Past*. Political Economy of the World-System Annuals. Boulder, CO: Paradigm Pubishers, 2005.

XXVII. Tabak, Faruk. *Allies as Rivals: The U.S., Europe and Japan in a Changing World-System*. Political Economy of the World-System Annuals, 27. Boulder, CO: Paradigm Publishers, 2005.

XXVIII. Grosfoguel, Ramón, Nelson Meldonado-Torres, and José David Saldívar. ed., *Latin@s in the World-System: Toward the Decolonization of the Twenty-first Century U.S. Empire*. Political Economy of the World-System Annuals, 28. Boulder, CO: Paradigm Publishers, 2005.

XXIX. Samman, Khaldoun, and Mazhor Al-Zo'by. eds., *Islam and the Orientalist World-System*. Political Economy of the World-System Annuals, 29. Boulder, CO: Paradigm Publishers, 2008.

XXX. Trichur, Ganesh K., ed., *The Rise of Asia and the Transformation of the World-System*. Political Economy of the World-System Annuals, 30. Boulder, CO: Paradigm Publishers, 2009.